Anthony C. Thiselton is Professor of Christian Theology at the University of Nottingham. He has previously taught at the Universities of Sheffield, Bristol, and Durham and is known internationally for his work on hermeneutics and the theory of interpretation. His previous books include *A Concise Encyclopaedia of the Philosophy of Religion* (Oneworld, 2002); *First Corinthians: A Shorter Exegetical and Pastoral Commentary* (Eerdmans, 2006); and *The Hermeneutics of Doctrine* (Eerdmans, 2007).

D1422252

To Rosemary

THE LIVING PAUL

An introduction to the apostle and his thought

ANTHONY C. THISELTON

First published in Great Britain in 2009

Society for Promoting Christian Knowledge
36 Causton Street
London SW1P 4ST

British Library Cataloguing-in-Publication Data
A catalogue record for this book is available from the British Library

ISBN 978–0–281–06110–5

1 3 5 7 9 10 8 6 4 2

Typeset by Graphicraft Ltd, Hong Kong
Printed in Great Britain by Ashford Colour Press

Produced on paper from sustainable forests

Contents

Preface and acknowledgements   vii

Timeline of Paul's apostolic ministry   viii

Abbreviations   x

1 A first obstacle to appreciating Paul: Paul and Jesus   1

2 A second obstacle to appreciating Paul: an 'immense cut' – new creation   11

3 Apostle to the Gentiles (1): traveller and missionary-pastor   20

4 Apostle to the Gentiles (2): traveller, pastor, letter-writer   29

5 Jesus Christ in Paul   38

6 Paul's view of God and its Trinitarian implications   49

7 Paul's view of the Holy Spirit   58

8 Paul's view of humanity   67

9 Human alienation and Paul on sin   75

10 The work of Christ and being 'in Christ'   82

11 Justification and the law   92

12 Why the Church?   101

13 The ministry of the word   110

14 Baptism and the Lord's Supper or Eucharist   117

15 Paul's ethics and views on Christian lifestyle   126

16 Cosmic and human destiny and the present: resurrection, judgement, and the *Parousia*   135

17 Paul and postmodernity   148

Contents

Bibliography   163

Index of biblical and related references   175

Index of authors   182

Index of subjects   184

Preface and acknowledgements

I am very grateful to SPCK for suggesting this excellent title on Paul, and for approving the direction of this book. I have long wanted to write something which makes Paul accessible, but without undue oversimplification. In order to bring Paul alive for today, the publishers encouraged me to write on Paul and Jesus; Paul and women; his warmth and sociability; his working with co-workers; and his relation to postmodernity. Yet they wanted readers to see him as a creative thinker, who also faced practical pastoral problems. Paul appears here as Apostle to the Gentiles: as traveller, missionary-pastor, letter-writer, and theologian. But we wish to concentrate on Paul's theology, as well as including other aspects of his life and practice.

The text aims at succinctness and conciseness, especially since the publishers requested a limited word-length. I have kept footnotes to a minimum. They provide documentation for information, and to preserve academic integrity. After writing many books on hermeneutics, I am very glad to add this book on Paul to my two on a single Pauline epistle. My teaching career began with Pauline theology in 1964, and this remains a central concern.

I am very grateful to Mrs Karen Woodward, my University Secretary, for patiently and carefully typing the whole manuscript, as well as helping with the indexes. My wife, Rosemary, and Mrs Sheila Rees gave their help with this book, for which I thank them. My hope and prayer is that many will read Paul as a living voice for today. Perhaps this remains an exercise in practical hermeneutics, but with no theory, only Paul.

Anthony C. Thiselton
Professor of Christian Theology
University of Nottingham, UK

Timeline of Paul's apostolic ministry

c. 33–34	Conversion and call on the road to Damascus (Gal. 1.15–16)
[Tiberius is Emperor]	
c. 34–37	Paul's ministry or retreat in Arabia and Nabataea (Gal. 1.17)
c. 36–37	Paul's stay in Antioch (Acts 11.25–26)
[Gaius becomes Emperor in 37]	
37–38	Paul's escape from Damascus (probably ruled by Aretas IV) (2 Cor. 11.32–33)
37–38	Paul's two-week stay in Jerusalem with Peter (Gal. 1.18)
38–47	'The missing years' and Paul's early ministry in Cilicia and Syria (unrecorded)
[Claudius becomes Emperor in 41]	
46–47	First missionary journey (Acts 13—14); with Barnabas, in Cyprus and Asia Minor
47–48	Second visit to Jerusalem; Apostolic Council (Gal. 2.1–10; Acts 15)
48–50	Second missionary journey, with Silas: Asia Minor; the advance to Greece: Macedonia and Achaia (Acts 16—17)
50–52	Ministry in Corinth (Acts 18.12–18; Gallio, Proconsul, date-inscription at Delphi)
51–52	Paul writes 1 Thessalonians (probably the earliest letter)
52	Most, but not all, view 2 Thessalonians as from Paul, written shortly afterwards
52–55	'Third missionary journey', based on stay in Ephesus; probably writes Galatians
53	Paul writes 1 Corinthians in response to oral reports, letter, and delegation
[Nero becomes Emperor in 54]	
55	Takes 'the collection' to Ephesus, Troas, and Macedonia and Corinth

55	Less likely but alternative date for writing Galatians; second stay in Corinth
55–56	Possible date for 2 Corinthians (some view chapters 1—9 and 10—13 as two letters)
56–57	Writes Romans; arrival in Jerusalem with collection; imprisonment (Acts 20—21)
56–58	Imprisonment in Caesarea (Acts 24—26). Perhaps Paul wrote Philemon; some think that Philippians and possibly Colossians may have been written then
59	Paul's voyage to Rome
59–62	Paul under house arrest in Rome. Many think that he wrote Philippians; some ascribe Colossians to this period; a minority think that Paul probably wrote Ephesians
From 62 onwards	Most think that Paul was martyred under Nero; a few speculate about a visit to Spain; some ascribe 1 and 2 Timothy and Titus to this period, but most view these as written by a disciple of Paul
c. 64–65	The latest likely date of Paul's life, unless he was released and went to Spain

Abbreviations

AV	Authorized Version
JSNTSup	*Journal for the Study of the New Testament*, Supplement Series
NEB	New English Bible
NIGTC	New International Greek Testament Commentary
NovTSup	*Novum Testamentum*, Supplement Series
NRSV	New Revised Standard Version
Phillips	J. B. Phillips, *The New Testament in Modern English*
RSV	Revised Standard Version
SBL	Society of Biblical Literature
SBLDS	Society of Biblical Literature Dissertation Series
SNTSMS	Society of New Testament Studies Monograph Series
VCSup	*Vigiliae Christianae*, Supplement Series
WUNT	Wissenschaftliche Untersuchungen zum Neuen Testament

1

A first obstacle to appreciating Paul: Paul and Jesus

Very many people, perhaps even millions, view Jesus of Nazareth with admiration and respect, but see Paul as the founder of a different system of doctrine and the inventor of established churches. They regard Jesus as a religious idealist, who taught a simple religion of love and tolerance; they regard Paul very differently, as one who imposed his ideas onto others, and who, unlike Jesus, undervalued women and the marginalized of society. This constitutes a first obstacle to understanding and appreciating Paul as he really was, and can be for us today. Three kinds of writers have driven a false divide between Paul and Jesus, and have exaggerated their differences.

Three kinds of problematic approaches

(1) One group emerged originally from the nineteenth-century liberalism of Albrecht Ritschl and his influential heir in the early twentieth century, Adolf von Harnack (1851–1930). Ritschl and Harnack found Christian doctrine unappealing. Harnack argued that Jesus taught only three 'simple' truths: the kingdom of God, the brotherhood of all, and the infinite value of the human soul. If this were true, a gap opens at once between Jesus and Paul. Harnack believed that Paul, more than anyone else, set about changing this simple religion and the teaching of Jesus into a complex system of doctrine. He drew on 'Hellenistic' or Greek metaphysics to transform the teaching of Jesus into a complicated system of beliefs.

(2) A second group of scholars claimed to approach Jesus and Paul from a strictly value-neutral 'historical' perspective. The most important often include Jewish scholars, although they also include some mainly American writers. A forceful recent representation of this view may be the Jewish scholar Hyam Maccoby

(1924–2004).[1] Maccoby states that it was Paul who founded Christianity, not Jesus. Paul invented the 'myth' of Jesus' divinity. A more careful Jewish writer, H. J. Schoeps, recognizes that Paul remains proud of his Judaism, and criticizes liberal approaches. He does not simply see Paul as heavily influenced by Greek ideas, and concedes that Paul was educated largely in Jerusalem under Rabbi Gamaliel, and followed the moderate theology of Rabbi Hillel. But he distinguishes between 'Hellenism' and 'Hellenistic Judaism'. The problem, he urges, is not that Paul was influenced by Greek culture, but that he was influenced by Greek-speaking Judaism. This conveyed a distorted understanding of the law, in which the law became isolated from the covenant. Here lies a crucial difference between Paul and Jesus, Schoeps argued, which vitiates Paul's work.[2] Finally, another well-known Jewish scholar, Geza Vermes, argued that Jesus is not to be identified with 'the Christ of the Church'.[3] The Church worships the Christ of Paul, who believes primarily in the exalted Christ (Phil. 2.5–11), rather than in the earthly Jesus of Nazareth.

(3) Recently a group of American scholars have fallen partly into both of these two categories, but follow their own agenda. John Dominic Crossan, Robert Funk, and others, think of themselves as value-neutral 'historical' scholars, and (like the second group) try to approach Jesus of Nazareth without any theological assumptions. In 1985 Funk founded the 'Jesus Seminar' at the Society of Biblical Literature in America. They included such sources as the non-canonical Gospel of Thomas. Jesus emerged, they claimed, as an itinerant sage, or a 'Galilean deviant', and a teacher of aphorisms, influenced by Greek Cynic moral philosophy. This picture is sharply criticized by N. T. Wright, Richard Bauckham, and James D. G. Dunn. Dunn calls the resultant 'Jesus' 'the Neo-Liberal Jesus', like that of the first group.[4]

---

[1] Hyam Maccoby, *The Mythmaker: Paul and the Invention of Christianity* (London: Weidenfeld and Nicolson, 1986).

[2] H. J. Schoeps, *Paul: The Theology of the Apostle in the Light of Jewish Religious History*, trans. H. Knight (London: Lutterworth Press, 1961), throughout.

[3] Geza Vermes, *Jesus the Jew: A Historian's Reading of the Gospels* (Philadelphia: Fortress Press, 1973), p. 17.

[4] J. D. G. Dunn, *Christianity in the Making*, vol. 1: *The Remembered Jesus* (Grand Rapids and Cambridge: Eerdmans, 2003), pp. 58–65; cf. John Dominic Crossan, *The Historical Jesus: The Life of a Mediterranean Jewish Peasant* (San Francisco: Harper, 1991); and N. T. Wright, *Jesus and the Victory of God* (London: SPCK, 1996).

A response to these approaches

In fact, however, it is false to claim that Paul knows *only* the exalted Christ, who is Son of God, but has no interest in the earthly Jesus of Nazareth. A purely 'historical' knowledge alone failed to impress Paul as a Jew. Paul admits that he once knew Christ 'from a human point of view', but knows him no longer in this way (2 Cor. 5.16). He is referring here to a purely human way of *belief*, not of a human *Jesus*. One writer has said that a 'fleshly' kind of knowledge differs from a 'fleshly' kind of Christ. Eduard Schweizer rightly sees Jesus as 'The man who fits no formula'.[5] One cannot begin with pre-conceived categories, or even 'titles', and try to make Jesus fit them; rather, Jesus shapes the categories, titles, and expectations which he uses.

David Wenham provides a comprehensive account of this issue in his book *Paul: Follower of Jesus or Founder of Christianity?*[6] He begins by showing that Paul used many of the stories and sayings of Jesus. Even the payment of ministerial stipends offers one of many examples (Matt. 10.10, par. Luke 10.7; cf. 1 Cor. 9.14). Jesus' sayings on divorce offer another (Matt. 5.27–28; 19.3–9; Mark 10.2–12; Luke 16.18; cf. 1 Cor. 7.10). The institution of the Lord's Supper is found in Mark 14.22–25; Matt. 26.26–29; and Luke 22.14–20; and set out in 1 Cor. 11.23–26. Wenham recognizes that parallels do not necessarily imply conscious dependence. But in this case there are so many, beginning with Jesus' announcement of the kingdom (or reign) of God and the time of fulfilment. Herman Ridderbos makes the same point. He exclaims, 'The general character of Paul's preaching is materially altogether in harmony with the great theme of Jesus' preaching the coming of the kingdom of heaven. What Jesus proclaims as the "fulfilment of the time" (Mark 1.15) is almost word for word identical with what Paul terms "the fullness of the time" (Gal. 4.4).'[7]

The fulfilment of Jewish expectation becomes a central theme in Jesus, Paul, New Testament eschatology (about the end-times) and

---

[5] Chapter heading in E. Schweizer, *Jesus*, trans. D. E. Green (London: SCM Press, 1971), pp. 13–52.

[6] David Wenham, *Paul: Follower of Jesus or Founder of Christianity* (Grand Rapids and Cambridge: Eerdmans, 1995), pp. 34–70.

[7] Herman Ridderbos, *Paul: An Outline of His Theology*, trans. J. R. de Witt (London: SPCK, 1977), p. 48. Cf. Herman Ridderbos, *Paul and Jesus: Origin and General Character of Paul's Preaching of Christ*, trans. David H. Freeman (Philadelphia: Presbyterian and Reformed Publishing, 1958), esp. pp. 59–89.

'apocalyptic'. It loomed large in the thought of the Qumran community, who produced the Dead Sea Scrolls. Jesus fulfilled the hopes and expectations of the many who looked to God's promises, declared in the Hebrew Bible or Old Testament. 'That the Scriptures might be fulfilled' (Mark 14.49) becomes a common theme in the first three Gospels. Matthew regularly sees the ministry of Jesus in this way (Matt. 1.22; 2.15, 17, 23; 8.17; 12.17; 13.35; 21.4; 25.54; 27.9 and 35). Paul also agrees that with the coming of Christ the law is fulfilled (Gal. 5.14); that now is the time of God's favour (2 Cor. 6.2); and that this is the dispensation of the fulfilment of the time (Eph. 1.10, assuming it is Pauline or perhaps by the Pauline disciple).

In spite of his focus on the exalted Lord, Paul includes a number of details about the earthly life of Jesus. He knows that Jesus was human (Rom. 5.15; 1 Cor. 15.21), and this becomes part of an Adam parallel or typology. Jesus was a Jew (Rom. 9.5), 'born of a woman under the law' (Gal. 4.4), and was descended from Abraham (Gal. 3.16), of the lineage of David (Rom. 1.3). Jesus had brothers (1 Cor. 9.5), one of whom was James (Gal. 1.19). His ministry was especially among the Jews (Rom. 15.8). In terms of earthly character, Paul refers to 'the meekness and gentleness of Christ' (2 Cor. 10.1), and recalls his self-description as 'meek and lowly in heart' (Matt. 11.29). He refers to his 'endurance' and 'obedience' (2 Thess. 3.5; Rom. 5.19), which are clearly references to his earthly state, and difficult to apply only to Christ as exalted Lord. In addition to the institution of the Lord's Supper (or Holy Communion), Paul speaks of Jesus as the Passover Lamb, who was really crucified (1 Cor. 5.7; 1 Cor. 2.8; Gal. 3.13). Paul asserts, 'God sent his Son in the likeness of sinful flesh' (Rom. 8.3). Further, 'He has reconciled you in the body of his flesh through death' (Col. 1.22). Both statements refer to the earthly Jesus.

Transforming grace in Jesus and in Paul

When we read of Paul's proclamation of justification by grace through faith, we may ask: Is this in any way different from the central message of Jesus? This proclamation remains central in Rom. 1.17 and Romans 1—8, as well as in Galatians, 1 Corinthians, and elsewhere in the Pauline writings. Jesus' parable of the Pharisee and the Tax Collector, the parable of the Prodigal Son, and the parable of the Good Employer and Day Labourer make precisely the same point as Paul. In the parable of the Pharisee and the Tax Collector (Luke 18.9–14), the story was addressed to those who trusted in themselves instead of God. The presence of Semiticizing tendencies in the language (vv. 11, 12, 13) and the use of an Aramaic idiom (behind the Greek) further assure us that the parable was not a later addition to the words of Jesus.

The Pharisee was a devout Jew, who understandably recalls his works of supererogation as he comes into the presence of God to worship ('I fast twice a week'; 'I give tithes of all that I possess'). People regarded the tax collector badly, and marginalized him from society, for he had various devices for defrauding the public. He smote his chest or heart as the perceived seat of sin, to express deepest contrition. The Pharisee stands in a prominent position, and recites his 'good works'; the tax collector stands at a distance, and implores God's mercy. The latter, to the amazement of the audience, is declared 'justified' (Greek, *dedikaiomenos*), rather than the devout and dutiful Pharisee.[8] We cannot know that the Pharisee was hypocritical. Indeed it would undermine the point of the story if he was. The tax collector was overwhelmed by a sense of his distance from God and his overwhelming need for mercy.

The three parables of the Lost Coin, the Lost Sheep, and the Lost Son (Luke 15) convey a similar point. The elder son (Luke 15.11–32) appears like the Pharisaic critics of Jesus. It does not seem to the elder son to be fair that the younger son, who has been selfish, defiant, estranged, and alienated, should receive a welcome back and his father's extravagant welcome. The parable is a vindication of God's mercy and grace to the undeserving. But we need not depend only on Luke. Matthew 20.1–15 tells the parable of the Good Employer and Grumbling Workers. The employer agrees to pay a fair day's wage to those whom he hires at the beginning of the day. This amount is 'right and fair' (Matt. 20.4). But he still looks for more labourers up to five o'clock ('the eleventh hour'). When the time comes for final payment, each receives a whole day's wage. How much more, the audience wonders, will go to those who have borne the heat of the day? They, too, receive a day's wage, and the hearers are outraged. Ernest Fuchs comments that Jesus could easily have produced a

---

8 On the details see Joachim Jeremias, *The Parables of Jesus*, trans. S. H. Hooke (rev. edn, London, SCM Press, 1963), pp. 139–44.

bland sermon on justification by grace. But he tells a story that makes everyone *feel* deep down the scandal of justification by grace alone. 'Such grace is unfair,' the workers and audience cry! By telling a dramatic story in this way, Jesus lets his audience come to terms with the offence or stumbling-block of pure grace, where love and sheer generosity eclipse all questions of justice and fairness (cf. 1 Cor. 1.18–25).

If we turn to Mark, the earliest Gospel, Jesus is like a physician who has to heal not those who are already well, but the sick and needy (Mark 2.17). Even the parable of the Servants in the Vineyard (Mark 12.1–11; cf. Matt. 21.33–44 and Luke 20.9–18) is unusually in the form of an allegory, which vindicates the offer of the gospel to the poor. The vineyard of God will be given to 'others' (Mark 12.9). The Jewish leaders mistreat the prophets (the earlier messengers) and finally kill the Son. Therefore God gives his vineyard to outsiders, who have no just claim to possess it.

Paul has a close parallel to each of these themes. With regard to the sending of the Son and heir, we have already noted, 'God . . . sent his Son in the likeness of sinful flesh to deal with sin . . . so that the just requirement of the law might be fulfilled in us' (Gal. 4.4; cf. Rom. 8.3). The Gentiles enter into the Jews' inheritance (Romans 9—11). Wenham observes that the words are parallel in Jesus and Paul 'at almost every point'.[9] Paul observes: 'All have sinned and fall short of the glory of God: they are now justified by his grace as a gift' (Rom. 3.22–25). 'God proves his love for us in that while we still were sinners, Christ died for us' (Rom. 5.8). This says the same as Jesus does in comparing himself with a physician, in speaking of the tax collector and Pharisee, and the Good Employer and the Day Labourer.

Jesus and Paul on love

It is not even true to suggest that Jesus' well-known sayings about love have no parallel in the sayings in Paul. Matthew tells us that the golden rule of love to the neighbour fulfils all the law and the prophets (Matt. 7.12; cf. Luke 6.31; cf. also Matt. 22.34–40, Mark

---

[9] Wenham, *Paul, Follower of Jesus*, p. 136.

12.28–34, and Luke 10.25–28). Jesus says that we must put ourselves last after God and others (Matt. 20.25–28; Mark 10.42–45; Luke 22.24–27). Jesus showed far more respect to women and outsiders or the marginalized than most Jewish teachers or rabbis (Luke 10.38–42). He welcomed children (Matt. 18.1–6; Mark 9.33–42; Luke 18.15–17).

Paul tells us that love is the content of the law of Christ (Gal. 6.2). He exhorts us, 'Owe no one anything but to love one another; for one who loves another has fulfilled the law. The commandments are summed up in this word, "Love your neighbour as yourself." "Love does no wrong" ' (Rom. 13.8–10). Faith has to be worked out in love (Gal. 5.6). To be rooted in Christ is to be rooted in love (Col. 2.7; cf. Eph. 3.17). Love is 'the fruit of the Spirit' (Gal. 5.22; cf. Rom. 15.30).

This is not at all confined to Galatians and Romans. The greatest vision of the supremacy of love comes in 1 Corinthians 13. Some argue that Paul did not compose it, in view of its measured and poetic style and vocabulary. But Paul may have composed it at a time other than during the process of dictating the letter. Almost every phrase reflects attitudes in the Church at Corinth, so perhaps Paul composed it before he dictated the letter, or when he had broken off dictating, perhaps overnight. In contrast to many in Corinth, Paul exclaims, 'Love waits patiently; love shows kindness. Love does not burn with envy; does not brag – is not inflated with its own importance. It does not behave with ill-mannered impropriety; is not preoccupied with the interests of the self; does not become exaggerated into pique; does not keep a reckoning up of evil . . . never tires of support, never loses faith, never exhausts hope, never gives up' (my translation in two commentaries, to convey the verbal and dynamic nature of the Greek, and to follow its meaning closely but idiomatically, 1 Cor. 13.4–7).[10] I also explore this in Chapter 15, on ethics and lifestyle. This directly addresses a community where some showed jealousy and boasting (1 Cor. 3.3); some showed arrogance (5.2); some were impatient to show off their own gifts (14.26, 27); some showed impatience and rudeness at the Lord's Supper (11.21–22); some manipulated the

---

[10] Anthony C. Thiselton, *First Corinthians: A Shorter Exegetical and Pastoral Commentary* (Grand Rapids and Cambridge: Eerdmans, 2006), p. 217; and Anthony C. Thiselton, *The First Epistle to the Corinthians: A Commentary on the Greek Text* (Grand Rapids: Eerdmans, and Carlisle: Paternoster Press, 2000), pp. 1046–60.

legal system to take advantage of poorer or more vulnerable fellow Christians (6.1–6); and others asserted their own beliefs (whether right or wrong) at the expense of fellow Christians (8.13). The examples could be extended.

Paul even maintains that although faith and hope are of first importance, only love remains permanent and lasts for eternity. He writes, 'If I have all faith . . . but do not have love, I am nothing . . . Love never ends . . . There is faith, hope, and love, but the greatest of these is love' (1 Cor. 13.2, 4, 13). Even the reference to 'faith that can move mountains' occurs both in Jesus and in Paul (Matt. 17.20; 1 Cor. 13.2).

Women in Jesus and Paul

The respect which Jesus showed to women is well known. Mary Magdalene was the first to carry the news of the resurrection; Jesus engaged in witty conversation with the 'Syro-Phoenician' woman; Jesus talked with the Samaritan woman at the well.

Nevertheless Paul also acknowledged the leadership role of women. If Paul had really been a misogynist, F. F. Bruce observes, would Priscilla and Aquila willingly 'have risked their necks' for Paul's life (Rom. 16.3–4)?[11] Bruce adds that Paul was sociable and gregarious (like Jesus), and delighted in the company of both men and women. He treated women as persons: he commended Phoebe as deacon of the church at Cenchreae, and calls her 'pre-eminent' and 'our sister' (Rom. 16.1, 2). Junia is 'pre-eminent among the apostles' (Rom. 16.17), and E. J. Epp has decisively shown this to be a female name, not the masculine form, Junias.[12] Euodia and Syntyche had a difference of opinion, but 'they struggled beside me in the work of the gospel' (Phil. 4.3). Persis, Tryphosa and Tryphaena are 'beloved in the Lord' and worked as co-workers with Paul (Rom. 16.12). Paul asks the Roman church to send his greeting to Rufus' mother, who is 'a mother to me also' (Rom. 16.11). This speaks much about Rufus' mother and about Paul. Julia and all the saints receive Paul's greetings (Rom. 16.15). The Pauline authorship of Romans 16 is not doubted.

---

[11] F. F. Bruce, *Paul: The Apostle of the Free Spirit* (Exeter: Paternoster Press, 1977), p. 457.

[12] Eldon Jay Epp, *Junia: The First Woman Apostle* (Minneapolis: Fortress Press, 2005), p. 80 and throughout.

In 1 Corinthians 11 Paul commends the church for observing the tradition of women leading in public prayer and 'prophesying' (11.2). We shall later argue that this means not delivering a private message, but publicly proclaiming the gospel in a pastoral and applied way. In 1 Cor. 11.11–12 Paul writes, 'Woman is not independent of man, or man independent of woman . . . Man comes through woman' (i.e. by birth from a mother). In 1 Cor. 7.1, 'It is well for a man not to touch a woman' is a quotation from a slogan used sometimes at Corinth; these words are not Paul's view. He breaks new ground beyond anything written by men in the world of Paul's day when he suggests that sexual intimacy may give pleasure to men and women equally (7.3–5).[13] Other ancient writers assume that women simply give pleasure to men. He shows pastoral concern for separated or divorced couples (7.12–16); for unmarried girls (1 Cor. 7.25–31, 36–38).

In 1 Cor. 14.33–36 Paul seems to contradict what he says in 1 Corinthians 11 by enjoining silence in worship on the part of women. Some regard these verses as a non-Pauline interpolation. Others implausibly contrast 'speaking' and 'chattering', which the Greek does not sustain. Probably this is a special case of sifting true prophecy from false 'prophecy', where in the early Church a self-styled 'prophet's' lifestyle was thought to be a test of whether or not their 'prophecy' was authentic. We can envisage, then, situations where women might say, 'That's not prophecy. You should see how my husband behaves at home.' If domestic recrimination crept in, we can understand why Paul prefers silence in public, not least to avoid gossip and further recrimination.[14]

Paul's warm friendships, and care for 'the weak'

That Paul was warm-hearted and sociable cannot be doubted from the evidence of the epistles. Stephanas, Fortunatus, and Achaicus 'refresh Paul's spirit' as they bring a little piece of Corinth to him when they visit him in Ephesus (1 Cor. 16.15–18). Paul describes Titus as his brother (2 Cor. 2.13), and Timothy as his 'beloved and faithful child in the Lord' (1 Cor. 4.17).

---

[13] Thiselton, *The First Epistle to the Corinthians*, pp. 498–512.
[14] Thiselton, *The First Epistle to the Corinthians*, pp. 1146–62.

Paul is also a defender of the socially vulnerable and less secure Christians, whom others at Corinth call 'the weak'. Although the elitist 'strong' may be technically right in claiming, 'No idol in the world really exists' (1 Cor. 8.4), some who are 'weak' or insecure still have scruples, and, Paul declares, 'by your "knowledge" those "weak" believers for whom Christ died are destroyed' (8.11). 'If food is a cause of their falling, I will never eat meat' (8.13; 9.15; cf. 10.23–28).

Paul's pastoral burden was such that 'I am again in the pain of childbirth until Christ is formed in you' (Gal. 4.19). Paul evokes such affection and love from the Galatians that when he suffered with his eyes (or perhaps suffered epilepsy), 'you would have torn out your eyes and given them to me' (Gal. 4.15; cf. 6.11, 17). It is fashionable today to emphasize that Paul did not pastor the churches as a lone, freelance, individual, but with co-workers. These included especially Barnabas, Timothy, Silas (or Silvanus) and Titus, but not these alone.[15] Moreover Paul refused to don the cloak of a professional, paid, rhetorician or orator. The Corinthians were ashamed that he was not a professional lecturer, but Paul preferred to labour with his own hands as a manual worker, lest he should become beholden to rich patrons in the church. Paul binds himself, his gospel and his lifestyle closely to that of Jesus and to the apostolic tradition prior to Paul.[16] The myth that he was a lone, grumpy, woman-hater, who founded a religion different from that of Jesus, is an illusion, or indeed a 'myth'. Paul even followed Jesus in speaking of the kingdom or reign of God (Rom. 14.17; 1 Cor. 4.20; 15.50; Col. 1.13; 1 Thess. 2.12). But normally he used language (not content) more appropriate to the Graeco-Roman world.

---

[15] W. H. Olrog, *Paulus und seine Mitarbeiter* (Neukirchen: Neukirchener, 1979); R. Banks, *Paul's Idea of Community* (Peabody: Hendrickson, 2nd edn 1994), pp. 49–63 and 149–58.

[16] Anders Eriksson, *Traditions as Rhetorical Proof: Pauline Argumentation in 1 Corinthians* (Stockholm: Almqvist & Wiksell, 1998).

2

A second obstacle to appreciating
Paul: an 'immense cut' –
new creation

A second obstacle stands in the way of fully understanding and appreciating Paul as a figure that lives for us today. Some years ago Johannes Weiss argued that 'between us and the real Paul there stand all kinds of hindrances to a true understanding' of Paul, of which the chief obstacle is 'an immense cut' which runs through Paul's thought.[1] Weiss writes, 'The two parts of his life are sharply separated . . . by his conversion; on one side there is only error, sin, and flesh; on the other is life, Spirit, truth and righteousness . . . Does he not belong to those choleric natures for whom there is an "either-or", who always observe things in their sharpest and most exclusive aspects?'[2] Does Paul not write only for those who have experienced a sudden, complete, decisive, conversion, and does he not overstate a contrast between 'formerly' and 'now', on the grounds of his unusual experience and personality?

Many readers of the Bible today have not experienced Paul's kind of call and conversion. Are Paul's writings still relevant to them? Paul's 'formerly' and 'now' refers not so much to autobiography or to human psychology, but to God's *new creation*. Whether they have experienced a sudden conversion or a gradual process of renewal, *all* Christians have shared together in God's act of new creation. Paul writes, 'If anyone is in Christ – new creation' (no verb in the Greek, 2 Cor. 5.17).

[1] Johannes Weiss, *Earliest Christianity*, trans. F. C. Grant (2 vols, New York: Harper Torch Books, 1959), vol. 2, p. 399 and pp. 442–6.
[2] Weiss, *Earliest Christianity*, vol. 2, p. 412.

New creation and apocalyptic

Technically Paul is explaining the Christian life in terms of what is called 'apocalyptic'. This is found in the Old Testament (or Hebrew Bible) and in Jewish and Christian writings of Paul's time. Old Testament, Jewish, and New Testament apocalyptic writings urged that the kingdom (or reign) of God would not arrive by means of human effort alone. Only God could bring about a new order of being. Obedience to the law could not achieve it. Even God's special anointing of a prophet, priest, or king fell short of what was really needed. This is not unreal, or 'myth'. Is Christianity simply about reforming human persons, or is it about how we can appropriate God's act of new creation in Christ, even if we still remain ordinary, fallible, human beings? Rightly, J. Christiaan Beker declares: 'Paul's apocalyptic message needs a new hearing in the church for the sake of the vitality of the church of our times.'[3] What motivates Paul's passionate concern is not human capacities or their biography, but the triumph of Christ. Alexandra Brown also uses similar language. She speaks of transformation through the cross, and of the 'creation of a new world'. By contrast, many Corinthian Christians 'think they already "have it" '.[4]

It is crucial to realize that Paul can speak of new creation and a new world (or a new order of existence) without implying that Christians instantly enter God's promised future without more ado. Whiteley suggests an excellent analogy.[5] It is like being transferred, he says, from the icy cold into a warm room. The heat is a *decisive* force; it cannot be reversed. But as someone stands in front of a roaring fire or even a radiator, that person *still suffers* from frozen joints or from pockets of cold. They feel the decisive heat, and know that eventually they will be warm through and through. But it remains a steady *process*, even though the warmth and the cold represent two kinds of forces or 'orders of existence'.

[3] J. Christiaan Beker, *Paul's Apocalyptic Gospel: The Coming Triumph of God* (Philadelphia: Fortress Press, 1982), p. 11; cf. J. C. Beker, *Paul the Apostle: The Triumph of God in Life and Thought* (Edinburgh: T. & T. Clark, 1980), pp. 3–182 and throughout.

[4] Alexandra R. Brown, *The Cross and Human Transformation: Paul's Apocalyptic Word in 1 Corinthians* (Minneapolis: Fortress Press, 1989), p. 96 and p. 30; cf. pp. 1–64.

[5] D. E. H. Whiteley, *The Theology of St. Paul* (Oxford: Blackwell, 1964, 2nd edn 1971), pp. 126–7.

A second analogy is widely used. The Christian is like a drowning person who has been 'saved' from a sinking ship. But they are not instantaneously wafted to land. They have been saved from the sinking craft (salvation is past). A lifeboat is steadily bringing them to the shore (present continuous process of being saved). They *will* be saved when the lifeboat brings them safely to the shore, to *terra firma* (future salvation). And C. Anderson Scott built a whole book on Paul around these 'three tenses of salvation'.[6]

Paul has no romantic idealism about 'having been saved', as if nothing better still lay in the future. He insists that 'two orders', two ages, or old and new creation both influence Christians. Thus he and many other Christians still suffer hardships, suffering, failures, disappointments, and setbacks. He three times prayed that a 'thorn in the flesh' would be removed – J. B. Phillips translates this as 'a physical handicap', and NEB as 'a sharp physical pain' (2 Cor. 12.7). Yet he was left to bear it with the words, 'My strength is made perfect in weakness' (2 Cor. 12.7–9). In 2 Cor. 11.23–29 Paul speaks of suffering many imprisonments, countless floggings, being beaten with 39 lashes no fewer than five times, and beaten with wooden staves, being stoned, suffering shipwreck three times, suffering danger from bandits and kidnappers, enduring hunger, thirst, and inadequate clothing.

In contrast to some in the church at Corinth, to whom Alexandra Brown refers, Paul sees himself like a battered gladiator fighting for his life in the arena, while the Corinthians lounge in the tiered seats above the arena to applaud or boo in response to the struggling apostles. Paul writes: 'We are put on display as the grand finale, as those doomed to die as a spectacle . . . We are roughly treated and have no fixed abode, labouring with our hands . . . We are abused . . . We have become, as it were, the world's scum and the scrapings from everyone's shoes' (1 Cor. 4.9–13, my translation).[7] Creation awaits God's final future redemption, for which it 'cranes its neck', or 'waits with eager longing' (Rom. 8.19).

---

[6] C. Anderson Scott, *Christianity according to St Paul* (Cambridge: Cambridge University Press, 1927).

[7] Thiselton, *First Corinthians*, p. 74; cf. Thiselton, *The First Epistle to the Corinthians*, pp. 359–65.

It is time perhaps to say a little more about 'apocalyptic'. This term denotes a type of approach which can be found both in the Old Testament and in Jewish and Christian literature from the close of the Hebrew Bible until the end of the first century. The apocalyptists did not place their confidence in human progress, as if each generation was bound to be better than the last. The world, they believed, and humankind had passed the point at which self-improvement could answer human problems. God alone will bring into existence a new order, or a new creation, sometimes called the new age, or the last days. But they also stressed that God worked in and through history, to bring about his purposes.

In the Bible, the book of Daniel offers an example of this principle. God's independence of human reform appears as 'a stone cut without (human) hands' (Dan. 7.13). Ezekiel speaks of new life and the 'resurrection' of dry bones through the Spirit (chapter 37), while Gog and Magog represent hostile cosmic forces over which God alone triumphs (Ezekiel 38—39). Parts of Isaiah look forward to a new creation (Isa. 2.4; 4.2–6; 9.2–3; 24.1–27; 37.31–32; 65.17–25; 66.1–24). Isaiah declares, 'I am about to create new heavens and a new earth; the former things will not be remembered' (Isa. 65.17). Joel looks forward to the 'last days' when God will pour his spirit not on chosen individuals, but upon 'all flesh', or all kinds of people including 'male and female' (Joel 2.28–29). Zephaniah also looks to 'the great day of the Lord' (Zeph. 1.9–18). An apocalyptic outlook characterizes most of Zechariah 9—14, which regularly speaks of 'that day' (Zech. 14.1–8). In the New Testament Mark 13.24–36 (with its parallel in Matt. 24.23–31 or perhaps further), 1 Cor. 15.12–20, 1 Thess. 4.13—5.8, and much of Rev. 4.1–11; 17.9–18; 21.3–5, provide some well-known examples.

In Jewish literature *1 Enoch* 37–71 (*The Similitudes of Enoch*), the book known as *The Testament of Moses*, and after Paul's time *The Apocalypse of Baruch* and 4 Ezra (or 2 Esdras) are among the better-known examples.[8] Apocalyptic influenced *Jubilees* and the *Sibylline Oracles*, showing that Greek-speaking Judaism was affected; but rather than stressing new creation, these books tend to emphasize God's

---

[8] Klaus Koch, *The Rediscovery of Apocalyptic: A Polemical Work on a Neglected Area of Biblical Studies and its Damaging Effects*, trans. Margaret Kohl (London: SCM Press, 1972).

dividing history into ages, and the reality of revelation and of the invisible world. Paul, like the apocalyptic writers, sees the world as the theatre or stage on which God performs his *public acts* of redemption and salvation according to his *sovereign* purposes.

Nevertheless, Christians, according to Paul, still live under the present order of creation. Indeed, what is done 'in the body' gives visible expression to Christian discipleship. Both the world and the body represent the gifts of a loving God, and are to be viewed positively. Yet the *new* creation has also broken into the world through Christ, and this now coexists with the old. For Christians the new creation becomes the decisive and transforming dimension of their lives. Whereas much preaching today consists of anecdotes about human life, Paul's preaching was mainly about God, Christ, and the Holy Spirit. Perhaps this is why we easily miss some of the sheer excitement of the gospel.

The old and the new

Some describe this coexistence of two world-orders as the *overlapping* of the old and new ages. Hence a new order of 'knowing' is required for 'spiritual things', which goes beyond conventional perspective. In 1 Cor. 1.18—2.16 Paul makes it clear that the message about the cross is 'folly' to those who judge with the criteria of the old order alone. The cross becomes a stumbling-block (1 Cor. 1.18, 23). Paul urges a need for transformation, by which and in which the Holy Spirit conveys 'the mind of Christ' (1 Cor. 2.16). The old way of knowing is 'the wisdom of the world', which God's wisdom makes foolish (1 Cor. 1.20).

Hence Munzinger suggestively calls for a 'world-switch' or radical perspectival shift in which Christians view everything differently through 'an epistemological [or way of knowing] revolution'.[9] He argues that Christians need 'a renewed mind' (cf. Eph. 4.23). This constitutes both an event and a process. The event takes place when the Christian becomes united with Christ as a new creation. But he or she may not necessarily be conscious of this moment. Initially the

---

[9] André Munzinger, *Discerning the Spirits: Theological and Ethical Hermeneutics in Paul* (SNTSMS 140; Cambridge: Cambridge University Press, 2007), p. 164.

undeserved grace of God and the prayers of others may sustain this initiation. But this becomes a steady process of living out what has happened. Paul describes the event as rescue 'from the power of darkness', or as being 'transferred . . . into the kingdom of his (God's) beloved Son' (Col. 1.13). This must then be implemented by cultivating 'the mind of Christ' (1 Cor. 2.16; cf. 3.1–4), and L. S. Thornton has suggested an analogy. If a new plant or tree is grafted onto the old, there is a unique moment of grafting. But after this the two organisms become increasingly interactive and inseparable.[10] Alexandra Brown comments about some in Corinth: 'A transformation of consciousness has already occurred. Yet the transformation has been incomplete . . . their appropriation . . . of that calling is what Paul brings into bold relief . . . The gospel must be preached again.'[11]

It is true, then, that 'an immense cut' runs through Paul's thought. However, first, this concerns new creation, or the new order of being, and is not a psychological reflection of his conversion experience. Second, it does not tie everything to a dramatic event, as if to discount the long process of acquiring the mind of Christ, or, to return to earlier analogies, to discount the process of thawing out pockets of ice, or the process of travelling in a lifeboat. Paul's 'conversion' was unique in constituting also his call to preach the gospel to the Gentiles. Paul tells his readers how this took place on his way to Damascus, as he was seeking to persecute the Christian community (Gal. 1.13–17; cf. Acts 9.1–19; 22.3–16, and 26.12–18). Paul's words 'God . . . set me apart before I was born and called me through his grace' (Gal. 1.13) remind us of the terms of Jeremiah's call: 'Before I formed you in the womb I knew you, and before you were born I consecrated you; I appointed you a prophet to the nations' (Jer. 1.5). Like the apocalyptists, Paul saw his call as the act of God alone. As Johannes Munck and others have rightly argued, this call came 'out of the blue' without any preparation.[12] The utterance, 'It is hard for you to kick against the goads' (Acts 26.14) has nothing to do with a

---

[10] L. S. Thornton, *The Common Life in the Body of Christ* (London: Dacre Press, 1942; 3rd edn 1950), pp. 62–4.

[11] Brown, *The Cross and Human Transformation*, p. 30.

[12] Johannes Munck, *Paul and the Salvation of Mankind*, trans. Frank Clarke (London: SCM Press, 1959), pp. 11–35.

troubled conscience, but is a proverb meaning 'From now on you will have no discharge from the service that I, Christ, have laid on you.'[13]

The coexistence of the old order means that there is no short-cut which allows Christians to avoid growth and suffering. The Christian still experiences weakness, fallibility, suffering, and death. The cross and resurrection constitute the gateway to the new world. The Holy Spirit, new life, resurrection with Christ, and new creation characterize this. Nevertheless, together both worlds make their impact on the Christian before the last day and final resurrection of the body, even if the impact of the new order of existence is decisive and determinative. Paul is well aware of this ambiguous situation. He writes, 'Not that I have already reached the goal, but I press on . . . Beloved, I do not consider that I have made it on my own, but . . . I press on toward the goal' (Phil. 3.11–14).

Preaching to Greeks and the 'two ages'

The sharp cut between 'formerly' and 'now' is further softened by Paul's use of Greek and Graeco-Roman terminology to express his apocalyptic gospel. He is deeply indebted to Greek-speaking Judaism and to the Greek Old Testament or Septuagint. If he is to be Apostle to the Gentiles, it is virtually unintelligible for Paul simply to proclaim, 'The new age has dawned', or 'The kingdom of God is here' (cf. Mark 1.15), even if such language immediately resonates with Jerusalem Jews. The same gospel must be clothed with concepts that the Gentiles, 'God-fearers' (devout Gentiles) and Greek-speaking Jews could readily understand. This is another reason why Paul lives for us today. We, too, understand words such as 'Lord', 'salvation', and 'turn from' and 'turn to'. We can appreciate his careful use of Roman rhetorical forms (e.g. 1 Cor. 15.1–58) and his analogies from everyday life, which are almost as numerous as the parables of Jesus.[14] We can appreciate his social metaphor of 'adoption', and the buying and selling of slaves (Rom. 8.14; Gal. 4.6; 1 Cor. 6.20). His major concept of reconciliation, as removing estrangement or a barrier between two persons, may

---

[13] Munck, *Paul and the Salvation of Mankind*, p. 21.

[14] Herbert M. Gale, *The Use of Analogy in the Letters of Paul* (Philadelphia: Westminster Press, 1964).

have no explicit ancestry in the Old Testament, but it has a very contemporary ring (2 Cor. 5.20). We understand what it is to be heir to a will (Gal. 3.15—4.7), and to wait for the fulfilment of a promise. This requires trust in the faithfulness of God (Rom. 3.3; 1 Cor. 1.9; 2 Cor. 1.18; 1 Thess. 5.24).

Paul is concerned that the word of God should be 'near', or accessible (Rom. 10.8). In Christ God becomes 'thinkable' or 'conceivable'. To this end Paul no longer lives for himself (2 Cor. 5.15). He attempts to bring into accord the concepts of the Hebrew Bible and the earlier apostolic preaching with language and ideas which retain a currency in the Graeco-Roman world. Yet nothing compromises his proclamation of new creation (2 Cor. 5.17). Because Christians are under the new order, but have not yet become fully free of the old, Paul emphasizes the role of the Holy Spirit and of prayer in the context of our human weakness.

Paul's humour

We conclude this chapter with reference to one of Paul's uses of humour, which is still fully intelligible to the modern world, yet shows that God's grace is everything, and that even Paul is deprecating about his 'weakness'. It would be exceptionally heroic, we can imagine, for someone to be 'first over the wall' when one's army was besieging a city. The defenders would pour down burning oil and heavy stones on the heads of those who climbed the siege-ladders and sought bravely to be first over the wall. In 2 Corinthians 11 and 12 Paul is comparing his 'weakness' with the supposed self-glory of counterfeit apostles. Paul regarded the boasting-game as foolish. Still, he says, if you must know, I will boast of 'weakness'. He says in effect, I was first over the wall, all right, but in the other direction. When King Aretas or his troops were pursuing me, I was first to be let down in a basket over the wall of Damascus, to get away safely (2 Cor. 11.30–33). The audience would have appreciated this Pauline twist to a well-known example of bravery.

What emerges is a warm and human Paul, who is good at communication and recognizes the processes of growth in the Christian life, and yet who preserves what is important about apocalyptic. As J. Louis Martyn, Alexandra Brown, and others, rightly suggest, Paul uses 'performative' speech (or dynamic language, which constitutes action) to proclaim the transforming power of God.[15] It does something in the very saying of it; it does not merely describe. This is also known as a 'speech-act'; as Brown writes, 'Through the folly of the cross', Paul's language functions for 'God's destruction of the old world . . . and creation of the new world'.[16] This both preserves the contrast between two orders of existence, and allows for the steady process of transformation to 'the mind of Christ'.

---

[15] Brown, *The Cross and Human Transformation*, pp. 31–64; cf. John L. Austin, *How to Do Things with Words* (Oxford: Clarendon Press, 1962), on performatives.
[16] Brown, *The Cross and Human Transformation*, p. 96; cf. pp. 31–148.

3

Apostle to the Gentiles (1): traveller and missionary-pastor

Paul's life up to the first missionary journey

Before his call or conversion Paul had been a native of Tarsus, the leading city of Cilicia in Asia Minor. Greek was spoken there, especially for trade and business. Tarsus was less than ten miles from the sea, or just five miles from its lagoon-like harbour. Like Corinth, Tarsus became a busy, bustling, centre for shipping and trade. Paul learned there the craft of leatherwork (including tent-making), and this embraced shoes, wineskins, and much else. Welborn urges that the Greek word for his trade denotes a maker of stage properties.[1]

Tarsus probably included about 75,000 inhabitants, and attracted many cosmopolitan visitors. The land around it was fertile, and through a pass in the Tarsus Mountains it had an outlet for trade with the East. Mark Antony and the Romans had secured the city against pirates, and after Augustus, many of its more prominent residents received Roman citizenship. All of this stood Paul in good stead for his extensive travels and encounter with Corinth, which shared many of the characteristics of Tarsus, although on a larger scale. Like Corinth, Tarsus had a provincial academy, and temples to a plurality of pagan deities. Like Corinth, its people were regarded as flamboyant and verging on the arrogant.

We do not know how soon Paul was sent to Jerusalem to be trained in the Scriptures and in Judaism as a Pharisee. Willem van Unnik has argued that 'brought up in this city' (namely in Jerusalem, Acts 22.3)

---

[1] L. L. Welborn, *Paul, the Fool of Christ: A Study of 1 Corinthians 1—4 in the Comic-Philosophic Tradition* (London and New York: T. & T. Clark International/Continuum, 2005), pp. 11–12.

applies to his boyhood.[2] He learned more of Hebrew and Aramaic from Gamaliel, and it is widely assumed that the threefold legacy of Jerusalem, Greek-speaking Jews and Gentiles, and Rome, all contributed to his ministry. In addition to visits to the Jerusalem Temple, Paul would have regularly worshipped in Jewish synagogues. In the synagogue he would probably have heard and read the Hebrew Bible with the Targums, which were Aramaic glosses on, or paraphrases of, the Hebrew text. Many Jews would be more fluent in Greek than in Hebrew or Aramaic. Paul was proud of this Jewish heritage, and as a devout Jew had 'violently persecuted' the early Christians as a dangerous and heretical sect of Judaism (Gal. 1.13). But he also knew enough of the Greek-speaking Jewish and Gentile worlds later to use concepts that were readily understandable among Gentiles.

Immediately after his call and conversion, Paul went away 'at once into Arabia' (Gal. 1.17). This included a large area east of Syria and Israel. Both Greek and Aramaic were spoken south-east of Damascus. We cannot be certain whether this visit took place as a retreat for prayer and reflection or whether Paul soon began to engage in missionary proclamation of the gospel. Working backwards from his encounter with the Proconsul Gallio in Corinth around AD 52 (or 51) we follow Jerome Murphy-O'Connor in estimating this visit to Arabia in AD 33 or 34.[3] Eventually Paul must have preached, for opposition forced him back to Damascus, probably from AD 34 to 37. Galatians 1.23 recounts how he 'proclaimed the faith he once tried to destroy'. The stay in Damascus was interrupted by Paul's first visit to Jerusalem in AD 36 or 37, and here he stayed with Peter for a fortnight. In spite of Paul's protestations to the Galatians that he did not learn the gospel from *human* sources (Gal. 1.11, 12), Paul must have spent this time familiarizing himself with Jesus' earthly life and passion, and with earliest apostolic preaching. As C. H. Dodd drily comments, when Paul met Peter, 'We may presume they did not spend all their time talking about the weather.'[4]

---

[2] Willem C. van Unnik, *Tarsus or Jerusalem: The City of Paul's Youth*, trans. George Ogg (London: Epworth Press, 1962); cf. also Ronald F. Hock, *The Social Context of Paul's Ministry: Tentmaking and Apostleship* (Philadelphia: Fortress Press, 1980).

[3] Jerome Murphy-O'Connor, *Paul: A Critical Life* (Oxford: Oxford University Press, 1997), pp. 7–22.

[4] C. H. Dodd, *The Apostolic Preaching and its Developments* (London: Hodder & Stoughton, 1936), p. 26.

The years 36 or 37 to 46 are often known as 'the hidden years', at the end of which Paul visited Jerusalem a second time, probably around AD 52 (Gal. 2.1). We know little about these hidden years, except that most see the persecutions and trials listed in 2 Cor. 11.23–33, which included floggings, markings, and imprisonment, as belonging to this period.

Cyprus and Asia Minor

After this time Barnabas looked for Paul (perhaps as a result of conversations with Peter, or on hearing of Paul's outreach work) and found him in Tarsus (Acts 11.25, 26). Acts recounts Paul's stay in Antioch for a whole year, where he proclaimed the gospel and shared in pastoral oversight of the church (11.26). Antioch was the seat of government for the Roman province which combined Syria and Cilicia. Syrian Antioch was the third city of the Empire, exceeded only by Rome and Alexandria, and it boasted a population of probably half a million. Here the church found a 'base' for its early outreach. Many turned to God (cf. Acts 11.20), and some had come from Cyprus, so it is not surprising that the Church (in Jerusalem) commissioned Barnabas and Paul to undertake 'the first missionary journey', as it is often called, based chiefly in Cyprus. Paul did not go as an individual 'freelance' missionary, but as a commissioned representative of the churches of Jerusalem and Antioch with co-workers, after prayer and the laying on of hands (Acts 13.1, 2).

Paul called on his Greek-speaking background and knowledge of the Greek Bible or Septuagint. The visit (with Barnabas) resulted in conversion for Sergius Paulus, Proconsul of Cyprus, but also a confrontation with Elymas, a pagan magician (cf. Acts 13.4–15). After Cyprus, they took the gospel to Perga, Pamphilia, and Antioch of Pisidia, all in Asia Minor. It is difficult to exaggerate the importance of Paul's knowledge of Greek, even for this 'first' missionary journey. Chilton calls the Septuagint 'the seedbed of Paul's life'.[5] The great centres of Greek-speaking and Diaspora Judaism far outnumbered the relatively small population of Aramaic-speaking Jews. Christopher Stanley has undertaken a careful study of Paul's respective use of

---

[5] Bruce Chilton, *Rabbi Paul: An Intellectual Biography* (New York and London: Doubleday, 2004), p. 14.

Hebrew and Greek Bibles and their variant texts. He concludes, 'His primary text is clearly the Greek translation known today as the "Septuagint" (LXX)', or sometimes a variant of the Septuagint or LXX.[6]

Acts portrays the mission of the gospel in successive stages: first to the Jews of Jerusalem and Judaea (Acts 1—5); second, to Greek-speaking Jews (6.1—8.40); third, to Jews and Gentiles of Antioch and Asia Minor; fourth, to Greece itself; and fifth and finally to Rome. Luke identifies the importance of the 'Hellenists' in 6.1—8.40; and then of the mission to the Gentiles, culminating in the Council of Jerusalem in Acts 15. Paul preaches the gospel 'to the Jews first' (Rom. 1.16), and in his first and second missionary journey preaches first in the synagogues, and then to the Gentiles (Gal. 1.16). Greek-speaking Judaism served as his 'base', and he preached in the synagogues of Thessalonica, Philippi, Ephesus, and Rome. The importance of the Septuagint is underlined by the legend of its origin in the *Letter of Aristeas*. Allegedly King Ptolemy of Egypt sent Aristeas to gather 72 elders from Jerusalem, who completed the Greek translation from the Hebrew in 72 days. The Septuagint places the books of the Old Testament in a different order, and includes the 'Apocryphal' books of Intertestamental times. It culminates with the prophecy and apocalyptic of Isaiah, Jeremiah, Ezekiel, and Daniel, and projects a more 'universalist' theology than the Hebrew Bible.

Greek-speaking Jews in Rome, Alexandria, Antioch, and Thessalonica had their own Hellenistic-Jewish literature. This included the Wisdom of Solomon, 2–4 Maccabees, the writings of Philo of Alexandria and Josephus, the *Letter of Aristeas*, and later the *Sibylline Oracles*, *2 Enoch*, and other writings. Typically the Wisdom of Solomon (which belongs to the Apocrypha and finds a place in Roman Catholic Bibles) has material like the synagogue sermons of many Greek-speaking Jewish centres. Written perhaps around 40 BC it speaks of the folly of idolatry, and of its consequences in immoral conduct (for example, in Wisd. 14.8–14 and 15.1–6). Some draw attention to similarities with Paul in Rom. 1.18–32, when he turns to lack of 'excuses' on the part of the Jew as well as the Gentile (Rom. 2.1–24; cf. Rom. 3.23). And 4 Maccabees (*c.* AD 18–100) has a typically

---

[6] Christopher D. Stanley, *Paul and the Language of Scripture: Citation Technique in the Pauline Epistles and Contemporary Literature* (SNTSMS 69; Cambridge: Cambridge University Press, 1992), p. 254.

Hellenistic emphasis on the supremacy of reason, although it underlines the place of righteous suffering and the atoning effect of the blood of the martyrs (4 Macc. 6.28–29; 17.21). Paul would be closely familiar with these themes, although his concept of resurrection stands in sharp contrast to the notion of 'immortality' in the book of Wisdom.

Henry Chadwick declares that the works of Philo 'throw more light on the words of Paul . . . than any other single non-Christian source'.[7] Paul may not have read his writings at first hand, but Philo was broadly Paul's contemporary and a great influence. Philo wants Greeks and Romans to admire the best in Judaism, and he tries to be loyal to both; he sees Moses as the archetypal philosopher, who even anticipated Plato at many points. He regularly allegorizes the Septuagint: God, as a spiritual being, does not 'plant' trees in Eden, and Adam cannot 'hide' from God. God plants 'virtues' (Gen. 2.8; 3.8), and 'Adam, where are you?' does not imply divine ignorance. God belongs to Plato's realm of perfection. In common with synagogue sermons, Philo attacks idolatry, as many Stoics did. Some phrases can be found in both Paul and Philo. We see 'as if in a mirror' (1 Cor. 13.12); we have our citizenship in heaven (Phil. 3.20); and we know God 'even as I have been fully known' (1 Cor. 13.12). Josephus is less important for Paul, because he partly postdates him (*c.* 37–100), and many of his writings are historical. But he gives us first hand knowledge of the Pharisees and Qumran, and uses the Septuagint in his work *The Antiquities of the Jews*.

We have recounted Paul's travels up to the end of the first missionary journey. We should note, though, that he is as much a *pastor* as he is a missionary on the move. In the face of hostility at Iconium, Barnabas and Paul 'remained there for a long time' (Acts 14.3). After success but also stoning in Derbe, they returned to Lystra and Antioch, and 'strengthened . . . the disciples, and encouraged them to continue in the faith' (Acts 14.21, 22). They 'appointed elders for them in each church' (14.23). When they returned to Antioch, they reported to the church (14.25, 26). After the Council of Jerusalem Paul and Barnabas visited believers 'in every city where we proclaimed the word of the Lord' (Acts 15.36). Paul spent further

[7] Henry Chadwick, 'St. Paul and Philo of Alexandria', *Bulletin of the John Rylands Library* 48 (1966), p. 287; cf. pp. 286–307.

time in Syria and in Cilicia with Silas (1 Thess. 1.1). He experienced 'daily pressure' from his 'anxiety for all the churches' (2 Cor. 11.28); Paul then sought to revisit the churches of Asia Minor.

Mention has been made of the Council of Jerusalem (Acts 15), which the latest scholarship dates around AD 48–9. Elders called the conference to produce a common policy upon the basis on which Gentiles could become or remain Christians. Were they, in effect, first to become good Jews, observing all the Jewish laws, including circumcision and dietary laws? Paul and Barnabas were representatives who spoke (Acts 15.2–3 and 12), as were Peter (vv. 7–11) and James (vv. 13–21). The speeches told of God's welcome to the Gentiles and its scriptural warrant. In the end the apostles did not impose circumcision and all dietary laws, but only those to which Jewish Christians were sensitive.

The advance to Greece

As Paul revisited the churches, the Holy Spirit began blocking his progress through illness and other means, pressing him onwards towards Troas on the coast. The 'second missionary journey' was well under way, and Paul received, in both senses, a 'vision' for Greece. He dreamed of 'the man of Macedonia' (northern Greece) who beckoned to him to cross the sea. This might well have been Luke, since Acts begins here to speak of 'we', as it narrates this journey. Timothy, Silas (or Silvanus), Luke, and Paul crossed to Europe, and arrived in Samothracia. They at once visited Philippi and Thessalonica, the two most important towns of Macedonia.

The party stayed 'for some days' in the Roman colony of Philippi (Acts 16.12). Lydia was baptized, and they stayed in her home. But their encounter with a fortune-telling slave girl provoked hostility and attack. Paul and Silas were beaten, flogged, and thrown into prison (Acts 16.22–24). Luke's 'take' of the episode in Acts 16.31 suggests Paul's humour; according to Luke an earthquake blew open all the prison doors, and in reply to the jailer's question, 'What must I do to be saved?' Paul exploited a double meaning by replying 'Believe on the Lord Jesus and you will be "saved"'! Next day the magistrates released Paul, but Paul protested that as Roman citizens, they should not have been flogged. The magistrates apologized, and the group returned to Lydia's home.

The next stage of travel in Greece was to journey to the synagogue in Thessalonica. The largest city in Macedonia, Rome had granted it autonomy and its own city-rulers. We have an account of events in 1 Thessalonians, as well as in Acts 17.1–15. Paul proclaimed the gospel for three weeks every Sabbath in the synagogue. Many became Christians, but other Jews were jealous and provoked a riot. They dragged Jason, Paul's host, to the officials, who demanded bail for Paul's good conduct or his departure. That night the Christians sent him off to Beroea, presumably to ensure Jason's safety. There the Jews were more receptive to his message, and many came to faith in Christ. But Jews came from Thessalonica to destabilize the situation. Silas and Timothy remained, but Paul was escorted to Athens, the capital of Achaia, or southern Greece.

Paul's visit to Athens and especially to Corinth forms the climax of this 'second missionary journey'. Paul was disturbed at the city's being 'full of idols' (Acts 17.16), and addressed Epicurean and Stoic philosophers on Mars Hill, near the Areopagus – a plaque marks the spot today. He congratulated them on their devotion, and spoke of the one God, who created the world. Many Stoics would share this belief, but when Paul proclaimed the resurrection, this was a different matter. Many scoffed, although some were persuaded. The little verse 'After this Paul left Athens and went to Corinth' (Acts 18.1) covers a long, arduous journey on foot, of some forty or fifty miles, since it is unlikely that he went by sea.

Corinth

The road passed through Eleusis and Megara, which was the seat of Socratic philosophy after the death of Socrates in Athens. According to 2 Cor. 1.19, Timothy and Silvanus seem to have rejoined Paul now. He would have reached Megara on the first nightfall. The first part of the second day of his journey brought Paul into dangerous country (cf. 2 Cor. 11.26), but later he would reach the Corinthian *territorium*, where he would have seen a jostling, busy, crowd, some clearing up after the Isthmian Games. As he neared the city, the towering height of Acro-Corinth, formerly the citadel and site of the temple to Aphrodite, would have dominated the view. Corinth was a busy, bustling, cosmopolitan port-city. In 146 BC the city had rebelled against Rome, and the Roman general Mummius sacked the city. However, in 44 BC Julius Caesar refounded it as a Roman colony, mainly for the veterans from his legions. It also served as a magnet for trade and business, for which many freedmen, freed-women, and slaves came for work and entrepreneurial opportunities. With its own port facing east (Cenchreae) and another facing west (Lechaeum), it had become the gateway for trade and business between Ephesus and Asia Minor to the east, and Rome and Italy to the west.

Furthermore, Corinth stood on an isthmus that controlled the north–south route between Macedonia (northern Greece), and the Peloponnese, or southern Greece. It stood at the cross-roads of trade routes. Compared with ancient but sleepy Athens, with dreams of a once glorious past, Corinth had become the place to make or to lose a quick fortune. Trade was so prosperous that the city regularly used the *diolkos*, or paved way, between the two harbours, which enabled lighter ships to be transported across the isthmus on rollers to avoid time lost in unloading and re-loading. Many things ensured its wealth, self-sufficiency, and competitiveness. It produced large quan-tities of bricks, clay tiles, and terracotta artefacts; the Pereine Springs guaranteed a large water-supply; the Isthmian Games, held every two years, promised a huge influx of tourists. Much depended on the out-come of Paul's preaching here.

Paul understandably came in 'fear and trembling' (1 Cor. 2.1–5), but determined to shun audience-pleasing rhetoric, in favour of an honest proclamation of the cross. Many viewed the message of the cross as folly (1 Cor. 1.18–25). But the household of Stephanas were 'the first converts of Achaia', as well as Crispus and Gaius (1 Cor. 1.14–16; 16.15). Many Jews opposed him, but many Gentiles accepted his message. Perhaps this underlined his resolve to go 'to the Gentiles' (Acts 18.6–10). Paul stayed with fellow Jewish Christians who were of the same trade, Aquila and Priscilla. They had probably been expelled from Rome by the edict of Claudius, and were already believers.

The Corinthian church contained those who would prefer that Paul lectured as a professional rhetorician. But he did not want to be beholden to wealthy patrons (1 Cor. 9.3–18). So he laboured in a small workshop (about 13 ft × 8 ft), probably on the hottest side of the market forum, where Aquila and Priscilla would have had sleeping-quarters above the ground floor. Here he preached and gossiped the gospel to his customers for 18 months. He was a pastor as well as a travelling missionary. Murphy-O'Connor calls Corinth 'a wide-open boom town'.[8]

Many of the problems which later arose in 1 Corinthians show the self-sufficiency, complacency, and competitiveness of the church in Corinth. But Paul remained in Corinth for a year and a half including the period of the Isthmian Games (probably AD 51). He stayed until the Jews made a united attack on him and took him before the tribunal (Acts 18.12). The Proconsul Gallio refused to implement the charges, so the Jews took it out on Sosthenes. Paul eventually sailed with Priscilla and Aquila to Ephesus, leaving from Cenchreae. From Ephesus Paul travelled to Caesarea and then again to Jerusalem. His pleas in 1 and 2 Corinthians about a collection of money for the poor in Jerusalem show his concern to remain in solidarity with the 'mother' church.

The second missionary journey had accomplished huge results. It had been eventful and often very dangerous. Paul had endured imprisonment and persecution, but he had established the gospel in the strategic centres of a cosmopolitan and trading population in Philippi, Thessalonica, and especially Corinth. An inscription found in modern times concerning the Proconsulship of Gallio dates this visit to Corinth.

---

[8] Murphy-O'Connor, *Paul: A Critical Life*, p. 108.

4

Apostle to the Gentiles (2): traveller, pastor, letter-writer

Letter-writing at Corinth

At Corinth Paul also began writing several of his extant letters. These included 1 Thessalonians, and Galatians (depending on geographical and historical factors), and perhaps 2 Thessalonians, if we assume that it was written by Paul.

In 1 Thessalonians Paul shows his pastoral concern for the community which he had to leave before he wished to do so. The letter would be read aloud to the assembled church, although some copies would also be made.[1] Possibly Paul dictated it to Silas, to Timothy, or to a scribe or secretary. Paul thanks God for them, and writes to them as a model church (1.1–10). Hardship and persecution came his way, but on his part Paul tenderly cared for them like a gentle nurse (2.1–20). Timothy has at last brought good news of their faith, steadfastness, and love; and, Paul asserts, 'Night and day we pray most earnestly that we may see you face to face' (3.10; cf. 3.1–3). He urges that their lifestyle may be 'holy', and that they do not grieve for Christians who have died, as if they would miss participation in the end events (4.1–14). They will be raised with Christ at the *Parousia*, or final coming, and 'so we will be with the Lord for ever' (4.17; cf. 4.15—5.11). Finally he adds some last exhortations, including necessary patience with the weak (5.14), and adds a prayer for blessing and greeting (5.12–28).[2]

The date of Galatians is a matter of debate. Depending on whether 'Galatia' means the original Galatian territory which stretched north

---

[1] E. Randolph Richards, *Paul and First-century Letter Writing: Secretaries, Composition, and Collection* (Downers Grove: InterVarsity Press, 2004); and Jerome Murphy-O'Connor, *Paul the Letter-Writer: His World, His Options, His Skills* (Collegeville, MN: Liturgical Press, 1995).

[2] Cf. Ernest Best, *A Commentary on the First and Second Epistles to the Thessalonians* (London: A. & C. Black, 1972).

to the Black Sea (the 'North Galatian' theory) or the area already visited by Paul in Phrygia (the 'South Galatian' theory) the letter is either later or belongs this period. Probably most scholars favour the 'South Galatian' theory (and thus the earlier dating of the letter), because it fits Roman nomenclature. Paul mentions Barnabas who was with him on the first missionary journey, and some references would fit closely with the Acts account of his first missionary journey (Acts 14.11–19; Gal. 2.1 and 4.14). A detailed discussion of this well-known controversy is provided by F. F. Bruce.[3] It has been said that Galatians stands in relation to Romans as a quick draft to a finished product. Bruce regards Galatians as probably earlier even than 1 and 2 Thessalonians, written as the admission of the Gentiles was becoming *the* burning question on the eve of the Jerusalem conference of Acts 15. But many date it later, and the arguments on both sides are not entirely conclusive. Some argue that Paul's allusion to Jerusalem in Gal. 2.1–10 refers to the Jerusalem Council, in which case Galatians postdates it.

Paul states his astonishment that Christians are turning away from the genuine gospel, and insists that his 'gospel' came by true revelation from God (Gal. 1.6–24). It was recognized as authentic by the 'core' apostles, James, Peter, and John (2.1–10). Admittedly Peter seemed to vacillate at Antioch, but Paul insisted that union with Christ meant freedom 'from the works of the law' (2.11–20). The Galatians, or many of them, seem irrational, almost hypnotized, failing to recognize that to be put right with God by grace through faith makes the law, in this sense, a passing thing (3.1–6). This is all part of God's long-standing purpose. We can see the principle in Abraham, before the law came through Moses. Christ himself is 'cursed' on the cross by the law (3.7–29). Galatians 4 and 5.1–14 press home the argument that Christians are 'free' sons or children of the promise, who come to God by grace and faith, not by the Jewish law. Galatians 5.13— 6.24 adds a series of practical exhortations. This is Paul's most passionate letter, because the heart of the gospel is at stake. He will reformulate these ideas, however, with greater precision and detail in Romans.

---

[3] F. F. Bruce, *The Epistle to the Galatians: A Commentary on the Greek Text* (NIGTC; Grand Rapids: Eerdmans and Exeter: Paternoster, 1982), pp. 3–18.

Second Thessalonians is regarded as Pauline by many, including Best, but not by all writers. Best comments that the phrasing and vocabulary of 1 Thessalonians was fresh in Paul's mind, although he had to address new problems.[4] This is even more likely if Paul kept a copy of 1 Thessalonians. The church faced opposition (2 Thess. 1.4–6); they misunderstood Paul's teaching about the Day of the Lord (2.1–12); and it was reported that some Christians were indolent and disruptive (3.6–15). But Paul expresses satisfaction with this community, although he corrects these misconceptions.

All this was probably written from Corinth from AD 50–1 or 52 at the latest. Paul left for Ephesus in AD 52, and went on to Caesarea and Jerusalem, leaving Aquila and Priscilla at Ephesus (Acts 18.19–23).

The third missionary journey and letter-writing at Ephesus

The so-called 'third missionary journey' takes place mainly in Ephesus and its surrounding territory. But this is more a pastoral revisitation than a missionary journey, beginning in the spring of AD 53. Ephesus was the leading city of Asia, from where Paul visited Phrygia. Luke recounts an unusual phenomenon of those Christians at Ephesus who had somehow missed out on Christian teaching about the Holy Spirit, and received instruction and the laying on of hands by Paul (Acts 19.1–7). He spoke for three months in the synagogue, and then in the lecture-hall of Tyrannus, probably when it was too hot to be used by its owner. Luke says that he continued this for two years (Acts 19.10). Luke records great success in Ephesus, including the burning of books on magic. He also recounts the minor riot of silversmiths, who accused Paul of damaging their trade and the reputation of Ephesus (Acts 19.23–41). Paul left Ephesus for Macedonia, exercising pastoral care for three months (Acts 20.1–3). After facing plots against him and travelling in the region, Paul returned to Ephesus, giving counsel to many.

---

[4] Best, *A Commentary on the First and Second Epistle to the Thessalonians*, pp. 58–59; cf. Charles A. Wanemaker, *The Epistles to the Thessalonians: A Commentary on the Greek Text* (Grand Rapids: Eerdmans and Carlisle: Paternoster, 1990), pp. 57–60.

To Paul in Ephesus came an oral report of the church in Corinth from Chloe's people (1 Cor. 1.11), supplemented by a letter from Corinth (1 Cor. 7.1; cf. 8.1) and the welcome visit from Corinth of Stephanas, Fortunatus, and Achaicus (1 Cor. 16.17). They provided, as it were, a little piece of Corinth, and so 'refreshed my spirit' (16.18), especially since Stephanas was Paul's first convert in Achaia.

The reports and the letter gave concern, but were mixed. Paul wrote 1 Corinthians in AD 53 or 54 (at the latest in 55) first to re-proclaim the message of the cross and its incompatibility with 'splits' (Greek, *schismata*) in 1 Cor. 1.18—2.5. These were not theological divisions, but personality-centred power groups.[5] This epistle has no less about undeserved grace than Romans: without Christ they are nothing. The wisdom of the Spirit issues in the mindset of Christ (2.5–16). Ministers should be neither overrated nor neglected (3.5–21). Some moral issues are straightforward and call for change, where necessary. In those days 'going to law' involves the manipulation of a less wealthy fellow Christian (5.1—6.20). Other ethical issues are more complex grey areas, including marriage and remarriage and 'food offered to idols'. The circumstances have to be taken into consideration (7.1—11.1). Paul then turns to other questions of worship, including attire, the Lord's Supper, and spiritual gifts (11.2—14.40). 'Prophecy' probably means pastorally applied preaching of the gospel, as we suggested above.[6] Paul then gives a masterly treatise on the resurrection, which forms the climax and crown of the epistle and addresses several grounds of doubt (15.1–58).[7] Finally Paul discusses the collection, forthcoming visits, and exchanges of greeting (16.1–20). This letter gives a varied and practical insight into Paul's concern for the gospel, and his pastoral and mission strategy.

Some date Colossians in this period, depending on whether Paul was in prison during this time in Ephesus (Col. 4.3, 10, 18). Dunn acknowledges that the decision is difficult, but in the end calls it 'late

---

[5] Thiselton, *The First Epistle to the Corinthians*, pp. 107–223; Thiselton, *First Corinthians*, pp. 38–49; David R. Hall, *The Unity of the Corinthian Correspondence* (London and New York: T. & T. Clark International, 2003), pp. 3–50; cf. also Welborn, *Paul the Fool of Christ*.

[6] Thomas W. Gillespie, *The First Theologians: A Study in Early Christian Prophecy* (Grand Rapids: Eerdmans, 1994), esp. pp. 178–263.

[7] Karl Barth, *The Resurrection of the Dead*, trans. H. J. Stenning (London: Hodder & Stoughton, 1933), pp. 17–18, and 113, 115, and 190–201.

Paul', before the emergence of a 'post-Pauline' theology.[8] Likewise we do not know whether Philemon was written from Caesarea, Ephesus, or Rome, though Onesimus, his runaway slave, came from Colossus.

We know, however, that Paul spent three years of hard toil at Ephesus, from where he undertook short journeys to proclaim the gospel and to strengthen the churches. Those who do not place Galatians in the period of the second journey at Corinth place it here at Ephesus. The silversmiths' riot may have occurred when Paul was trying to write. It is likely that the Second Epistle to the Corinthians followed from here, although many divide 2 Corinthians 1—9 from 2 Corinthians 10—13, and recall Paul's 'previous letter to Corinth' (1 Cor. 5.9), making four letters in all. Although 2 Corinthians is a deeply personal letter, we do not know (as the Corinthians would have done) its precise circumstances. Paul expresses his thanks to God and his relief: 'Thanks be to God, who in Christ always leads us in triumph', but the triumph is God's act in Christ (2 Cor. 2.14). Paul admits, 'We were so utterly, unbearably crushed, that we despaired of life itself. Indeed, we felt that we had received the sentence of death' (Phillips paraphrases: 'the end of our tether'), so that we should rely 'not on ourselves but on God who raises the dead' (2 Cor. 1.8–9). He does not represent a mixture of 'yes' and 'no' (1.17–21). There were good reasons why he did not visit Corinth (1.23—2.11).

As in 1 Corinthians, Paul asserts that the Holy Spirit gives life, but that this does not exempt apostles from suffering and hardship. 'We are afflicted in every way, but not crushed; perplexed but not driven to despair; persecuted but not forsaken; struck down, but not destroyed; always carrying in the body the death of Jesus, so that the life of Jesus may also be made visible in our bodies' (2 Cor. 4.8–10). The Christian life, as well as Paul's, is marked by death and suffering in this world, but by life and resurrection in the new order. Thus, 'the One who raised the Lord Jesus will raise us also with Jesus' (4.14). The great difference between the two orders is that 'What can be seen is temporary; but what cannot be seen is eternal' (4.18). For we walk

---

[8] James D. G. Dunn, *The Epistles to the Colossians and to Philemon: A Commentary on the Greek Text* (Grand Rapids: Eerdmans and Carlisle: Paternoster, 1996), pp. 39–40.

by faith not by sight (5.2). Paul's aim is to be pleasing to God. 'If any-one is in Christ, [as we saw, the Greek has no verb] – a new creation' (5.17). In ministry 'we are ambassadors for Christ' (5.20), whether in honour or dishonour, good repute or ill (6.8). The Corinthians are to follow the example of Christ, who 'though he was rich, yet for our sakes became poor' (8.9).

At chapters 10—13, 2 Corinthians changes key. Paul considers the claims of 'the false apostles' and their self-commendation. Self-promotion was typical of Corinth. But, as for me, states Paul, 'If I must boast, I will boast of the things that show my weakness' (2 Cor. 11.30), like Paul's escape at first over the wall (11.33). His 'thorn in the flesh' (or sharp physical pain) is a sign of authentic apostleship. Unlike the false apostles the essence of apostleship is to be a trans-parent window through which we all can see the cross, not human 'success'.[9] God's grace is sufficient for the true apostle; God's power is made perfect in weakness (12.9). Paul concludes, 'Test your-selves . . . put all things in order . . . agree with one another' (13.5, 11).

Towards the close of this period of the so-called third missionary journey, Paul reflected that he had now planted the gospel in strategic centres of Asia Minor (especially Ephesus), Macedonia (especially Thessalonica), and Greece proper (especially Corinth) (Rom. 15.19, 23). His eyes now looked towards Italy and Rome, and even beyond it to Spain (Rom. 15.23–24; 16.28). He would carry the gospel westward, using Rome as his 'base', as Ephesus had been for Asia Minor. He therefore wrote the Epistle to the Romans, to confirm his 'gospel', to prepare the Roman church for his coming, and to commend Phoebe and other friends. This epistle, however, was not written from Ephesus. Paul had returned to Corinth, from where he wrote Romans. For a long time Paul had wanted to visit Rome (Rom. 1.10–13), but had been prevented from doing so. Now he writes this letter before he journeys to Jerusalem (Rom. 15.25). Before arriving in Rome, he has to go to Jerusalem with the collection from Greece and Macedonia, for the relief of poor Christians (15.25–27).

---

[9] Jeffrey A. Crafton, *The Agency of the Apostle: A Dramatistic Analysis of Paul's Response to Conflict in 2 Corinthians* (JSNTSup 51; Sheffield: Sheffield Academic Press, 1991), esp. pp. 61–4; cf. Murray J. Harris, *The Second Epistle to the Corinthians: A Commentary on the Greek Text* (NIGTC; Grand Rapids: Eerdmans, 2005); and Margaret E. Thrall, *A Critical and Exegetical Commentary on the Second Epistle to the Corinthians*, 2 vols (Edinburgh: T. & T. Clark, 1994 and 2000).

He probably spent three more months in Corinth (cf. Acts 20.1–6). Phoebe probably took the letter to Rome. It was written between AD 55 and 59, probably in 56.

We shall consider Romans in detail when we examine Paul's teaching on justification and election. Meanwhile, by way of summary, we note that Rom. 1.18—4.25 places both Jew and Gentile in a dire state without the grace of God. But by grace and promise, God counts believers as right with him through Jesus Christ. Paul here expounds his introductory theme, 'He who is righteous by faith shall live' (Rom. 1.17). Then in 5.1—8.39 he expounds union with Christ or being 'in Christ' as an outworking of this. He turns to the implications for Israel, and for Jew and Gentile, in 9.1—11.32, culminating in praise for God's faithfulness and sovereignty over history (11.33–36). Finally, he speaks of the outworking of the gospel in everyday terms.[10]

It is not surprising that parallels with 1 Corinthians were perhaps recalled in Corinth, and parallels with Galatians are strong, where Paul first sets out these common themes. According to Luke, a plot against Paul meant that he left Corinth for Troas (accompanied, as usual, by co-workers, who this time included Sopater, Timothy, and probably Luke, among others (Acts 20.3–6). Paul preached in Troas, and after stopping in Lesbos sailed to Mytilene and then to Miletus. There elders from Ephesus met him, and he preached his farewell sermon to them. We cannot think of Paul as a harsh and insensitive controversialist or misogynist when we read that (according to Luke), 'There was much weeping . . . they embraced Paul and kissed him, grieving . . . that they would not see him again' (Acts 20.37–38).

The party then set sail first for Cos and Rhodes, and then went on to Tyre. Christians there urge Paul 'through the Spirit . . . not to go to Jerusalem' (Acts 21.4). But they saw Paul on board ship to Caesarea, where Agabus again said through the Spirit that Paul would be bound in Jerusalem and handed over to Gentiles (21.11). Paul expressed his willingness to die there. Luke tells us that the Jerusalem Christians warmly welcomed Paul (21.17), and praised God

---

[10] See C. E. B. Cranfield, *A Critical and Exegetical Commentary on the Epistle to the Romans*, 2 vols (International Critical Commentary; Edinburgh: T. & T. Clark, 1975 and 1979); and James D. G. Dunn, *Romans 1—8* and *Romans 9—16* (Dallas, TX: Word Books, 1988).

for what had been achieved through Paul (21.20). The collection would have shown that Paul's Gentile communities stood in solidarity with them; and this ends the so-called third missionary journey. Paul exhibited his sensitivity towards Jerusalem Christians and Jews, and this involved him in going to the Temple and taking a vow. But Paul's being in the Temple outraged some Jews.

From Jerusalem to Rome

Luke recounts events which cannot be reconstructed from Paul's epistles (Acts 21.27—25.12). By way of summary, according to Luke's narrative, Jews from Asia provoked mob violence, and tried to kill Paul. He was saved only by the intervention of the Roman Tribune and his soldiers. The Tribune placed Paul in protective custody, and allowed him to address the crowd. Paul again stated his loyalty to Judaism and recounted his call as a Christian (22.3–23). But when he mentioned the Gentiles, the crowd again erupted. The Tribune took Paul to the barracks and had him flogged and examined. Again, Paul raised his inherited Roman citizenship. Jews took a pledge to have him killed; but Paul's nephew heard of the plot, and the Tribune ordered two centurions to take 200 soldiers and 200 auxiliary spearmen to escort Paul safely to Caesarea, and to report to the Governor, Felix. Paul gave his defence to Felix, but, hoping for a bribe and to please the Jews, Felix kept him in jail for two years at Caesarea.

Some suggest that Paul wrote some of the 'prison epistles' from Caesarea during this time, perhaps including Colossians and/or Philippians. We shall postpone a consideration of these letters, however, until we consider Paul's view of Christ in Chapter 5. After two years Festus succeeded Felix as Governor. Jews continued threats and violence, and Festus, for the sake of the Jews, gave Paul the option of having another trial in Jerusalem, or making appeal to the Emperor. The climax of this narrative is Paul's appeal to the Emperor, who would now have been Nero (Acts 25.12). Punctuated by further Pauline speeches and testimony before King Agrippa (Acts 26.1–29), Acts chapters 27 and 28 recount Paul's hazardous journey from Caesarea to Rome, including the experience of a dangerous storm near to Crete, and a shipwreck at Malta. After a three-month delay, Paul sailed to Italy, and finally reached Rome. Luke says that Paul remained there for two whole years, proclaiming the kingdom of God and teaching about Christ 'without hindrance' (Acts 28.31).

If he was released, Paul would have gone on to Spain. We do not know what occurred. Many consider that Paul wrote Philippians and Colossians, and perhaps even Ephesians and possibly the letters to Timothy and to Titus, from Rome. It is credible that an older and semi-confined Paul was concerned for church order and stability, rather than his earlier themes. All we know for certain is that he proclaimed the gospel and pastored the church from Jerusalem to Rome, facing death-threats and suffering persecution and hardships. Nevertheless he obeyed his call to be Apostle to the Gentiles. Most centres in the Empire had heard the gospel, and its echoes remain.

5

Jesus Christ in Paul

If we want to avoid making Paul seem dead and remote, the worst thing is to imagine that he simply ascribes to Christ a number of creedal titles, such as 'Lord', 'Christ', 'Son of God', and so on, as if he were a theologian checking a 'correct' view of the person Jesus Christ. This is a long way from the truth. Usually the terms arise from practical experience, even if they also imply a state of affairs.

Jesus Christ as Lord

Paul's favourite term for Jesus Christ is 'Lord' (Greek, *Kyrios*). But, as many have pointed out, what *Lord* means in practical terms is most clearly seen in Paul's correlative term *slave* or *servant*. To call Christ one's *Lord* means to be wholly at his disposal. Bultmann sees that it implies Christian freedom, for under Christ's Lordship, Christians no longer bear responsibility for themselves; for their well-being is the responsibility of their Lord, at whose disposal they are and to whom they belong. Bultmann declares that the Christian 'no longer belongs to himself (1 Cor. 6.19). He no longer bears the care for himself . . . yielding himself entirely to the grace of God . . . "None of us lives to himself, and none of us dies to himself. If we live, we live to the Lord; and if we die, we die to the Lord. So whether we live or die we are the Lord's" (Rom. 14.7–8).'[1] This, Bultmann says, implies true freedom, for the slave can commit his or her welfare simply to the Lord.

What did being a *slave* imply in the world of Paul's day? At one extreme, a slave was regarded simply as a 'thing' (Latin, *res*), or as a property. Many slave-owners or 'lords' were harsh, and treated their slaves ruthlessly as their personal property, to do with as they

---

[1] Rudolf Bultmann, *Theology of the New Testament*, trans. K. Grobel, vol. 1 (London: SCM Press, 1952), p. 331.

wished. At the other extreme, however, many Stoics, 'God-fearers', and other 'good' pagans could be humane, and employ literate or numerate slaves to manage their estates or their businesses while they indulged in city-politics, personal pleasures, or other interests. If a slave had a 'good' master, slavery could be attractive. It was possible to rise high, and to earn enough pocket-money to begin life again as an honoured freedman or freedwoman, perhaps in one's thirties.[2] For this reason, some who fell on hard times deliberately sold themselves into slavery, alongside prisoners captured in war, or people who had committed crimes. Everything depended on who the lord or master would be. If they were fortunate, the master's name and reputation would guarantee them a better status and a higher security against thieves or kidnappers than ever they could have had as poor free-men, left to rely simply on their own resources.

Paul sees Christ as the most generous, loving, and kind of all masters or *lords* at whose disposal it was possible to be. With Christ as his Lord, a Christian no longer worried about himself. Even if he were to die, his wife (or spouse) and children would remain the re-sponsibility of his *Lord*. As we shall see, coming to faith means being freed from unwanted bondage to evil powers beyond one's control, to enter into 'belonging' to Jesus Christ. We shall discuss this further when we view Paul's notion of redemption.

It is no mere coincidence that Paul uses the phrase '*my* Lord' (not '*our* Lord') in Phil. 3.8, where he speaks of his conversion.[3] For at his call, Paul realized that *God* had exalted Jesus Christ, and had vindicated the claims of the earliest Christian community by raising Christ from the dead. The Lordship of Christ derives its practical cur-rency from the obedience and surrender of his followers; yet it does not *depend* on this. This is only half of the truth about Lordship. Some Christians sing, 'We build him a throne', and this underlines the practical *currency* of Christ's Lordship. But Christ would not cease to be *Lord* if all of his people turned away in disobedience. For Paul

---

[2] Dale B. Martin, *Slavery as Salvation* (New Haven: Yale University Press, 1990), pp. 63–8 and throughout; Thiselton, *First Epistle to the Corinthians*, pp. 562–5; Thomas E. J. Wiedemann, *Greek and Roman Slavery* (London: Croom Helm, 1981); and L. A. H. Coombs, *The Metaphor of Slavery in the Writings of the Early Church* (Sheffield: Sheffield Academic Press, 1998), pp. 21–94.

[3] Joachim Jeremias, 'The Key to Pauline Theology', *Expository Times* 76 (1964), p. 28; cf. 27–30.

asserts: *God* declared Jesus Lord by his resurrection from the dead (Rom. 1.4). At the resurrection God enthroned Christ as messianic king.

Both of these two distinct aspects form part of what it means to confess Christ as Lord. The practical aspect, which gives the confession currency in daily life, may be called the personal or 'existential' aspect. The aspect which underlines God's enthronement of Christ, however humans may respond, grounds the confession in reality, and may be called the reality or 'ontological' aspect. In terms of both aspects one older writer calls this 'the one audible profession of faith which Paul requires' and 'a summary of Christian preaching' (1 Cor. 12.3; 2 Cor. 4.5).[4] If this is so, and it does seem to be the case, the confession cannot be a simple assent to a head-content, or to a right belief about Jesus Christ. It implies not less than this; but more. It involves trust, involvement, surrender, obedience, reverence, and grateful love. It is not simply a matter of ascribing the right 'title' to Christ.

Paul speaks of God 'who raised Jesus our Lord from the dead' (Rom. 4.24), where he links it closely with a formula which probably goes back to the apostolic church before Paul writes. In Rom. 4.25, he adds, Christ 'was handed over to death for our trespasses and was raised for our justification'. Paul inherited this, although the Lordship of Christ became central to him not least because of the manner of his call in which Christ was revealed as exalted by God. In Paul's writings it occurs in various contexts. One is that of *devotion* or *worship*, as Werner Kramer and others have observed.[5] In the context of the *Lord's Supper* or the Eucharist, for example, Paul speaks of 'the cup of the Lord' (1 Cor. 10.21); 'I received from the Lord' (11.23); 'the Lord's death' (11.26); 'judged by the Lord' (11.32); and, as is well-known, 'the Lord's Supper' (11.20). The Aramaic form *Maranatha* (16.22), meaning 'May the Lord come', is almost certainly a prayer, as it is in Rev. 22.20 and in one of the earliest Christian writings, *Didache* 10.6.

Another context concerns practical *conduct*. Paul discusses how 'to please the Lord' (1 Cor. 7.32), which is parallel to 'to serve the Lord' in Rom. 12.11. 'The work of the Lord' (1 Cor. 15.58; 16.10) is

---

[4] Scott, *Christianity according to St Paul*, pp. 249–50.
[5] Werner Kramer, *Christ, Lord, Son of God*, trans. Brian Hardy (London: SCM Press, 1966), pp. 161–73.

central to the Christian life. The collection concerns the Lord's work (2 Cor. 8.5, 19). Lifestyle depends on the will of the Lord (1 Thess. 1.6). The Lord enables the Church to grow in love (1 Thess. 3.12–13), and gives to Paul his apostolic role (2 Cor. 10.8; 13.10). Romans 14.8, as Kramer argues, concerns the living of the Christian life, and 2 Cor. 5.6, 8, concerns the nature of Christian existence. Finally, in 1 Cor. 6.13 'the body' belongs to the Lord. The body, as Ernst Käsemann urges, makes visible obedience to the Lord communicable and credible.[6]

A third context concerns the *Parousia*, the last events, or eschatology. Paul regularly speaks of 'the day of the Lord' or 'the *Parousia* [Coming or Presence] of the Lord' (1 Thess. 5.2; 1 Cor. 5.5; 1 Thess. 4.15; 5.23). He also speaks of the 'revealing of the Lord' or of the Lord's epiphany, or of his descent (1 Cor. 1.7; 1 Thess. 4.16; 1 Cor. 4.5). Although Christ remains 'Lord' in the present, the future will bring a *public* revelation of what is now perceived in faith only by the Church, and as Lord, Christ will assume the role of universal Judge. We shall argue that Paul's concern continues in later epistles.

Clearly both the Old Testament and Hellenistic-Jewish thought also lie in the background. There is no conflict with monotheism in the Old Testament, because Paul subsumes his high doctrine of Christ into his focus on God. Today Neil Richardson and James Dunn are among the many who make this point.[7] We need not depend solely on the fact that the title 'Lord of all' is a Jewish formula used of Yahweh or the God of Israel, although many argue for the importance of this. Wilhelm Bousset, followed by Rudolf Bultmann, long ago urged the role of the term in the Greek-speaking Church.[8] But even if it can be shown that Paul uses the language of the Greek-speaking Church to communicate the gospel, Whiteley rightly comments, 'Nothing must be allowed to obscure the fact that it was his [Paul's] Christology which called his language into use, rather than his words which gave rise to his Christology.'[9] In terms of his view

---

[6] Ernst Käsemann, *New Testament Questions of Today*, trans. W. J. Montague (London: SCM Press, 1969), p. 135.

[7] Dunn, J. D. G., *The Theology of Paul the Apostle* (London: T. & T. Clark, 1998), pp. 252–60.

[8] Wilhelm Bousset, *Kyrios Christos: A History of the Belief in Christ from the Beginnings of Christianity to Irenaeus*, trans. John Seely (Nashville: Abingdon, 5th edn, 1970).

[9] Whiteley, *The Theology of St. Paul*, p. 102.

of Christ, the central theme remains that of 'belonging' to Christ, and hence of trusting him not with fear, but with confidence.

Because Lordship is associated with the resurrection of Christ as the climax of his work, many emphasize that *kyrios* (Lord) carries implications of Christ's being *rightful* Lord. We have seen this aspect in Rom. 1.3–4 and 10.9, but it also occurs in the preaching of Acts 2.36. There is probably an implicit contrast with 'Caesar is Lord', which was used perhaps later in the Empire as a rival confession to test the loyalty of early Christians. Paul's use of 'Lord' may owe much also to its high significance in the Old Testament, as an ascription to God. This did not distance Paul from Jesus and the Gospels, although in the first part of the twentieth century Bousset implied this view. Paul did not differ from earliest Christians. Nevertheless, he did much to make this a favourite key term. He applies it to Jesus over 200 times.

Messiah, Last Adam, and Son of God

Paul also uses 'Messiah' and 'Man' or 'Last Adam'. By the time of Paul's letters he often uses 'Christ' as a proper name. But sometimes he uses *Christos* as the Greek equivalent to 'Messiah' in Jewish thought; 1 Cor. 1.23 should be translated: 'But we proclaim a crucified Christ, to the Jews a stumbling-block (*skandalon*).' The Hebrew word *Mashiah* is *Christos* in Greek, and means 'the Anointed One', that is, anointed by the Holy Spirit to bring in the kingdom of God. Where Paul addresses the issue of Jewish identity in Romans 9, Dunn points out that it makes sense to translate 'the Christ' (Rom. 9.3–5; cf. Rom. 13.9, 10; 15.2–3), 'with *Christos* still bearing its titular force'.[10] Clearly in Rom. 5.15–19 and in 1 Cor. 15.21–22 Paul refers to Christ as the 'Last Adam'. He writes that as in Adam all die, so in Christ shall all be made alive. Christ is head and representative of a new humanity, just as Adam was head and representative of the old, natural, humanity.

As bearing the image of God, Adam is the prototype of Christ, 'the type of the one to come' (Rom. 5.14). Like other early Christians, Paul quotes Ps. 8.6 in this context: 'you put him in charge over the works of your hands'. In Phil. 2.5–11 Christ becomes 'Adam in reverse'. Adam saw equality with God something to be grasped at; but

---

[10] Dunn, *The Theology of Paul the Apostle*, p. 199; cf. pp. 197–9.

Christ did not seek it, and emptied himself. Therefore Adam was humbled, but Christ was exalted. These passages emphasize both the humanness of Jesus; but also his cosmic and representative significance. Paul takes some of the speculation about Adam found among his contemporaries (for example, in Philo), but uses it to focus on the human and representative character of Christ. Christ is humanity as God intended it to be.

Perhaps the same dual emphasis comes in Paul's use of 'human being' or 'man'. *Man* may perhaps be a Greek rendering of the Hebrew 'Son of Man'. In Dan. 7.13 the term stresses the human character of a cosmic figure, even though he comes 'with the clouds of heaven', and receives 'dominion and glory and kingship'. This language is close to that of 1 Cor. 15.25–28, where all enemies are put under Christ's feet. But the passage begins: 'Since death came through a human being, the resurrection of the dead has also come through a human being' (1 Cor. 15.21). This is clearer still in one of the later epistles, namely in Col. 1.22. Paul writes, 'He has now reconciled (you) in his fleshly body through death', while in Col. 2.9 he writes, 'For in him the whole fullness of deity dwells bodily (Greek, *sōmatikōs*, in an embodied way).' This must refer to the humanity or humanness of Jesus Christ, as well as to divine indwelling.

To understand Paul's use of 'Son of God' it is wise first to ask about Aramaic and Hebrew uses of 'Son of God' before we turn to alleged parallels in Greek religion. Speaking of the two worlds of meaning which we meet, N. T. Wright has given this detailed consideration.[11] The Hebrews used the term 'Son of' especially in connection with David the King in 2 Samuel 7 and Psalm 2, where they looked forward to one who bore the character and role of David, but to a degree which would outstrip him. This became a messianic title. Quite contrary to the use of 'Son of God' in the Greek mystery religions, it resisted any tendency to turn Christianity into a private cult. 'Son of God' acquired cosmic significance, eclipsing its application to the Emperors Augustus or Nero.

It is likely that Paul inherited the thought expressed in Rom. 1.3–4 from early apostolic tradition, where God declares Jesus Christ to be Son of God, largely but not entirely because of the resurrection.

---

[11] N. T. Wright, *The Resurrection of the Son of God* (London: SPCK, 2003), pp. 723–38.

Dunn rightly observes, 'We should not speak here of an "adoption-ist" Christology . . . a taking into sonship of one who was not previously "son".'[12] In 1 Thess. 1.9, 10, Paul recalls how his readers 'turned to God from idols to serve a living and true God, and to wait for his Son from heaven, whom he raised from the dead – Jesus'. Many regard this as a summary of Paul's preaching to the Gentiles. When he recalls his call and conversion, Paul states that God was pleased 'to reveal his Son to me' (Gal. 1.16). The passage about the handing over of the kingdom concerns Christ as Son of God, in 1 Cor. 15.25–28. Lest we should imagine that this features only in earlier epistles, we find it in 'God has transferred us into the kingdom of the Son of his love' (Col. 1.13).

The cosmic or universal Christ

The cosmic significance of Christ for the whole world emerges most of all in Colossians. Clearly the church at Colossae was concerned about how faith in Christ related to the widespread belief that human destinies were controlled by 'principalities and powers', namely forces beyond human control, or angelic beings. Paul assured them that Christ fully disclosed God's sovereignty and purpose: Christ is all, from first to last. Christ is the goal towards which the whole created order moves. Christ embodies the creative thoughts of God. Paul writes, 'He (Christ) is the image of the invisible God, the firstborn of all creation; for in him all things in heaven and on earth were created, things visible and invisible, whether thrones or dominions, rulers or powers – all things have been created through him and for him' (Col. 1.15–18). The Greek may mean both *beginning* and *chief* or *first* or *main principle*. It may carry echoes of Gen. 1.1 and Prov. 8.22, seeing Christ as God's cosmic wisdom, which pre-existed the world. As God's 'image' Christ concretely embodies him, or makes God 'thinkable' or 'conceivable' (see p. 49).

This brings us finally to the incarnation and pre-existence of Christ in Paul. This is not confined to the well-known passage in Phil. 2.5–11. In 2 Cor. 8.9, Paul writes: 'You know the grace of our Lord Jesus Christ, that although he was rich, yet for your sakes he became

---

[12] Dunn, *The Theology of Paul the Apostle*, p. 243.

poor.' We have already looked at passages in which God 'sends' his Son (Rom. 8.3; Gal. 4.4). In 1 Cor. 10.4, we also noted, the rock that Moses struck was Christ, who is God's pre-existent wisdom. In 2 Cor. 3.17 Christ is seen as identified with the Holy Spirit who imparted a transient glory to Moses. But the clearest statement does come in Phil. 2.5–11, which Paul quotes and fully endorses, whether or not some see it as a non-Pauline interpolation. We shall consider this further at the end of this chapter. To the question whether the New Testament teaches Christ's deity, Cullmann asserts ' "yes" . . . on the condition that we do not connect the concept with later Greek speculations about substance and natures'.[13] It is not that Paul rejects such language, but he avoids it, leaving open certain questions for later debates about substance and natures. Such language, John Robinson points out, may lead to emphasizing Christ's divinity at the expense of neglecting his true humanness in the incarnation, or to trying to arrive at a hybrid figure who is neither true God nor true man.[14] Paul concentrates on the practical currency of Christ as 'Lord', as divinely decreed by God.

Larry Hurtado rightly appeals to the place of Christ in very early Christian devotion.[15] He argues that much occurred in the short period between the resurrection of Jesus and Paul's call, let alone in the 18 years before his earliest extant epistle. In Rev. 19.10, the angel forbids John to worship him, but in Rev. 5.9–14 the heavenly elders worship not only God, but also the Lamb. In Paul, baptism is in Christ; prayer is through Jesus Christ; and hymns concern Jesus. He is closely associated with worship of God. This transcends Jewish conceptions of such divine agents as Wisdom, Word, and Glory, which could be accommodated to Jewish monotheism.[16] We consider Paul's view of God in the next chapter.

Dunn has also wrestled with this question. He points out that Paul interchanges certain functions between Christ and God; for example, the 'judgement seat of God' (Rom. 14.10) is the 'judgement

---

[13] Oscar Cullmann, *The Christology of the New Testament*, trans. J. G. Guthrie and C. A. M. Hall (London: SCM Press, 1963), p. 306.

[14] John A. T. Robinson, *The Human Face of God* (London: SCM Press, 1973).

[15] Larry W. Hurtado, *Lord Jesus Christ: Devotion to Jesus in Earliest Christianity* (Grand Rapids and Cambridge: Eerdmans, 2003).

[16] Cf. also Larry W. Hurtado, *One God, One Lord: Early Christian Devotion and Ancient Jewish Monotheism* (London: SCM Press, 1988).

seat of Christ' (2 Cor. 5.10). Paul even adapts the Jewish *Shema* (Deut. 6.4) to attribute the Lordship of the one God to Jesus Christ.[17] But Christ is 'mediate' Creator of the universe in more than one passage. This forces upon us the question asked by Athanasius and Basil. Are Christ and the Spirit creatures, that is, beings that were *created*, or not? Clearly Christ and the Spirit belong to the order of *uncreated* beings with God the Father, not to the order of creation such as angels, powers, and humans. In this sense, Paul gives us all the ingredients for a rounded Christology. Later generations may put these ingredients together in different ways. But when Paul focuses on the Lordship of Christ, his view of Christ is primarily one of *relationship* rather than 'titles'. The same is true of Paul's view of Christ as human, and Christ as God. We meet God in and through Christ, and when we look at Christ, we see what 'being human' really means. Rather than asking: 'Was Christ truly human?' we look at Christ and in this light can ask, 'Are we truly human?' This will be the subject of Chapter 8. Meanwhile, Paul presupposed the pre-existence of Christ and reverenced him as *Kyrios*. He deepened and adapted the view of Christ that eventually found its way into our creeds.[18]

In Chapter 3 we postponed a closer look at the 'prison' epistles (Philippians, Colossians, and Philemon, possibly with Ephesians). They shed special light on Paul's view of Christ, but are difficult to fit with certainty into the chronology of Paul's life. Certainly Colossians is relatively late, as is Ephesians if we assume a Pauline authorship, which remains a matter of debate. I see reasons to accept it as authentic. But in every case we cannot be certain whether the 'prison' from which they are written refers to Caesarea, Rome, or perhaps even Ephesus.

There are strong arguments for Rome and Caesarea. Philippians may have been written from prison in Caesarea (Acts 23.35), where there was a Roman garrison, which matches 'the praetorium' of Phil. 1.13. Acts suggests that Paul's imprisonment was at least for two years (24.27), and constituted 'open arrest' (Phil. 2.25–30 and 4.10–20; cf. Acts 24.23). On the other hand Paul does not mention 'the collection' in Philippians, which may imply a later date. In the case

---

[17] Dunn, *The Theology of Paul the Apostle*, pp. 252–60.
[18] A. Grillmeier, *Christ in Christian Tradition: From the Apostolic Age to Chalcedon*, trans. J. Bowden (London: Mowbray, 1965), p. 13.

of Colossians the argument for Rome seems perhaps strongest, but we cannot be certain. Probably Philippians was written in 59–60, and Colossians in 60–1.

Philippians is a very personal letter. Philippi was an ancient and historic Roman colony, annexed by Rome in 168 BC, and Paul had made his first visit to Europe there (Chapter 3). Women played a prominent role in the church, beginning with Lydia and moving on to Euodia and Syntyche who worked with Paul in their struggle on behalf of the gospel (Phil. 4.2, 3). Paul gives thanks for the church and prays for it with joy and satisfaction (1.3–11; 4.10–20). Death for Paul is a real possibility. He writes, 'Living is Christ and dying is gain . . . my desire is to depart and be with Christ, for that is far better' (1.21, 23).

Yet Paul has one concern, namely that the Philippians 'do nothing from selfish ambition or conceit' (2.3). Concern for others rather than for self is demonstrated in Christ, 'who though he was in the form of God, did not regard equality with God as something to be exploited, but emptied himself, taking the form of a slave, being born in human likeness' (2.6, 7). Therefore God has exalted him as Lord and given him 'the name that is above every name . . . that . . . every knee should bend, in heaven and on earth and under the earth' (2.9, 10). Jesus is the supreme example of self-sacrificing humble service, but this would not make sense if Jesus Christ did not become 'incarnate', that is, took enfleshed or embodied human existence, but was also pre-existent, and not a created being. Hence God exalts him as Lord over the universe, not simply over the Church. This underlines our earlier point that God made him Lord, as well as 'Lord' in our practical experience. Additionally, he is Lord of the whole cosmos or universe. By AD 60 Paul had come to reflect on the momentous universal implications of Christ's Lordship over all, including non-human agencies or forces.[19] We may note in passing that the tone of Phil. 3.1–16 is different, but includes again, 'Not that I have already obtained this or have already reached my goal' (3.12). And 3.20 takes up the status of a Roman colony: 'Our citizenship is in heaven' (i.e. not here).

---

[19] Gerald F. Hawthorne, *Philippians* (Waco, TX: Word Books, 1983), esp. pp. 76–96; John B. Polhill, *Paul and his Letters* (Nashville: Broadman & Holman, 1999), pp. 164–79; and Stephen E. Fowl, *The Story of Christ in the Ethics of Paul* (JSNTSup 36; Sheffield: Sheffield Academic Press, 1990), pp. 49–102.

Colossians is even more cosmic in its ascription of Lordship to Christ. Many today see this as enhancing the Colossian Christians' confidence in their understanding of Christ, in contrast to cults around them. The church is probably predominantly Gentile, and founded by the Christian Gentile Epaphras (Col. 1.7). Colossae is a much smaller city than Philippi, Thessalonica, Corinth, or Ephesus. But the church 'shares the inheritance of the saints' (Col. 1.27). Paul prays for this church that God will give them spiritual wisdom (1.9), and that they may be strong (1.11). Colossians 1.15–20 is one of the highest expressions of cosmic Christology in the New Testament. Like John 1.1, 1 Cor. 8.4–6, and Heb. 1.1, Paul asserts Christ's involvement in creation, including 'all things in heaven and on earth, things visible and invisible . . . rulers and powers' (1.16). In Christ all things cohere or hold together (1.17). When he heard, 'Why have you persecuted *me*?' Paul began to see the Church as Christ's own body, and Christ is also the head of it (1.18). His resurrection makes him the first of the new order, and 'in him all the fullness of God was pleased to dwell' (1.18, 19). Through the cross 'all' can be reconciled with God (1.20).[20]

Clearly Christ is not a creature, nor a created being. The universe has come into being 'for' him. Jesus Christ is a cosmic principle of cohesion and animation, who holds the world together. He is the bodily representation of God. In Paul's mind Christ was equated with the Wisdom of God and the Word of God. This was seen in Judaism as the pre-existent agent of God, before the beginning of time. Yet the cross and resurrection remain pivotal for it all. Paul gives the glimpse of Christ's cosmic glory that he may 'present everyone mature in Christ' (1.28). In Christ are all the treasures of knowledge and wisdom (2.3). The so-called 'philosophy' at Colossae and Laodicea should cause them no anxiety. This is merely a man-made system, or 'a human way of thinking' (2.18), with petty legalistic formulae and an over-assessment of angels. Let the word of Christ, Paul urges, 'dwell in you richly' (3.16). The readers are to rejoice in Christ, and pray for Paul, as he prays for them (4.2–4). But the focus of the letter remains Christ, and his universal or cosmic glory.

---

[20] C. F. D. Moule, *The Epistles of Paul the Apostle to the Colossians and to Philemon* (Cambridge Greek Testament Commentary; Cambridge: Cambridge University Press, 1957); and Dunn, *The Epistles to the Colossians and Philemon*, esp. pp. 83–104.

6

Paul's view of God and
its Trinitarian implications

God, the Old Testament, and Christ

Paul inherited from the Old Testament and Judaism a concept of God as the *living* God. God is both active in the world and absolute *sovereign*. Paul's conversion and call, however, qualified this conception in at least two ways. First, God's revelation to Paul 'out of the blue' underlined God's undeserved *grace*. God shows initiating, sovereign grace. Paul saw himself as 'the least of the apostles, unfit to be called an apostle, because I persecuted the Church of God, but by the grace of God I am what I am' (1 Cor. 15.9, 10). Second, as he progressed in his knowledge of Jesus Christ and saw the intimate co-operation between God as Father and Jesus Christ as Son as joint agents, Paul discerned what we might call the '*Christlikeness*' of God; each bore the stamp of the other.

God's ways for Paul are 'unsearchable' and 'inexhaustible' (Rom. 11.33). He agreed with the Old Testament legacy that God is holy and 'other' or transcendent (cf. Isa. 6.2–5). *Through Christ* God, however, is also *approachable*, or in the words of Eberhard Jüngel today, also 'thinkable' or '*conceivable*'.[1] Through Christ God becomes a daily reality in Paul's life. God the Father is ultimately the Creator of the universe, but he created everything that exists through Christ (Col. 1.15–17; 1 Cor. 8.4–6; cf. Rom. 11.33–36). Paul knows God daily especially through prayer.

Neil Richardson rightly protests that while books and parts of books and articles on Paul's view of Christ abound, relatively few concern Paul's view of God. He finds this 'astonishing'.[2] Richardson

---

[1] Eberhard Jüngel, *God as the Mystery of the World*, trans. D. L. Guder (Edinburgh: T. & T. Clark, 1983), pp. 8–9 and 220–1; cf. pp. 287–8 and 376–82.
[2] Neil Richardson, *Paul's Language about God* (JSNTSup 99; Sheffield: Sheffield Academic Press, 1994), p. 12.

cites Bultmann, Conzelmann, and Kümmel as giving hardly any space to this important subject in their respective *Theologies of the New Testament*. They simply assume that Paul repeats an Old Testament or Jewish view, without Christ's making much difference to his view of God. Admittedly more recently the situation has begun to improve, especially in the light of works by L. Hurtado and H. Moxnes, but otherwise the trend mostly remains.[3]

From the first Paul addresses *prayer* to God. He writes in what is probably his earliest extant letter, 'We always give thanks to God for all of you in our prayers, constantly remembering before our God and Father your work of faith and labour of love' (1 Thess. 1.2, 3; cf. Rom. 1.8; 1 Cor. 1.4–9; Phil. 1.3–11; Col. 1.3–8; the regular 'thanksgiving' forms in Paul's letters). He adds, 'We also constantly give thanks to God for this, that when you received the word of God . . . you accepted it not as a human word, but as what it really is, God's word' (1 Thess. 2.13). Paul pleads, 'May our God and Father himself and our Lord Jesus direct our way to you' (3.11). This continues in 2 Thessalonians. The author writes, 'We must always give thanks to God for you' (2 Thess. 1.3). He continues, 'We always pray for you, asking that our God will make you worthy of his call' (1.11), 'We must always give thanks to God for you' (2.13), and 'God our Father . . . comfort your hearts' (2.16, 17).

Paul refers many times to God in 1 and 2 Thessalonians. The Christians at Thessalonica are 'beloved by God' (1 Thess. 1.4), confirming that God shows love (cf. Deut. 7.7, 8; John 3.16; 1 John 3.1). Paul speaks of their faith as directed to God (1.8), their turning from idols to God (1.9), the gospel of God (2.2, 9) and approval by God or being pleasing to God (2.4). God is their witness (2.5), and they must be 'worthy of God' (2.12). Timothy is a co-worker for God (3.2; cf. 3.9; 4.1, 3, 7, 8, 9, 14; 5.9, 18, 23). If we may cite 2 Thessalonians as written by Paul we may add 2 Thess. 1.2, 4, 5, 8, 12; 2.4, 11, 15, 16; and 3.5.

Nevertheless the main epistle for references to God is probably Romans. Paul offers his credentials to the Christians in Rome largely in the hope that they will support him and provide his 'base' for his mission to Spain. Leon Morris undertakes some word-counts. After

---

[3] See Hurtado, *One God, One Lord*; and Halvor Moxnes, *Theology in Conflict: Studies in Paul's Understanding of God in Romans* (NovTSup 53; Leiden: Brill, 1980).

the and *and*, he writes, 'Paul's next most frequent word in this epistle is *Theos*, "God".'[4] Moxnes also implies this. Morris counts 153 occurrences of the word. Paul speaks of God's nature (Rom. 1.23); his faithfulness (3.3); his truth (3.4); his patience (2.4; 3.26); and goodness (2.4; 11.22). God is 'the God of hope' and 'the God of peace' (15.15, 33; 16.20). God may also show wrath and severity (1.18; 3.5; 9.22; 11.22). It is sometimes supposed that wrath denotes absence of love, or is the opposite of love. But the opposite of love is not wrath, but indifference, as most parents know well. The more one loves a child, the more one may show anger at the child's attempt at what would bring self-destruction.

Neil Richardson sees Romans 9–11 as addressed to Gentile Christians at Rome about Israel's role on the stage of world history, which forms the theatre of God's dealings with the world. Paul first expresses his grief that physical Israel has largely not recognized the Messiah of Israel. In chapter 9 he also asks who are the true children of God who are heirs to God's promises (9.8–11; cf. Isa. 10.20–23; 11.1, 16). God is not unjust (9.14), but everything depends on God's mercy, not on human will (9.16). God is like a potter, who moulds the clay (9.20–22, which reflects Jer. 18.5–9). Paul cites Hos. 2.1, 25 and Isa. 10.22–23 from the Septuagint, with small changes to make his point clearer.[5] He then cites Isa. 8.14 and 28.16 (LXX), as Cranfield argues, with small changes 'to bring out more sharply the sovereignty of God's purpose'.[6] There is a critique of 'zeal for God', which was a prominent theme in Jewish piety (1 Macc. 2.27, 54; Sir. 48.2).

Grace, experience, and narrative

Paul provides more distinctive material when he turns to the theme of the *grace* of God. Richardson argues that 'the grace of God' does not occur in the Septuagint.[7] In strictly linguistic terms this may be

---

[4] Leon Morris, 'The Theme of Romans', in W. Ward Gasque and Ralph P. Martin (eds), *Apostolic History and the Gospel: Presented to F. F. Bruce* (Exeter: Paternoster Press, 1970), p. 250; cf. pp. 249–63.

[5] Stanley, *Paul and the Language of Scripture*, pp. 109–19.

[6] Cranfield, *The Epistle to the Romans*, vol. 2, p. 486; cf. Dunn, *Romans 9–11*, p. 554.

[7] Richardson, *Paul's Language about God*, pp. 74–5.

true as an explicit assertion about the English *grace*. But the LXX does speak of Noah's finding *grace* (Greek, *charis*) in the eyes of the Lord (Gen. 6.8); of Abraham's finding *charis* in God's eyes (Gen. 18.3); and many similar references (e.g. Exod. 3.21; Judith 10.8, etc.) even if the NRSV translates it *favour* not *grace*. The Old Testament does speak of God as 'gracious' in adjectival construction. A major point in Paul's argument is that 'There is a remnant chosen by grace. But if it is by grace it is no longer on the basis of "works", otherwise grace would no longer be *grace*' (Rom. 11.5, 6). Romans 10 and 11 combine to say that all comes from the grace of God (Hebrew, *chēn*; Greek, *charis*), not from human striving or 'zeal'.[8]

We mention one more epistle to correct the impression that God remains less prominent than Christ in Paul's thinking. In 1 Corinthians, 'God is the head of Christ' (11.3), and, 'All things come from God' (11.12). Further, when all things have been subjected to God in Christ, 'the Son himself will also be subjected to the one who put all things in subjection under him (i.e. God), so that God may be all in all' (15.28). These passages are so well known that they are often called 'subordination' passages. Hurtado concludes that they are inherited from 'Palestinian' Jewish Christians and underline God's ultimate sole agency.[9]

How can we speak, as the creeds seem to do, of the co-equality of the Holy Trinity, when Paul writes in this vein? Some convincingly argue that it was all too easy for the church at Corinth to cherish intimacy with Christ as Lord, while neglecting the supposedly more remote or distant figure of God. They also appeal to the analogy of Hellenistic mystery cults. Paul seeks to correct such a view. Cerfaux compares the 'mystery' of God as all in all with Eph. 1.23, which he regards as Pauline.[10] Further, such passages as Col. 1.15–20 (cf. the previous chapter, p. 44) also complement Paul's view.

Against widespread misunderstanding today, Paul does not separate the action of the God of the Old Testament and Israel from that

[8] Richard H. Bell, *Provoked to Jealousy: The Origin and Purpose of the Jealousy Motive in Romans 9—11* (WUNT 2.63; Tübingen: Mohr, 1994); and Richard H. Bell, *The Irrevocable Call of God* (WUNT 2.184; Tübingen: Mohr, 2005).

[9] Hurtado, *One God, One Lord*, p. 96.

[10] L. Cerfaux, *The Church in the Theology of Paul*, trans. G. Webb and A. Walker (New York: Herder & Herder, 1959), p. 317.

of Christ. In fact he sees creation itself as the joint work of God the Father and the Son, although in that agency of co-creation each has different roles. Explicitly in Col. 1.16 Paul writes, 'In Christ all things in heaven and earth were created', and lists the visible and invisible orders of being. But this is because 'the fullness of God was pleased to dwell in him' (1.19). Theologians tend to speak of God the Father as ultimate or first cause (Greek, *ek* or *ex*, from); but of Christ or God the Son as mediate Creator (Greek, *dia*, through). In 1 Cor. 8.6 Paul states exactly the same thing: 'There is one God, the Father, *from* whom (Greek, *ek* or *ex*) are all things . . . and one Lord, Jesus Christ, *through* whom (Greek, *dia*) are all things, and *through* whom (*dia*) we exist.' Paul is not alone in the New Testament in making the distinction, and in calling Christ 'mediate' Creator of the universe. John declares, 'All things came into being *through* (*dia*) him (Christ),' and that he was God (John 1.1, 3). Hebrews asserts, '*Through* him (*dia*, Christ) he (God) made the worlds' (Heb. 1.2; cf. 1.2–4).

To recite the creeds, with their strong assertion of the Holy Trinity, may suggest that Paul is now remote from such beliefs, as if to reinforce the notion that later doctrine did not arise directly from the New Testament. In Paul, however, *the Trinity is partly grounded in everyday experience*. In Rom. 8.26 he admits that 'we do not know how to pray as we ought'. But, he adds, it is the Holy Spirit who inspires us to pray, and who helps us in our weakness. The Spirit inspires us to offer our prayer to God as our Father (8.15–16), and we offer prayer through Christ. In the daily, ordinary, experience of prayer, all three Persons of the Trinity are directly involved. *Prayer is offered to God the Father, inspired by God the Holy Spirit, through Christ our Lord*, God's Son. The Spirit enables our prayers to be articulate and intelligible to God, just as Christ makes God conceivable and thinkable to us.

The narrative of Jesus Christ, however, even more strongly offers a ground for belief in God as Trinity. At one level, Paul avoids tritheism, or belief in three separate Gods, because he shares the Jewish creed that 'There is no God but one' (1 Cor. 8.4; cf. Deut. 4.15–20; 6.4; 10.12; 26.10). On the other hand, Jesus Christ is exalted as Lord by God the Father, and was raised from the dead by the Spirit (Rom. 1.3, 4; 8.11; 1 Cor. 15.4, 44; Phil. 2.9–11). As the Church Fathers pointed out (especially Athanasius and Basil in the fourth century) in Paul neither the Son nor the Spirit is a created being. They referred especially to 1 Cor. 2.10–16; 12.4–8; and 2 Cor. 13.14 to argue that both the Son of God and the Holy Spirit co-work with God the Father to bring us the blessings of the revelation of God's own mind (1 Cor. 2.14–16), the gifts of the *charismata* (1 Cor. 12.4–8), and that which God alone can give (2 Cor. 13.14).[11]

Although he does not explicitly mention it, Paul would have known, perhaps through apostolic tradition, that when Jesus Christ was baptized, Father, Son, and Holy Spirit were involved: the Father spoke of Jesus' obedience; the Spirit descended upon him; and Jesus expressed his solidarity with God's people. Paul was explicit, however, about Christ in the wilderness wanderings of Israel. Israel drank from the rock, which, in Paul's view was Christ (1 Cor. 10.4; cf. Exod. 17.2–7); and the church at Corinth must not follow Israel in putting Christ to the test (1 Cor. 10.9; cf. Exod. 32.1–6), but must rely on the faithful God (1 Cor. 10.13).

Approachability of God and the Trinity

Nothing makes Paul seem more remote than the mistaken notion held often today that since 'God put forward (Jesus) as a sacrifice of atonement (or means of meeting, expiation, or propitiation)' (Rom. 3.25), God stands at a distance from the suffering and death of Jesus Christ. Against such a mistaken concept, Paul declares, 'God was in Christ, reconciling the world to himself' (2 Cor. 5.19). One of the problems perhaps lies with the word 'sent', as in God's 'sending his own Son . . . to deal with sin' (Rom. 8.3), or 'God sent his Son . . . in order to redeem those who were under the law' (Gal. 4.4, 5). But God's being the sovereign, initiating cause does not imply that God distanced himself from what he set in motion. What does Paul mean when he speaks of the cross as the fruit of the *love* of *God*? Jürgen Moltmann characteristically writes: '*A God who cannot suffer cannot love. A God who cannot love is a dead God.*'[12] If, for Paul, God is *Christlike*, we cannot separate the experiences and love of each from

---

[11] Michael A. G. Haykin, *The Spirit of God: The Exegesis of 1 and 2 Corinthians in the Pneumatomachian Controversy of the Fourth Century* (VCSup 27; Leiden and New York: Brill, 1994), pp. 59–169.

[12] Jürgen Moltmann, *The Trinity and the Kingdom of God: The Doctrine of God*, trans. Margaret Kohl (London: SCM Press, 1981), p. 38 (my italics).

the other too sharply. The notion that God cannot suffer stems from a later philosophical and doctrinal demand to mark off God from his creatures, and to ascribe a static 'perfection' to him. The heresy called 'patripassianism' makes God endure passively as if at the receiving end of human actions. But, on the contrary, God-in-Christ voluntarily and sovereignly chooses to limit his options, by his active will. This does not compromise his sovereignty. Only Jesus Christ physically suffers on the cross; but God co-suffers with him.

What are we to say about Jesus' cry of dereliction from the cross? Moltmann again offers a profound comment. He writes, 'It is only as the One who forsakes [Christ], who surrenders the other, that the Father is still present. Communicating love and responding love are alike transformed into infinite pain.'[13] The innermost life of Father, Son, and Spirit, he urges, is at stake, as the Father 'loses' his dear Son. Yet the resurrection through the Spirit by God becomes also a reality. Paul hardly ever speaks of one event without speaking of the other. To ignore this becomes once again to risk a non-Pauline tri-theism, as if God the Father, Son, and Holy Spirit are not really one. We shall comment further when we consider the atonement in Paul.

In one sense Paul does not write extensively about God to the churches because 'God is the fundamental presupposition of Paul's theology', though 'the word "God" itself occurs 548 times in the Pauline corpus'.[14] Dunn claims that Paul's view of God is 'axiomatic' and often 'taken for granted' and shared with 'Jewish affirmations about God'.[15] This is true when we consider God's creation and sovereign power (Rom. 1.19, 20; cf. 1 Tim. 1.17; 2.5; and Ps. 8.9); God as Judge (Rom. 3.5; cf. Isa. 33.2); God as searching human hearts (Rom. 8.7; cf. 1 Chron. 28.9); God as exercising his will (1 Cor. 1.1; 2 Cor. 1.1; Col. 1.1; 1 Thess. 4.3; cf. Ps. 40.8); God giving life to the dead (Rom. 4.17; cf. Isa. 26.19); God's glory (Rom. 6.4; cf. Isa. 6.3); the righteousness of God (Rom. 1.17; cf. Isa. 7.17); his eternity (2 Cor. 4.16; cf. Isa. 57.15) and his 'goodness' (Rom. 3.12; cf. Ps. 53.1). But the work of creation, alluding to Gen. 1.1—2.3, Paul sees as a matter of 'the glory of God in the face of Jesus Christ' (2 Cor. 4.6). It is the result of shared double (or triple) agency (Col. 1.15–17). Christ holds all

---

[13] Moltmann, *The Trinity and the Kingdom of God*, p. 80.

[14] Dunn, *The Theology of Paul the Apostle*, p. 28.

[15] Dunn, *The Theology of Paul the Apostle*, p. 29.

things together lest they fragment into nothing, even if God was the originating cause (1 Cor. 8.6). The distinctiveness of Paul's thought emerges most clearly when we consider God's love and grace, and his revelatory and saving acts. In 1 Cor. 1.18—2.5 'God' is frequent and emphatic; yet the central theme is that of Christ's cross.

That God's 'wisdom' should be focused on the cross was regarded as 'folly' by the world and even by the Jews, for whom it is a scandal and a snare. Paul rejects the sophistry and audience-pleasing rhetoric that the church in Corinth expects, because a simple preaching of the cross most closely accords with God's will and purposes in Christ. Even the power of God becomes, in the eyes of others, a 'weakness' (1 Cor. 1.18, 19, 23; 2.1–5). Paul rejects the claims of the 'Christ group' in 1.10–12, who used the figure of Christ as a divisive slogan and as a cult-hero to whom they had special access, rather than the Jesus of the cross. Paul then proceeds to say that God can be 'known' only through the Holy Spirit (2.6–16). 'God's wisdom' turns out to be 'the mind of Christ', conveyed and revealed through the Holy Spirit. One major problem at Corinth was that many seem to have divorced both Christ and the Holy Spirit from God the Father, the Almighty. Hence Richardson comments, 'The cross is the key to Paul's language about God in this section.'[16]

Basil the Great viewed doxology as critical to distinguishing the uncreated order of Father, Son, and Holy Spirit from the created order of humanity, angels, and powers, and for this alluded to Paul. He cited especially 1 Cor. 2.10–16 and 12.8. At the end of Romans Paul writes, 'Now to God, who is able to strengthen you . . . according to the command of the eternal God . . . to the only wise God through Jesus Christ, to whom be glory for ever' (Rom. 16.25–27). In 11.36 he declares, 'To him (God in Christ) be glory for ever.' He speaks of 'the will of our God and Father, to whom be glory for ever and ever' (Gal. 1.5). We may compare: 'To him be glory in the church by Christ Jesus' (Eph. 3.21) and 'To whom be glory for ever and ever' (2 Tim. 4.18). In Paul's thought neither Christ nor the Holy Spirit are 'created beings'. (Hence in our creeds Christ is 'begotten not made'; and the Spirit 'proceeds' from the Father.) These three alone therefore can receive worship or glory, although most frequently

---

[16] Richardson, *Paul's Language about God*, p. 134.

God alone receives worship as Father 'through' Christ, in the power of the Spirit.

For Paul, Christians are 'sons' of the Father in the derived sense of sharing the Sonship of Christ. God is pre-eminently the Father of Jesus. God is Father of Christians in several distinct senses. First, 'We ourselves, who have the firstfruits of the Spirit . . . wait for adoption . . .' (Rom. 8.24). Second, fatherhood denotes Fatherly care, and ultimate creation of life. Third, God is 'the Father of mercies' who showers his children with gifts that are for their corporate good (2 Cor. 1.3). In Eph. 3.14–15 fatherhood is said to derive from God as Father. Paul sees God as Father of Jesus in an absolute sense (Col. 1.13). A confirmation of this lies in Paul's borrowing of Jesus' own Aramaic term for 'Father' in Rom. 8.13 and Gal. 4.6: 'When we cry "Abba! Father!" it is that very Spirit bearing witness with our spirit that we are children of God.'

The claim of Joachim Jeremias that this is almost in effect a nursery term denoting intimacy is highly controversial.[17] Nevertheless, the relation involved is an intimately close, caring, and welcoming one. In Rom. 5.7 Paul says, 'God's love has been poured into our hearts through the Holy Spirit, who has been given to us.' In the later epistles attributed by some to Paul, but at least reflecting Pauline thought, God is called *Saviour* (1 Tim. 2.3; Titus 2.10, 13; 3.4). Ephesians calls God 'the Father of glory' (1.17). In Phil. 4.20, Paul declares, 'To our God and Father be glory for ever and ever.' The relationship of intimacy with God will be crucial when we look in Chapter 10 at the atonement and work of Christ. Romans 8.39 declares that Christians will never be separated from God's love.

We find admittedly no fully-fledged doctrine of the Holy Trinity in Paul, but Paul says enough about God, Christ, and the Holy Spirit to see that all co-operate, and that none is a created creature. As Athanasius and Basil saw, Paul left open a view of God which logically demanded the conclusion that God is one, eternal, personal, sovereign, and Trinitarian. God's nature is seen from his actions, and those above all constitute sovereign grace and love. God's love is the very reason for our creation and subsequent redemption.

---

[17] Joachim Jeremias, 'Abba', in *The Central Message of the New Testament* (London: SCM Press, 1965), pp. 9–30; cf. James Barr, 'Abba Isn't Daddy', *Journal of Theological Studies* 39 (1988), pp. 28–47.

7

Paul's view of the Holy Spirit

Paul's view of the Holy Spirit is centred on *Christ*. Paul writes, 'Anyone who does not have the Spirit of Christ does not belong to him' (Rom. 8.9). 'Because you are children, God sent the Spirit of his Son into our hearts, crying "Abba! Father!"' (Gal. 4.6). The Holy Spirit is the Spirit of Christ, who reproduces Christ's attitude to God within Christians. The Spirit reveals Jesus Christ, and being 'in' Christ is the criterion of receiving the Holy Spirit.

Ambiguity of 'spirit'

Yet we need to distinguish between different uses of the word *spirit* (Greek, *pneuma*). In Rom. 12.11 does the Greek behind the English (*tō pneumati zeontes*) mean 'be fervent in spirit' (AV), describing a human quality, or 'be aglow with the Spirit' (RSV)? Does it mean 'ardent in spirit' (NRSV) or 'aglow with the Spirit' (REB)? The Greek of the first century did not distinguish here between capital letters (or Uncials) and lower case (or miniscules). Paul sometimes uses the Greek word *pneuma* to refer to the human spirit, but more usually and more theologically to refer to the Holy Spirit of God or the Spirit of Christ. Sometimes the word denotes a psychological state: 'we have not received the spirit of bondage' (Rom. 8.13), but more characteristically refers to the Spirit of God (Rom. 8.14; 2 Cor. 3.3).

Our first point of substance (apart from the Spirit's intimate connection with Christ) concerns Paul's continuity with, and difference from, the Old Testament ideas of the Spirit. The Septuagint Greek word *pneuma* and the Hebrew word *ruach* can both mean Spirit of God, the human spirit, or wind or even breath. Human beings cannot make the wind blow, nor can they rival the life-giving creative energy that comes from God. The Spirit therefore can enable humans to do what they cannot do in their own strength. When it is said, 'The Egyptians are human, not God, and their horses flesh, not spirit' (Isa. 31.3), the verse calls attention to their fragility and weakness, in contrast to God's power. Judges recounts how the Spirit of the Lord came upon Gideon, and equipped him for his super-human task (Judg. 6.34). Contrary to the notion of a gentle dove, the Spirit of the Lord 'rushed on' Samson, and 'he tore a lion apart barehanded, as one might tear apart a kid' (Judg. 14.6). The Spirit 'rushed on' Samson, and his ropes melted away (Judg. 15.14). Then he massacred a thousand men with the jawbone of an ass. Isaiah recounts that the Spirit of the Lord protected Israel from marauding bandits (Isa. 63.14).

All this is very different from the notion of 'the Spirit' as a gentle influence. In Ezekiel *ruach*, Spirit, occurs more than 40 times. The Spirit lifts the prophet as the Spirit did Elijah, to enable him to see visions and revelation (Ezek. 3.12; 8.3; 11.1; 37.1). Through the agency of the Spirit, the community of the remnant of Israel received new life or 'resurrection' (Ezek. 37.1–14). The Spirit even enables dry bones to come to life. The Old Testament looks forward to 'the New Age' or new world-order, when the Holy Spirit will be poured out on 'all flesh', or on all kinds of people (Joel 2.28).

Paul inherits all this thinking. Several Pauline passages on 'gifts of the Spirit' presuppose all this. But there is also a radical difference. Paul knows that in the 'last days' the Spirit will be a communal or corporate gift for all the people of God, and that he will be intimately connected with, and derived from, Christ. Scholars often write that the Spirit in Paul is 'Christocentric, communal, and eschatological', that is, a gift given in the last days to all kinds of people through Christ. Moreover, this gift is permanent, not *ad hoc* or intermittent. Whiteley observes that for Paul the Spirit becomes 'the hallmark' of every Christian.[1] There are therefore two systems of thought at work. In the 'Christological' system, *all* Christians receive the Spirit to unite them with Christ. In the continuing Old Testament system, the Spirit is also given to chosen *individuals* to carry out certain tasks, which now are Christ-centred. Both perspectives and approaches remain valid for Paul. But the 'Christological' system comes into being with the completion of the work and ministry of Christ. In the Old Testament it remains only a hoped-for promise, to be fulfilled in the

---

[1] Whiteley, *The Theology of St. Paul*, pp. 124–6.

'last days', as Peter's sermon on the Day of Pentecost also states (Acts 2.17–21; cf. Joel 2.28, 29).

The Holy Spirit and Jesus Christ

This leads Paul to state emphatically that every Christian receives the Holy Spirit on the basis of belonging to Christ, or of being 'in Christ', but also that the Holy Spirit is the cause of our belonging to Christ. At first sight this looks like a paradox, if not a contradiction. But the context of thought is different in each case. Some years ago Albert Schweitzer called the Holy Spirit 'the life principle of His [Christ's] Messianic personality'.[2] From a logical and theological point of view Paul asserts: 'Anyone who does not have the Spirit of Christ does not belong to him' (Rom. 8.9). Again, 'Because you are children, God has sent the Spirit of his Son into our hearts, crying "Abba! Father!"' Sonship, we saw, derives from Christ's Sonship; hence Christians may use the word 'Abba' that Jesus used (Gal. 4.6). But at the level not of logic but of experience and life, Paul declares, 'No one can say "Jesus is Lord" except by the Holy Spirit' (1 Cor. 12.3).

Today some wrestle with the question whether they have received the gift of the Holy Spirit, in spite of times of failure. Paul states that it is impossible to be a Christian and not to receive the Spirit. Even to worry about it implies the action of the Spirit within. Many worry needlessly about Jesus' reference to 'blasphemy against the Holy Spirit' (Mark 3.28–30; par. Matt. 12.31–32), when simply to worry about this proves that the Spirit is at work. The context concerns refusal to recognize good, and to call it evil. Certainly if we pray at all, this is a sign of the Spirit's action, for we have seen that Paul believes that prayer is prompted by the Holy Spirit (Rom. 8.26, 27).

In 1 Cor. 12.3 Paul defines the action of the Holy Spirit as issuing in trust and obedience to Christ as Lord. The negative implications of this come in the difficult first half of the verse: 'No one speaking by the Spirit of God ever says "Let Jesus be cursed"' (1 Cor. 12.3). It was traditionally assumed either that this referred (1) to negative evaluations of the earthly Jesus, or (2) to accepting his atoning work

---

[2] Albert Schweitzer, *The Mysticism of Paul the Apostle*, trans. W. Montgomery (London: A. & C. Black, 1931), p. 165.

through the cross but not the resurrection, or (3) to an ecstatic utterance, without due accompanying reflection, or (4) that it reflected the utterance of a Jew.[3] But Bruce Winter has recently offered a better explanation. Excavations have led to discovery of 'curse' tablets near to Corinth, which contain 'curse prayers' to pagan deities concerning rivals in love or business. The Greek has no verb and may either mean 'curse' (active) or 'be cursed'.[4] Paul probably says that the Spirit would never lead anyone to pray, 'May Jesus curse this or that rival in business or in love.' In any case, the Holy Spirit comes not only at the beginning of the Christian life, but as the basis and ground of our whole Christian life. According to the REB translation, the Spirit not only is 'the source' of Christian life, but also directs its 'course' (Gal. 5.25).

According to James Dunn, Rom. 8.9, 10 *excludes* the possibility both of a non-Christian possessing the Spirit and of a Christian's *not* possessing the Spirit.[5] This suggests a reappraisal regarding 'baptism in the Spirit' as an experience subsequent to that of becoming a Christian. In the same book, devoted to this subject, Dunn again comments, 'There is no alternative to the conclusion that the baptism of the Spirit is what made the Corinthians members of the body of Christ, that is, Christians' (1 Cor. 12.13).[6] This does not deny that a person may experience subsequent deepening of the action of the Holy Spirit, perhaps many times, rather than twice; but it suggests that Paul's term 'baptism in the Holy Spirit' is not an appropriate term for describing this, if we are faithful to Paul's use. Even as a metaphorical term, 'baptism' indicates normally the beginning of the Christian life. There is 'no thought of a *second* gift of the Spirit'.[7] Here Dunn also refers to 2 Corinthians 3.

The Holy Spirit, then, gives to Christians the same attitude towards, and ideally also the same intimacy with, God the Father that Jesus had. This is characterized by trust, confidence, reverence,

[3] Joseph A. Fitzmyer, *First Corinthians: A New Translation with Introduction and Commentary* (Anchor Yale Bible 32; New Haven and London: Yale University Press, 2008), p. 459.

[4] Bruce W. Winter, *After Paul Left Corinth* (Grand Rapids: Eerdmans, 2001), pp. 164–83.

[5] J. D. G. Dunn, *Baptism in the Holy Spirit* (London: SCM Press, 1970), p. 95.

[6] Dunn, *Baptism in the Holy Spirit*, p. 129.

[7] Dunn, *Baptism in the Holy Spirit*, p. 135 (my italics).

worship, and obedience. Christians may address God as Abba, Father, just as Jesus did (Gal. 4.6; Rom. 8.15). Like Jesus, Christians are also enabled to look towards the final end of God's purposes for the world. But because the 'end' has not yet come, Paul writes, 'We eagerly wait for the hope of righteousness' (Gal. 5.5). Elsewhere Paul asserts, 'We eagerly wait (Greek, *apekdechomenoi*) for adoption, the redemption of our bodies' (Rom. 8.23). To recall our earlier analogies (see pp. 12–13) we are still travelling in the lifeboat towards ultimate safety, or we still have pockets of ice as the fire warms us through. We pray in weakness, with inexpressible sighs or groans (Rom. 8.26–27). We press towards the goal (Phil. 3.11–14). The Holy Spirit implants within us a longing to see God's purposes fully fulfilled, and meanwhile strengthens our faith in time of hardship or doubt. One writer has devoted a small book to this theme.[8] The Spirit is even the agent of the Christians' final, future resurrection (Rom. 8.11).

Two special words underline this in Paul's writings. One is a metaphor drawn from manufacturing and finance. The Holy Spirit is both a foretaste or prototype of what is to come off the production line, and a down-payment, or deposit, or first instalment, which guarantees more to come (Greek, *arrabōn*, 2 Cor. 5.5). The second term that Paul uses is also a metaphor, drawn from agriculture or farming. The Greek word *aparchē* means the firstfruits of a crop, which guarantees more of the same kind to come. Many writers speak of the Spirit here as a 'break in' of the future. There is always more to come, and this is guaranteed. Becoming more holy means in this context 'to become what we are', or what God has made us in Christ.

The issue of the Spirit's indwelling in the Christlike or ethical life in Gal. 5.22–23 is well known. There Paul writes, 'The fruit of the Spirit is love, joy, peace, patience, kindness, generosity, faithfulness, gentleness and self-control.' Paul has previously drawn a contrasting picture of 'the works of the flesh', which include strife, jealousy, anger, and quarrels (5.20). The fruit of the Spirit should be manifest in 'those who belong to Christ' (5.24). Even if some of the positive qualities are shared among 'good' pagans, Paul argues that their basis and motivation are different. We consider this further in Chapter 15, on ethics and lifestyle.

---

[8] Neill Q. Hamilton, *The Holy Spirit and Eschatology in Paul* (Edinburgh: Oliver & Boyd, 1957).

Gifts of the Holy Spirit

This brings us to the second system of thought about the Holy Spirit, which Paul inherits. The gifts of the Holy Spirit are usually given to chosen individuals for specific tasks, but only within a communal or corporate framework, for the well-being of the whole community. The classic verse, which sums up Paul's approach, is 1 Cor. 12.7: 'To each is given the manifestation of the Spirit for the common good.' Paul explains that gifts of wisdom, healing, prophecy, or kinds of tongues are usually not given to the same person, but that the Spirit allots these gifts 'to each one individually, just as the Spirit chooses' (1 Cor. 12.11; cf. 12.8–10).

Some of these gifts remain open to more than one interpretation. Probably the most notorious is 'prophecy'. Many think of this as short inspired staccato utterances about specific churches or people. But 'prophecy' is an intelligible articulation of the message of the gospel and of Christian encouragement (1 Cor. 14.3, 4, 24–25). At least four or five writers, if not many more, argue convincingly that the basic meaning of prophecy is applied pastoral preaching of the main truths of the gospel, not some individually tailored 'message'. Thomas Gillespie gives perhaps the best account of this view, although there are others.[9]

Next to this, probably 'various kinds of tongues' is controversial. Certainly as Paul uses the term in 1 Corinthians 12 and 14, it is clear that 'tongues' are addressed not to fellow members of the congregation but to *God* (1 Cor. 14.2). It is also likely that when Paul alludes to the interpretation of tongues he refers to the person who speaks in tongues. There is no Greek word to imply 'someone' alongside the first speaker. Paul urges that the Christian who experiences wonderful, visionary things should be able to put what they have experienced into intelligible words to benefit the whole congregation. Up to this point he or she perhaps subconsciously or intuitively perceives the insight in question. Paul insists that the rest of the church needs to benefit through the use of intelligible speech (1 Cor. 14.1–19). Otherwise it is like blowing a military trumpet without its being a

---

[9] Gillespie, *The First Theologians*, esp. pp. 97–164; and Thiselton, *The First Epistle to the Corinthians*, pp. 956–70 and 1087–94 (cf. bibliography and comment, pp. 903–7 and 1077–81).

meaningful signal: it is mere noise (1 Cor. 14.7, 8; cf. 13.1). If we may speculate for a moment, Gerd Theissen, among others, believes that Paul's view of 'the secrets of the heart' is very close to our modern notion of the subconscious. Paul agrees that genuine praise can flow to God from the subconscious, but this may fail to benefit others (1 Cor. 14.4).[10] If they remain uninterpreted, tongues must be restricted to the private domain (14.2–5). But it is better for the tongues-speaker to pray to God for ability to articulate what he or she perceives (14.13–19).

The gift usually translated as 'the working of miracles' (1 Cor. 12.10, NRSV) is also controversial. We should not impose onto Paul the use of the Greek *dunamis* ('power' or 'force') as it is used in the first three Gospels. It may imply a supra-rational or even more than natural gift of God, but in the sense that anything that comes from the Spirit transcends, or lies beyond, nature. The Greek *energēmata dunameōn* really means 'effective deeds of power'.[11] Sometimes the Spirit's gifts seem to go beyond nature, but on the other hand we must not limit the Spirit's action to the spectacular. The Spirit in Paul and in John is self-effacing, serving to glorify Christ and build up the Church. Similarly, 'healing' finds its place among these gifts, but it is likely to include both normal processes and special acts. It is possible that today some stress the supernatural more than Paul does. This intensifies the problems of those who pray with faith, and yet remain technically 'unhealed'. Even Paul suffered eyesight problems (or even epilepsy), and bore his 'thorn in the flesh' (2 Cor. 12.7–9; Gal. 4.13–15; 6.11), although God revealed that his grace-in-weakness more than made up for it.

These phenomena are best explained at the communal level of the whole Church, rather than on an individual level. For this is Paul's frame of reference for speaking of the gifts of the Spirit. One example of this is the gift of 'faith'. In this context Paul is not speaking of justifying faith, which is given to every Christian, but of a special robust confidence in God, with which an individual can encourage the Church as a whole. Karl Barth offers an admirable comment on 'spiritual gifts'. He points out that many have 'counterparts

---

[10] Gerd Theissen, *Psychological Aspects of Pauline Theology*, trans. John P. Galvin (Edinburgh: T. & T. Clark, 1987), pp. 59–114 and 292–341.

[11] Thiselton, *The First Epistle to the Corinthians*, pp. 952–6.

in paganism', but that this does not in itself call them into question. However, he adds, 'What we are really concerned with is not phenomena in themselves, but with their whence? And whither?'

Is the Holy Spirit a 'person'?

Does Paul regard the Spirit as a 'person'? The word is analogical, in that God, or Christ, is more than 'a person' in the everyday sense of the term. Paul has a particular way of emphasizing this about the Holy Spirit. Sometimes he uses dynamistic, or less personal, language about the Spirit, as when he speaks of the Spirit's being 'poured out' like a liquid, or 'filling' people (Rom. 5.5; 2 Cor. 5.5; 1 Thess. 5.19; Eph. 5.18). More characteristically Paul uses the language of personal agency. For example, 'The Spirit *helps us* in our weakness; for we do not know how to pray as we ought' (Rom. 8.26). The Greek word used here, *sunantilambanetai*, is a strongly personal word. In the same passage the Spirit 'intercedes'. In 1 Cor. 2.10–16 the Spirit 'searches everything, even the depths of God' (2.10). He has an intimate knowledge of God, as God's Spirit (2.11). The Spirit 'teaches' God's ways (2.13), and gives to Christians 'the mind of Christ' (2.16).

The Holy Spirit in Paul is more than an impersonal 'force'. Modern thought is often unhelpful when it regularly speaks of 'spirituality' as if it were a human quality, rather than a mindset dependent on the action of the Holy Spirit. We may say, if we wish, that this interaction of imagery means that the Holy Spirit is '*supra*-personal', that is, more than, but not less than, personal. It is irrelevant to argue that no word for 'person' existed in the first century. This implies a word–concept exact match, and it has been shown that this is an error in linguistics.[12] Paul spoke of the Spirit in terms appropriate only to a personal agent, even if more is involved.

Paul does not identify the Spirit with the risen Christ. Some are misled by a false interpretation of 2 Cor. 3.17: 'Now the Lord is the Spirit.' The 'is' means 'denotes in the passage which I have quoted'; it is an exegetical 'is'. Paul is referring to Exod. 34.34, which recounts how Moses went in 'before the Lord to speak with him'. Paul interprets the veil of Moses (Exod. 34.35) as hiding his temporary and

---

[12] James Barr, *The Semantics of Biblical Language* (Oxford: Oxford University Press, 1961), pp. 216–46.

fading glory. Hence in 2 Corinthians he means: 'Now *Kyrios* (Lord) in this passage denotes the Spirit; and where the Spirit of the Lord is, there is liberty.' Taylor, Wright, Dunn, and Harris endorse this view.[13] But Paul does closely associate Christ and the Spirit, as we saw with reference to 1 Cor. 12.3 and similar passages. The Church is the body of Christ, over which he is also head. The Holy Spirit brings shared experience. We should render the word *koinōnia* in the Greek (2 Cor. 13.13; Phil. 2.1) 'being a shareholder', or 'participation in', rather than 'companionship with'; for the Spirit is the basis of our common life, in which we have become stakeholders or shareholders. In Ephesians 'the seal' of the Spirit is God's mark of ownership (1.13–14), but Christians also belong to Christ as their Lord.

As Athanasius and Basil saw, 1 Cor. 12.4–6 gives more than a hint of the Holy Trinity. Paul correlates as co-agents 'the same Spirit', 'the same Lord', and 'the same God' in terms respectively of gifts, service, and initiative or activation. This is co-joined with 1 Cor. 2.6–10, where the action of the Spirit leads to intimate knowledge of God and to 'the mind of Christ' (2.16). These passages also lead to 2 Cor. 13.13, where the grace of Christ, the love of God, and the *koinōnia* of the Spirit together come from a source beyond the created order. We conclude that Paul formulates the ingredients for a doctrine of the Holy Trinity.[14] But his main emphasis is less on doctrine, which is implied, than on practical experience. The Spirit inspires us to pray, comforts and strengthens us in times of doubt or hardship, makes Christ real to us and nurtures a Christlike mindset within us, and is our life-line to the world of God in Christ. Yet we saw from the Old Testament that he could equip Gideon and Samson for battle, and from 1 Corinthians 12 that he endows us with a variety of gifts. The Spirit has rightly been called 'the Beyond that is Within'.

---

[13] Harris, *The Second Epistle to the Corinthians*, pp. 310–13; Dunn, *The Theology of Paul the Apostle*, pp. 421–2; Vincent Taylor, *The Person of Christ in New Testament Teaching* (London: Macmillan, 1959), p. 54; and N. T. Wright, *The Climax of the Covenant: Christ and Law in Pauline Theology* (Edinburgh: T. & T. Clark, 1991), pp. 175–92.

[14] Haykin, *The Spirit of God*, pp. 59–169.

8

Paul's view of humanity

Paul does not set out a coherent view of humanity, as he does, for example, with the resurrection (1 Corinthians 15). He draws a distinction between God as Sovereign and Creator, and humanity as dependent and creaturely (Rom. 1.25). It is through Christ that God brings humanity into being (Col. 1.17). This implies that the very creation of humanity belongs to God's purposes of love. Being 'bodily' is a gift for humanity's good, and is not, as Plato argues, a source of regret. The body, as we shall see, makes discipleship visible and communicable.

Creatureliness and humanity in the image of God

Humankind shares the created universe with angels and powers (Rom. 8.38; Col. 1.16), or invisible forces. But humankind bears the image of God, as Paul inherited from Gen. 1.26, 27, and would have inferred from Ps. 8.5–8. Humanity receives 'dominion' as stewards over the animal and plant creation. This is not power to exploit animals and the world, but to accept responsibility for them. However, although Paul assumes the Old Testament view of humanity's creation in the image of God, humanity does not remain unsullied (see Chapter 9), and we can see the *unspoiled image* of God only in *Christ* (2 Cor. 4.4; Col. 1.15; 3.10). Therefore, as we noted, rather than asking the traditional question, 'Is Christ truly human?' Paul would have said that in the light of Christ we should first ask, 'Are *we* truly human?' Nevertheless, we may assume that, for Paul, being in God's image still includes rationality, dominion (or stewardship over the world, including the animal kingdom), and ability *to relate* to God and to others.

It is clear that Paul prizes human *rationality*. But this can be misused and abused, to serve the purposes of evil. The church at Thessalonica is not using rational judgement, and not using its mind, in the face of claims about the coming of Christ. They need a 'right mind' (1 Thess. 5.12, 14; 2 Thess. 3.15; cf. 2 Thess. 2.2). The Galatians have been seduced, or bewitched by Judaizing tendencies, so they need logically to reflect on the implications of the gospel (Gal. 3.1, 2). They are foolish. Paul prays that the Philippians will experience God's blessing on their minds and thoughts (Phil. 4.7). Sometimes the Greek word for mind (*nous*) means attitude or mind-set (1 Cor. 2.16), although often it simply means 'mind'. As Dunn and Bornkamm point out, the transformation of human existence is through a renewal of the mind (Rom. 12.2; cf. Eph. 4.23).[1] Christians are meant to *think*. But Paul rejects both a Platonist and 'Gnostic' view of the mind as a capacity connected with God and a 'higher' world. It is not a power for good in itself, but may be transformed into an essential tool for good. It becomes necessary, for example, to control irrational excesses of charismatic mysticism by clear, cool, sober, reflection on the part of the mind (1 Cor. 14.14–15; cf. Rom. 12.2).[2]

Paul, however, is no elitist who views humans as potential intellectuals. People *feel* and *will* as well as think. Hence *heart* (Greek, *kardia*) becomes important. Following Old Testament tradition, Paul uses the term to denote deep human feeling, an obstinate or determined will, or the core of one's being. Paul uses it more than 50 times, excluding Timothy and Titus. Paul feels sorrow in his heart (Rom. 9.2), and a person can be steadfast or determined in heart (1 Cor. 7.37), or Paul can pray that the peace of God may 'rule in your hearts' (Gal. 3.15). Nevertheless, the most 'modern' use of heart is to include what amounts to the *unconscious* or subconscious, as Theissen and Bultmann rightly argue.[3] To pour the love of God 'in our hearts' (Rom. 5.5) means 'through and through', including reaching aspects of the self of which we may be unaware. God 'searches the hearts' (Rom.

---

[1] Dunn, *The Theology of Paul the Apostle*, pp. 73–5; Günther Bornkamm, 'Faith and Reason in Paul' in *Early Christian Experience*, trans. P. L. Hammer (London: SCM Press, 1969), pp. 29–46.

[2] Cf. Robert Jewett, *Paul's Anthropological Terms: A Study of Their Use in Conflict Settings* (Leiden: Brill, 1971), pp. 358–90; S. K. Stowers, 'Paul on the Use and Abuse of Reason', in D. L. Balch and others (eds) *Greeks, Romans, Christians* (Minneapolis: Fortress Press, 1990), pp. 253–86.

[3] Theissen, *Psychological Aspects of Pauline Theology*, pp. 59–114 and 267–319; Rudolf Bultmann, *Theology of the New Testament*, vol. 2 (London: SCM Press, 1955), pp. 220–7.

8.27). Paul speaks of the secrets of the heart (1 Cor. 4.5; 14.25) and 'testing' hearts (1 Thess. 2.4). Mostly Paul uses 'heart' to mean 'in the core of one's being', as in, 'sent the Spirit to dwell in your hearts' (Gal. 4.6), 'The word is in your heart' (Rom. 10.8).

Paul's terminology

This at once raises questions about whether these terms 'mind', 'heart', and so on, denote 'parts' of people at all, or rather aspects or capacities of the whole human person. Paul believes in what today we call the psychosomatic unity of the whole person. Thus, surprisingly, but fully in accord with the Old Testament, there are few references to 'the soul' (Greek, *psychē*) as such, although more when the Greek word means 'life'. In Rom. 13.1 the AV translation 'Let every soul be subject to the higher powers' does not mean 'soul', but simply 'everyone'. The NRSV rightly has 'Let every person be subject . . .' 'Body' and 'soul' (as well as spirit) are *modes of a person's existence* in the physical public world. This is the world of either ordinary life or life in the spiritual, eternal, world. The term *psychē* does not usually carry special value in Paul; on the contrary, when it is used as an adjective (Greek, *psuchikos*) it should be translated either 'unspiritual' (1 Cor. 2.14, NRSV) or just 'ordinary'. It denotes being characterized by life or vitality, as animals may be. Its opposite 'spiritual', we shall see in 1 Cor. 15.42–44, means 'characterized by the Holy Spirit'. This is seldom a human quality.

The use of *psychē* to mean 'living creature' or 'ordinary person' is quite in harmony with the Old Testament, as Jewett and others claim.[4] The Hebrew term for 'soul' (*nephesh*) often means 'life' (Gen. 9.4; 19.17; 44.30; Exod. 4.19 and Lev. 17.14), and sometimes even denotes a dead body (Num. 9.6; 7.10). They risked their necks to save my *psychē* (Rom. 16.4; cf. 1 Thess. 2.8; Phil. 2.30) cannot mean 'soul', but denotes 'life'.

The term *flesh* (Greek, *sarx*) partly becomes a theological term in Paul, which we shall examine more fully in the next chapter. But it also serves as a term for neutral, creaturely, or vulnerable, human existence. It may denote the physical substance from which we are made.

---

[4] Jewett, *Paul's Anthropological Terms*, p. 356; cf. pp. 334–57.

'All flesh is not the same flesh' (1 Cor. 15.39) provides an example, where Paul refers to embodied life or bodily substance or material. Paul applies it there to animals as co-sharers of creation. Similarly, we noted that 'a thorn in the flesh' probably means 'a sharp physical pain' (2 Cor. 12.7, REB). Paul also refers to a weakness of the flesh (Gal. 4.13). This follows the Old Testament use of 'flesh' (Hebrew, *basar*). It inevitably takes on a further meaning in debates about circumcision (Rom. 2.28; Phil. 3.3, 4; Gal. 6.12, 13), where some 'boast in the flesh'. The phrase 'my natural kinsfolk' (Rom. 9.3) may mean 'Jews physically', or perhaps imply a little more.

'Flesh' denotes human vulnerability and fallibility, as when Paul (or a Pauline disciple) says, 'Our struggle is not against enemies of flesh and blood, but against the rulers . . . and powers' (Eph. 6.12). The words mean strong superhuman forces, not weak ones. This is like Job. 10.4, where God is asked, 'Have you eyes of flesh, to see as humans see?' or Isa. 31.3, 'The Egyptians are men, not God, and their horses flesh, not spirit.' The term here denotes human frailty. Even Christians can relapse into judging things by purely human (fleshly) standards (2 Cor. 11.18). Philemon v. 16 described Onesimus, the runaway slave, as both 'beloved in the flesh' (that is, as a man) 'and in the Lord' (as a Christian). The 'mind of the flesh' and similar uses will be considered in the next chapter.

Body is a very different matter. Ernst Käsemann rightly describes the body as a gift from God through which we can manifest our Christian discipleship and obedience to the Lordship of Christ *in the public, visible, world.* Thereby accepting Christ as Lord becomes communicable and credible, which it would not be if it were merely an 'inner' or 'private' matter.[5] This is close to the philosopher Wittgenstein's maxim that difficult concepts can best be understood by 'watching' what other people do in public. He calls this 'public criteria of meaning'.[6] Hence Paul appeals to the church at Corinth, 'glorify God in your body' (1 Cor. 6.20). (Some manuscript readings quite wrongly added 'and in your spirit', as in the AV.)

The notion in Christianity that somehow 'bodily' life is second best or of no interest to 'spiritual' people is at variance with Paul's

---

[5] Käsemann, *New Testament Questions of Today*, p. 135; cf. pp. 108–37.

[6] Ludwig Wittgenstein, *Philosophical Investigations* (German and English, Oxford: Blackwell, 1967), §54 (p. 27); cf. §§293–317 (pp. 100–4).

view. It comes from Plato, from many other Greeks, and from later Gnosticism. Paul readily uses athletic imagery about training the body (1 Cor. 9.24–27). He writes, 'Your bodies are members of Christ' (1 Cor. 6.17). 'Members' should be taken literally as body-parts, not metaphorically as if merely 'members' of a club. 'Body' is used for the Church, and this may derive from Christ's words, 'Why are you persecuting *me*?' (Acts 9.4; 22.7). In Rom. 12.1, Christians are to present their 'bodies' as a living sacrifice, which means 'themselves' in the visible and public domain. 'The body' is thus a temple of the Holy Spirit whether communally (1 Cor. 3.16–17) or individually (1 Cor. 6.19).[7] 'Body', some claim, has a binding force which enables humankind to share solidarity with one another and the animal kingdom. The body is also destined for resurrection (1 Cor. 15.33–49). 'God gives it a body, as he has chosen' (15.38). Here Paul means that mode of being which allows public communication, recognizability, and identity, even as 'heavenly bodies' function in non-earthly conditions. 'Spiritual' body does not contradict this, but refers (as we have claimed, and shall argue in Chapter 16) to being characterized by the Holy Spirit. Hence Paul agrees with the Corinthian slogan 'Food is meant for the stomach . . . and God will destroy both' (1 Cor. 6.13; the NRSV stops the quotation of the slogan too soon), but adds: 'The body is meant for the Lord, and the Lord for the body, and God who raised the Lord will also raise us' (1 Cor. 6.13–14).

Two controversial aspects of the human being have yet to be considered, namely *conscience* and *spirit*. While C. A. Pierce showed that conscience means primarily painful awareness of one's own wrong actions, and not, as the Stoics imagined, a divine directive about future conduct, others have since modified this view to allow for 'a good conscience' (2 Cor. 1.12; 1 Thess. 1.5; 3.9). In 1 Cor. 8.7, 10, 12, and 10.25–29 it verges on meaning *self-awareness*, stressing a security of conviction rather than necessarily a moral capacity as such. The Greek word for conscience, *syneidēsis*, at face value means a knowing-with, or co-knowing, as if another quality of the self considers the action of the self. At all events, it is not 'the voice of God',

---

[7] Albert L. P. Hogeterp, *Paul and God's Temple* (Leuven, Paris, and Dudley, MA: Peters, 2006), pp. 295–360, 379–86.

as some Greeks thought, for it may become damaged. It is probably somewhere between 'self-awareness' and 'conscience'.[8]

Spirit and bodily humanity

The problem about 'spirit' is that both the Greek and English cover two distinct things. They cover the human spirit as a human aspect, and the divine Holy Spirit as a person or agent. We noted this in the last chapter, where the REB translated Rom. 12.11 as 'be aglow with the Spirit', but NRSV as 'be ardent in spirit'. Paul's Greek comes to us in Uncials (capitals). The REB is more characteristic of Paul, but we cannot tell from the Greek. In fact the range of uses of 'spirit' includes (1) the human spirit; (2) a psychological use, as in 'spirit of bondage'; (3) seductive spirits (although Paul usually uses *daimōn* for this); and (4) the Holy Spirit or the Spirit of God.

Paul uses *human spirit* in closing greetings (Gal. 6.18; Phil. 4.23; Philemon v. 25). Usually 'your spirit' simply means 'you'. The use of poetic parallelism in 'My soul magnifies the Lord, and my spirit rejoices in God my Saviour' shows that soul and spirit are interchangeable (Luke 1.47). Paul writes, 'May your spirit, soul, and body be kept sound' (1 Thess. 5.23), to mean, 'May you be kept through and through.' The use of the adjective 'spiritual' (*pneumatikos*) shows that Paul's emphasis is on the Holy Spirit of God. 'We have received not the spirit of the world, but the Spirit who is from God' (1 Cor. 2.12) leads on to 'spiritual things' being what the Holy Spirit teaches (2.13) and spiritual people being those who are animated and characterized by the Holy Spirit (2.14–15). The same use marks the 'spiritual body' of the resurrection, which implies a self which is recognizable and identifiable publicly, but animated and characterized by the Holy Spirit. Paul is addressing the problem of moral transformation as the raised Christian enters God's immediate presence, rather than change into a non-material mode of existence.[9] There is a sharp difference between Paul and the Stoics. The Stoics thought

---

[8] Peter D. Gooch, 'Conscience in 1 Corinthians 8 and 10', *New Testament Studies* 33 (1987), pp. 244–54; H.-J. Eckstein, *Der Begriff Syneidēsis bei Paulus* (Tübingen: Mohr, 1983); C. A. Pierce, *Conscience in the New Testament* (London: SCM Press, 1965); and Thiselton, *The First Epistle to the Corinthians*, pp. 607–17 and 640–8.

[9] Thiselton, *The First Epistle to the Corinthians*, pp. 1258–81; and Wright, *The Resurrection of the Son of God*, pp. 342–56.

of the spirit as an immanent 'world-soul'; Paul thinks of spirit as a transcendent, holy, personal, agent, who is not a creature (cf. 1 Cor. 2.11–16).

Paul offers various intersections with, but also differences from, modern thought. The closest Paul comes to modern Western thought is his emphasis on the psychosomatic unity of humans and on our subconscious or unconscious. Self-deception is all too possible, as Sigmund Freud saw. He shares an understanding of the former with the Old Testament and Judaism: body affects mind, and mind affects body; they are a unity. The *heart* possesses secrets unknown even to the conscious mind, but known to God and open to the Spirit. But the word *spiritual* is used often today in a way incompatible with Paul. He would not have spoken of 'spirituality' as a vague human capacity for awareness of the divine, or to denote human religiosity, unless it was anchored in the Christlike work of the Holy Spirit. He would also not have denigrated *the body* in the name of Christian thought. Paul saw it as one of God's great gifts, and used it to communicate in part what Christian service and futurity meant.

We can take this further. Paul is not embarrassed or ashamed to urge Christians to rejoice in the physical aspect of sex. As we noted above (p. 9), and shall revisit in Chapter 15 on ethics, Paul was hugely ahead of his time in believing that women, as well as men, gained pleasure from this physical expression of love, rather than merely being a passive instrument for man's pleasure (1 Cor. 7.3–5). Paul shares the biblical view that love seeks the best for the other.

Similarly even money is also a gift, like the body, which provides a further opportunity to show publicly what one chooses to do with one's resources. Paul declares, 'I have learned to be content with whatever I have' (Phil. 4.11); 'I did not covet any man's silver or gold' (Acts 20.33). Not money itself but '*love* of money' is the root of all evil (1 Tim. 6.10). Some Christians, like Erastus, were public benefactors (a tablet about his donation still lies in the environs of ancient Corinth). The 'collection' expresses the mainly Gentile churches' concern for and solidarity with the poor in Jerusalem (1 Cor. 16.1–4; 2 Cor. 8.1–7). It is an expression of those who 'first gave themselves to the Lord' (2 Cor. 8.5). Paul's converts must 'do nothing from selfish ambition' (Phil. 2.3). Paul renounces ambition and personal power.

Paul rejoices in God and Christ rather than in human capacities. Yet he values and enjoins the use of the mind and thinking, and recognizes that the human heart enables us to feel deeply and passionately, as well as to conceal our motives and desires from us. He values the body as God's gift and vehicle of expressing our attitude to Christ. Perhaps most of all, being made in the image of God means that human beings have the capacity for relationships.[10] This includes men and women, Jew and Gentile, slave and free (Gal. 3.28) and friend and fiend. But above all it makes it possible to have a close relationship with God through Christ.

---

[10] Stanley J. Grenz, *The Social God and the Relational Self: A Trinitarian Theology of the Imago Dei* (Louisville: Westminster John Knox Press, 2001), pp. 267–303.

9

Human alienation and Paul on sin

There has been widespread misunderstanding of Paul's view of sin. Many see Paul as obsessed with the problem, often quoting Rom. 7.19. 'I do not do the good I want, but the evil I do not want is what I do.' They often assume that Rom. 7.7–24 is autobiographical, when in fact Paul is discussing the plight of humanity, not his own pilgrimage. Paul does not struggle with a bad conscience, as Stendahl long ago observed.[1]

Paul has a robust conscience. Even before his call and conversion he declares himself 'as to righteousness under the law, blameless' (Phil. 3.6), and Rom. 2.17—3.20 speaks not of a bad conscience, but of the failure of Israel as a people. In 1 Cor. 4.4 Paul declares that he has nothing on his conscience. He sees sin and guilt, or what it amounts to, in a different light from what many imagine. It receives an important place, but Paul knows of nothing against himself (1 Cor. 4.4).

Three aspects of sin

In contrast to many modern assumptions, sin is not primarily a series of acts performed by an individual, such as not telling the truth, or failing to love our neighbour. Paul is much more concerned with the *corporate or communal* state of humanity, and its alienation from God and from one another caused by misdirected desire.[2] He does indeed take over the Old Testament notion that one form of 'sin' is *missing the mark, failing*, or *committing a sin of omission*. The Hebrew Bible usually uses the word *chatta'th* for such misdemeanours (Gen. 4.7;

---

[1] K. Stendahl, *Paul among Jews and Gentiles* (London: SCM Press, 1977), pp. 78–96; reprinted from 'The Apostle Paul and the Introspective Conscience of the West', *Harvard Theological Review* 56 (1963), pp. 199–215.

[2] Tom Holland, *Contours of Pauline Theology: A Radical New Survey of Influences on Paul's Biblical Writings* (Fearn, Rosshire: Mentor, 2004), esp. pp. 96–9 on Romans 7.

18.20; Exod. 10.17; 32.30–34; Lev. 4.3; 16.16; Deut. 9.18; 1 Sam. 2.17;
Job 10.6; Pss. 25.7; 51.2; Isa. 6.7; 43.25; and over 250 other references).
In the Septuagint *hamartia* regularly translates the term, and in the
Pauline writings it occurs in Rom. 3.9; 5.12, 13, 26; 6.1, 2, 11; 7.7;
1 Cor. 15.58; and many times elsewhere. The Greek term also occurs
in Jewish literature: 4 Macc. 4.12; Wisd. 1.4; 2.12; 10.13; 11.23; Sir.
2.11; 3.3; 4.21; and elsewhere, sometimes in cognate forms. But this
is only one of three aspects of the phenomenon.

A second important word in the Hebrew Bible is *pāshaʿ*, in its
verbal form 'to rebel', or 'to transgress', and *peshaʿ*, 'transgression' (Amos
4.4; Prov. 8.21; Jer. 3.13; 1 Kings 12.19; 2 Kings 1.1; 3.17; Isa. 1.28;
46.4; 48.8; 53.12; Hos. 14.10; and elsewhere. It is used of nations
rebelling against kings, and Israel or people rebelling against God.
Two major Greek translations are *asebeia*, 'ungodliness', and *parabasis*, 'transgression'. The latter occurs in Wisd. 14.31 and other Jewish
literature. 'Transgression' (*parabasis*) can be found in Rom. 4.15; 5.14;
and elsewhere in Paul; 'ungodliness' (*asebeia*) is found in Rom. 1.18;
11.26; and elsewhere. These words primarily denote an act, but also
a state, in which those who commit ungodliness or transgression are
in a state of alienation from God and often from one another. The
Hebrew *peshaʿ* is also translated by *paraptōma*, 'misdeed' or 'trespass'
(2 Cor. 5.19; Rom. 4.25; 5.15; Gal. 6.1; Col. 2.13). This is a metaphorical extension of 'blunder', or 'false step'. But the Hebrew background
of 'rebellion' remains a contributory factor to the meaning of the word.
It occurs in Greek-speaking Jewish writings, for example in Wisd. 8.13;
10.2.

The third major Hebrew term is *ʿāwōn*, which means 'iniquity', 'guilt',
'a distorted state', or its consequences, including 'internal' results or
external punishment.[3] In the Hebrew Bible it occurs in Gen. 15.16;
Exod. 21.43; 2 Kings 7.9; Ps. 51.7; Hos. 9.7; Job 15.5; 20.27; Jer. 11.10;
and in many other references. In Gen. 4.13 Cain cries to God, 'My
ʿāwōn (punishment or guilt) is more than I can bear.' 'Internal'
punishment concerns the distortion, incapacity, or alienation of
the self consequent on failure or rebellion. 'External' punishment
occurs when God intervenes as Judge to impose some penalty. The
Septuagint and Greek Jewish literature have no precise equivalent, but

---

[3] Francis Brown (ed.), a revision of F. Brown, S. R. Driver, and C. A. Briggs (eds), *Hebrew and English Lexicon* (Lafayette, IN: Associated Publishers, 1988), pp. 730–1.

hamartia translates *'awōn* as well as *chatta'th* and *pesha'*. Paul usually uses paraphrases such as 'guilt', 'bondage', 'slavery', or 'alienation'. The power of sin becomes a way of expressing sin's resultant consequences, and especially particular uses of 'flesh', 'death', and even the 'wrath' of God. He uses various forceful metaphors such as 'sin deceived me and through it (the commandment) killed me' (Rom. 7.11). Unredeemed Israel or humankind is 'wretched' and involved in corporate powers that bring death (7.24). The result of wrongdoing is to be 'sold into slavery under sin' (7.14). Christians are 'delivered from bondage' (8.21). They must not become entangled 'again to a yoke of slavery' or bondage (Gal. 5.1).

One of Paul's arguably distinctive contributions, along with John, is to downplay the naive moralistic idea of sin as committing acts or missing the mark, and to emphasize the more serious concept of sin as *state*, which often involves bondage and alienation. Bondage, as Augustine and Luther saw, shatters the illusion that humanity can deal with the problem on its own. Alienation underlines the difficulty of calling upon God, if the problem of sin is unresolved. It becomes, in effect, a vicious circle, to which only the work of Christ offers a solution. On the basis of Christ's work, the Holy Spirit may begin a process which humanity cannot achieve on its own.

'Flesh' and bondage

Of the total uses of 'flesh' in Paul, W. D. Davies has noted that 56 are value-neutral, denoting materiality, physical structure, kinship, the sphere of present existence, or weakness; while 35 uses are ethical or theological, relating to bondage, to alienation, or to some other effect of sin.[4] We noted the former in our last chapter. Paul on occasion uses 'flesh' to denote all humanity in its distance from God: 'In me, that is in my flesh, no good thing makes its home' (Rom. 7.18). But today these words may convey a false impression to a modern audience. Paul is *not* repeating the view of Plato and many Greeks that humanity is wicked because it belongs to the material or transitory realm. He means that by nature he is part of that corporate

---

[4] W. D. Davies, *Paul and Rabbinic Judaism: Some Rabbinic Elements in Pauline Theology* (London: SPCK, 1958), p. 19.

structure which has failed to give God his due, and has even by impli-cation rebelled against him as sovereign, to whom worship and alle-giance is due. Whether humanity is aware of it or not, the attitude of this corporate structure (Paul calls it 'the mind of the flesh') is in effect at war (in a state of hostility) with God (Rom. 8.7).

Paul expresses this principle in various ways. He declares, 'We are under the power of sin', whether as Jews or as Gentiles (Rom. 3.9). The 'body' (i.e. the corporate structure) of sin is to be destroyed (Rom. 6.6). 'You were slaves of sin' (Rom. 6.6). Sin pays 'wages' like an em-ployer, but 'the wages of sin (which at first look promising) is death' (Rom. 6.25). This is universal to all humanity. Whether Jew or Gentile, 'there is no distinction, since all have sinned and all fall short of the glory of God' (Rom. 3.22, 23). So Paul presses into service for his argument the deceptive employer who pays 'wages' that turn out to be death (Rom. 6.23); a king who rules like a tyrant and forces his subjects to obey (Rom. 5.21); and a master who enslaves people and treats them harshly (Rom. 6.6). This 'objective' situation paints the picture conveyed by *'awōn* in vivid colours.

Paul's language is strong. It can seem to raise a difficulty for many in the modern world because he speaks of wrongdoing as bringing humanity under the 'wrath' of God. One writer has underrated this as a process of cause and effect in a moral universe. There is some truth in this, since often wrongdoing brings its own 'reward'. In the same way that hard piano practice brings the 'reward' of being able to play well without an additional external reward, so in this sense sin brings its 'reward' in the form of various inbuilt consequences. But Paul means more than this, as Alan Richardson explicitly stated.[5] God's wrath is 'revealed from heaven' (Rom. 1.18), because although humanity had recognition of God to hand, 'they exchanged the glory of the immortal God for images' (that is, self-made constructions) (1.23). This concept must be purged of any ideas of anthropomor-phic 'revenge'. But a loving parent is angry at self-destruction, while a careless parent remains indifferent to it. *The opposite of love is not anger, but indifference*, we earlier said (p. 51). An explanation in terms of natural processes runs the risk of making God appear less actively

---

[5] Alan Richardson, *Introduction to the Theology of the New Testament* (London: SCM Press, 1958), p. 76.

concerned. Moltmann sees emotion in God as at the heart of the Trinity, and fully reflected in the biblical writings.[6]

Human 'misery' and alienation

The modern reader can also find that Paul's attitude to the 'state' or stance of humans and to the 'Fall' raises problems. Action represents no more than a part of misdirected desire. Paul argues that evil is deeper than conscious action, but a disorientation of the self away from God. Wolfhart Pannenberg writes, 'The decay of the doctrine of original sin led to the anchoring of the concept of sin in *acts* of sin', and consequent theological 'failure'.[7] 'The term "misery" sums up our detachment from God. The term "alienation" has a similar breadth.'[8] Pannenberg explains that 'misery' is the lot of all who are deprived of the fellowship with God that is the destiny of human life and the source of blessing and well-being. Paul thus says, 'Wretched man that I am', when he contemplates such existence (Rom. 7.24). It is in this light that we see that Christ alone is fully human, for he does enjoy fellowship with God. The classical significance of Augustine, Pannenberg comments, is that he saw Paul's link between sin and its consequences more clearly than many of the other Fathers, and this was an 'extraordinary achievement'.[9]

The 'Fall', which seems such a problem for much modern thought, does not suggest that for Paul a historical Adam is the *cause* of human alienation and misery. He concedes that we all somehow share in Adam's loss, but as those who willingly follow the same path. However we understand 'Adam', humankind, apart from Christ, stands in solidarity with Adam, suffering destructive forces in which they share; on the other hand the new humanity 'in Christ' provides new creation and a new corporate solidarity. Thus *evil forces in the world are more powerful than isolated individuals*. Postmodern thought understands this well, in contrast to the individualism of modernity from Descartes and the secular Enlightenment onwards

---

[6] Moltmann, *The Trinity and the Kingdom of God*, pp. 31–52.

[7] Wolfhart Pannenberg, *Systematic Theology*, 3 vols, trans. G. W. Bromiley (Grand Rapids: Eerdmans and Edinburgh: T. & T. Clark, 1991, 1994, 1998), vol. 2, p. 254.

[8] Pannenberg, *Systematic Theology*, vol. 2, p. 178.

[9] Pannenberg, *Systematic Theology*, vol. 2, p. 241.

(discussed in Chapter 17). *No individual is isolated from forces of evil that stem from the 'Adam' solidarity.* Human misery *began* with Adam, just as blessing *begins* with Christ (Rom. 5.12–21). But to suggest that Adam *caused* individuals to sin conflicts with Paul's statement, 'death spread to all because *all* sinned' (Rom. 5.12), 'Death exercised dominion from Adam to Moses . . . but the free gift is not like the trespass, for . . . the grace of God abounded for the many' (Rom. 5.14–15). If we dissociate Adam from humanity's sin, it becomes more difficult to understand Christ's role as head of the new humanity, bringing the free gift of salvation. Paul sees a parallel and a contrast: 'Where sin increased, grace abounded all the more' (5.20).

The Judaism of Paul's day reflected a struggle between viewing Adam as a cause of sin and sin as the responsibility purely of the self alone. Like Paul, 4 Ezra (also called 2 Esdras) stresses the powerlessness of the law. Sin is universal (4 Ezra 3.35–36; 7.46, 68; 8.35); 4 Ezra declares, 'O Adam, what have you done! For though it was you who sinned, the fall was not yours alone, but ours also who are your descendants' (4 Ezra 7.117–118; cf. 116). It also says, 'A grain of evil seed was sown in the heart of Adam . . . and how much fruit of ungodliness has it produced up to this time' (4.30; cf. 3.21–23; 7.11, 12).[10] But *2 Baruch* has the very opposite approach. Famously an almost 'Pelagian' passage (that is, one that seems to deny original sin) reads: 'Adam is not therefore the cause, save only in his own self; but each of us has been the Adam of his own soul' (*2 Baruch* 64.19, cf. 15–18). Philo sees Adam as the rational principle, and Eve as the sensuous element in human nature (Philo, *De mundi opificio*, 56). This idea is not in Paul.

Williams tries to link the Rabbinic notion of an inherited 'evil impulse' (*yêtzer hâ-râ'*) with Paul on sin. But there is also 'an impulse to good'. Both impulses function after the 'Fall'. It is a description, but not an explanation. If it has any role, this is more likely to relate to humanity's divided self in Rom. 7.7–24.

Many see three versions of the 'Fall' of Gen. 3.1–34 in Rom. 1.18–32; Rom. 5.12–21; and Rom. 7.7–24. We may admit that Paul's attack on the moral effects of idolatry and his extensive lists of vices

---

[10] N. P. Williams, *The Ideas of the Fall and Original Sin: A Historical and Critical Study* (London and New York: Longman, Green & Co., 1929), pp. 79–80; cf. pp. 70–91; and also Davies, *Paul and Rabbinic Judaism*, pp. 32–5.

can be paralleled in the homilies of Greek-speaking Jewish synagogues. But Paul would have grown up with them and, even as a Christian, quotes this language as his own. It forms part of his argument that both Gentiles and Jews stand equally under the judgement of God and falling short of his purpose. He first condemns the Gentile world as standing in need of grace, and then turns to Jews in chapters 2 and 3 to say that they stand under the same judgement. Romans 5.12–21 considers the corporate status of humanity as bound up either with Adam and disaster, or with Jesus Christ and grace. If we deny that humanity is 'in Adam', we risk denying, by the same logic, new humanity 'in Christ'.

The technical term for this is the 'corporate solidarity' of humanity. It used to be difficult to explain this concept, since we have all inherited the individualism of the Enlightenment. But today everyone is familiar with the corporate solidarity of a football team where one member of a team can either (like Adam) cause an 'own goal', or (like Christ) score for the team, to whom the goal is credited. No one claims that the rules of the game are unfair. It means sharing the liabilities and advantages of the whole group.

Romans 7.7–24 underlines the inadequacy of the law to deal with sin. Indeed on occasion the very command *not* to do something provokes us even more strongly to do it (7.8–10). The law itself is spiritual (7.14), but given the condition of humanity, it merely shows a greater need for Christ. This is a careful outworking of Galatians 3, and Gal. 4.21—5.1. Sin has become a 'power'; and the one greater power is God in Christ and the Spirit. Paul is far from being introspective or gloomy. He does not discuss this subject for its own sake; but he concludes the chapter, 'Thanks be to God through Jesus Christ our Lord' (Rom. 7.25), who can deliver us from this capacity of death (7.24). Christ objectively deals with it; the Holy Spirit subjectively implements Christ's work.

10

The work of Christ and being 'in Christ'

The centrality of the cross

For Paul the cross of Christ became the focal point of everything. He defines the gospel message as 'the word of the cross' (1 Cor. 1.18). In Galatians he interrupts the usual words of greeting with 'from Christ who sacrificed himself for our sins' (Gal. 1.4). In 1.9 he exclaims: 'If we or an angel from heaven should proclaim to you a gospel contrary to what we proclaimed to you, let that one be accursed!' He tells the church in Corinth: 'In Christ God was reconciling the world to himself, not counting their trespasses against them' (2 Cor. 5.19). Paul declares, 'May I never boast of anything except the cross of our Lord Jesus Christ' (Gal. 6.14). Odysseus may glory in his cleverness; but Paul glories only in the cross of Christ.

Paul uses a variety of imagery and analogies to help his readers to understand the cross. In some passages he uses a mixture of substitution or participation: 'If many died through one man's trespass, much more surely have the grace of God and the free gift of the one man, Jesus Christ, abounded for the many' (Rom. 5.15). It is a matter of controversy whether Paul here speaks of substitution, participation, or representation, or elements of all three. But the simplest way of conveying this profound mystery to modern readers is perhaps to say that *Christ did for humanity what humanity was incapable of doing for itself*. In football it is all too possible for a player to substitute for another, and then for the whole team to be credited with the substitute's goal. He is substitute, representative, and participant. Paul writes, 'Through the obedience of the one, shall the many be constituted righteous' (Rom. 5.19); or 'One died for all' (2 Cor. 5.21).

In fact Paul uses other analogies or imagery; but most are related to specific aspects of human misdirected desire or alienation. Two images resonate with the modern world, for they are drawn from

everyday life. The first is especially relevant to an economic down-
turn and increasing debt in the closing years of the first decade of
the new millennium. A proposal to cancel developing countries' debt
also provides a ready parallel. Paul uses the image of a record of debt
'that stood against us'. Christ, he says, 'has set this aside, nailing it to
the cross' (Gal. 2.14). This was a familiar phenomenon in the world
of Paul's day. But it is no less familiar as common currency today.
Cancelled debt is an analogy familiar in hymns and in the Lord's Prayer.
It relates to the notion of sin as a debt. Anselm underlined that sin
is failing to give God due worship and obedience.

A second image from Paul is that of purchase-price or 'redemption' from slavery. Every Jew would be familiar with its use in the
Hebrew and Greek Bible. In the book of Judges, (1) Israel does evil;
(2) this provokes the Lord to anger; (3) God 'sells' Israel into oppression; (4) Israel then cries to the Lord; (5) God raises up a saviour
and *redeems* them from jeopardy (Judg. 3.7–11, 12–30). This cycle of
events results in 'peace' or 'salvation'. The Hebrew term for 'redeem'
and 'redeemer' (*go'el* and *gā'al*, or *pādāh*) occurs in Exodus (Exod.
6.6; 15.13; Pss. 74.2; 77.15), and in the second great saving event of
the return from exile (Isa. 43.1; 44.6; 47.4; 60.16). It also applies to
personal vindication or individual redemption (Job 19.25). *Go'el*
also means 'to do the work of a near kinsman', who can redeem
a near relative on their behalf. In substance, redemption means
redemption *from* a state of oppression or jeopardy; *by* a costly price
or redeeming action; *to* a state of security, freedom, or well-being.

Many today are familiar with redeeming a pledge temporarily
given to a pawnbroker or moneylender. A person then can pay a price
and receive the object back. In Exod. 21.30 when a man has earned
a death penalty for an act of negligence which led to someone's death,
a ransom could be paid in place of his death (*pādāh* is used). In Isa.
43.2–4 a prophecy of redemption points to the liberation of Israel.

Gentiles would also be familiar with this analogy. Adolf
Deissmann earlier cited the analogy of a 'purchase' of slaves for 'freedom' by pagan deities. He rightly referred to inscriptions at Delphi
and elsewhere.[1] More recently, however, Dale Martin and others have

---

[1] Adolf Deissmann, *Light from the Ancient East: The New Testament Illustrated by
Recently Discovered Texts from the Graeco-Roman World*, trans. L. R. M. Strachan
(London: Hodder & Stoughton, 1927), pp. 319–30.

shown conclusively that this misunderstands Paul's point. In Paul, the 'purchase' redeems humanity *from* an evil master, namely the powers of evil, not to be free and autonomous, but to the new lordship of a good master, Jesus Christ.[2] We noted in Chapter 5, when we considered Christ as Lord (*Kyrios*), that to belong to Jesus as Lord meant that he took over our care for us. The slave of a 'good' lord was actually better off, we said, than poor free people, who only had their own resources and status for security. To 'belong' to Christ involved the protection of his name, honour, and love. But the basis of this 'exchange of Lords' lay in Christ's act of redemption. It goes beyond the metaphor of purchase to ask, 'To whom is the price paid?' It is a metaphor of *cost*. Christ has paid the price of sin.

One of the most famous of Paul's allusions can be found in 1 Cor. 6.19, 20: 'You are not your own; for you were bought with a price.' Paul repeats this in 1 Cor. 7.22–23: 'A freed person belongs to the Lord . . . he or she is a slave of Christ. You were bought with a price; do not become slaves of human masters.' In Gal. 3.13 Paul declares, 'Christ redeemed us from the curse of the law'; and he adds, 'God sent his Son . . . in order to redeem those who were under the law' (Gal. 4.4, 5). Metaphorically the law itself is seen as an owner or 'lord', who places humanity in bondage to it. Here the aspect of sin most in view is that of a 'power' who places humanity into bondage. The law imposes a vicious circle of effects, which intensify human guilt, and the human situation of helplessness. 'Holy' as it is, the law is weak, in that it cannot remedy the human plight. It merely increases consciousness of sin and guilt. In common with the apocalyptists, Paul looks for new creation, rather than increased human reformation. Christians need 'redemption', even if the price is costly.

Sacrifice as substitution *and* participation

Cultic imagery, however, may need to be explained more carefully to modern enquirers. Paul writes, 'Our paschal lamb, Christ, has been sacrificed' (1 Cor. 5.7). The interpretation of 'For our sake he made him to be sin . . . so that in him we might become the righteousness

---

[2] Martin, *Slavery as Salvation*, pp. 63–8 and throughout; Thiselton, *The First Epistle to the Corinthians*, pp. 544–65.

of God' (2 Cor. 5.21) remains controversial, because this might well mean 'made him a sin-offering' for us. But the term does not necessarily mean this, and some would not agree that 'sacrifice' dominates Paul's thought to this extent. Some argue that it is difficult to decide on which view is right, because the Old Testament Hebrew behind the Greek, *chattā'th* and *'ashām* can mean 'sin' and/or 'sin-offering'. The same ambiguity characterizes Rom. 8.3: God sent his Son 'as a sin-offering' (Greek *peri hamartias*). As Murray Harris points out, the background is in Lev. 4.1–35 on sin-offerings and perhaps in Isa. 53.4–12, where 'the Lord laid on him (the Servant of God) the iniquity of us all'.[3] We may today find the sacrificial system hard to understand, but it is the *presupposition* of Paul's view of the cross and atonement. These verses include aspects of participation and representation, but also of exchange and substitution.

This brings us to Paul's legal or forensic imagery, which involves the notion of a penalty. Many years ago the Methodist scholar Vincent Taylor concluded a study of 'forensic' passages with the comment, 'Everyone desires a better word than "penal", but until we find it, we ought not to abandon it.'[4] One of the most widely known passages occurs in Gal. 3.13, 'Christ has become a curse for us', where Paul applies Deut. 21.23 to Christ: 'A hanged man is accursed by God.' In Romans the parallel, generally agreed, came from the shared apostolic teaching before Paul, but is readily endorsed by Paul. Jesus our Lord 'was handed over to death for our trespasses and was raised for our justification' (Rom. 4.25). Jeremias includes this with 'forensic' imagery, together with the image of the cancelled debt which we have already noted in Col. 2.14.[5] Whiteley contests the 'substitutionary' force of the standard passages (Rom. 8.3; 2 Cor. 5.21; Gal. 3.13), urging that they mean only 'one with the sinner'.[6] Although he probably underestimates the place of 'substitution' (or the 'for us' aspect, although 'for' is broad in meaning), Whiteley is rightly concerned that we do not forget our involvement with the cross. People do not simply gain its benefits as observers, rather than as participants (just

---

[3] Harris, *The Second Epistle to the Corinthians*, p. 452; cf. pp. 449–56.
[4] Vincent Taylor, *The Atonement in New Testament Teaching* (London: Epworth Press, 1940), p. 130.
[5] Jeremias, *The Central Message of the New Testament*, pp. 36–7.
[6] Whiteley, *The Theology of St. Paul*, pp. 134–40.

as we saw that even God is no mere 'observer' of the atonement). Christ's work is all-sufficient for us. We do not have to 'add' to it. But we are identified with it as those who also 'die with Christ', and are transformed by it. Dunn rightly insists that these verses 'remove sin from the sinner', and applies the weight of the sacrificial system to them, but he also speaks of 'the inadequacy of the word "substitution"'.[7] He does not say that 'substitution' is wrong; but that it is inadequate alone. Both aspects of the cross are true: Christ has dealt with sin totally; but we are not left to live as we lived before.

How does this tension arise? Even if some years ago, J. K. S. Reid has navigated through this maze helpfully. He contrasts: (1) 'a *rule of correspondence*', whereby *participation* or sharing applies to the atonement of Christ; and (2) 'a *rule of contrariety*', where Christ died as our *substitute* in our place.[8] Like James Denney, Reid is content with the line in a hymn, 'In my place condemned he stood.' But this is not the *whole* truth. The rule of *contrariety* applies where 'Christ wins those benefits for us who had himself no need of them.'[9] Because Christ died, we live; because he suffered, Christians are free to rejoice; because Christ was reckoned as guilty, we are reckoned as innocent. But the rule of *correspondence* also applies: we participate in Christ's death and resurrection; Christians have been 'raised with Christ' (Col. 3.1); 'If while we were enemies, we were reconciled to God through the death of his Son, much more, surely, will we be saved by his life' (Rom. 5.10). Both principles operate. The rule of correspondence saves us from looking at the cross as mere spectators, as if we were not involved. The rule of *contrariety* gives us full assurance: it has Christ who is the sole ground of acquittal or forgiveness, even if people fail or are half-hearted in their faith or involvement. A theology of substitution has sometimes been regarded as harsh and unattractive. But Christians need assurance that Christ died in *their* place. Admittedly this provides only part of the story. A Christian who does not participate in some way in dying and being raised with Christ is a contradiction in terms.

We must, however, take a step back, because there is a second way in which 'substitution' can be misunderstood. Not only is it an

---

[7] Dunn, *The Theology of Paul the Apostle*, pp. 218 and 223.
[8] J. K. S. Reid, *Our Life in Christ* (London: SCM Press, 1963), pp. 90–1 (my italics).
[9] Reid, *Our Life in Christ*, pp. 90–1.

'inadequate' description on its own; as we have noted, there is also the danger of separating too rigidly the work of God the Father from that of God the Son. Someone once remarked: 'Only a terrible father would send his son to do all the horrible work.' God did not 'send' Christ to suffer, and stand apart from it. The notion that God cannot suffer turns him into the Absolute of Plato, not of Paul. As we have already quoted from Moltmann, 'A God who cannot suffer cannot love.' God's grace, for Paul, is not the *fruit* of sacrifice, but the *root* of sacrifice. 'God was in Christ reconciling the world to himself' (2 Cor. 5.19). 'All this is from God, who has reconciled us to himself through Christ' (5.18). There is no thought in Paul of a grudging God being persuaded by Christ on the cross to give humanity a second chance. God 'sent' his Son because it was the shared purpose of God as Father, Son, and Holy Spirit.

The place of meeting as 'expiation' and/or 'propitiation'?

Before we explore 'participation' further, we must pause to examine one 'difficult' and controversial passage, namely Rom. 3.25. At least six views deserve serious respect: (1) The NRSV translates the verse, referring to Christ, as 'whom God put forward as *a sacrifice of atonement* by his blood, effective through faith'; (2) the REB has 'the means of *expiating* sin'; (3) J. B. Phillips, the AV, and the Anglican Book of Common Prayer have 'the means of *propitiation*' or simply '*propitiation*'; (4) Anders Nygren argues for *mercy-seat*; while (5) C. K. Barrett suggests '*expiatory agency*';[10] and (6) others suggest simply *place of meeting*, on the ground of its effect. All are divergent attempts to translate the Greek *hilastērion*, which occurs in the New Testament nowhere else except in 1 John 2.2; 4.10; and once in Heb. 9.5. Danker's classic *Lexicon* offers both 'expiation' and 'propitiation'.[11] We could cite more writers on each side of this debate. But the fact

---

[10] Anders Nygren, *Commentary on Romans*, trans. C. C. Rasmussen (London: SCM Press, 1952), p. 156; and C. K. Barrett, *A Commentary on the Epistle to the Romans* (London: A. & C. Black, 1962), p. 77.

[11] W. F. Danker (ed.), *Greek–English Lexicon of the New Testament* (based on Walter Bauer, W. F. Arndt, and F. W. Gingrich's *Lexicon*, 3rd edn, Chicago: University of Chicago Press, 2000), p. 474.

is that there are advantages and disadvantages for each term. Each needs to be explained. *Expiation* is a means of covering sin. Dodd compares it to using disinfectant. The advantage is that it avoids the notion of propitiating God, as if his favour needed to be bought, bribed, or at least won over. But its disadvantage is that it implies that the cross is a mechanism, not a matter of personal dealings. *Propitiation* has the advantage of being a personal word. But it has the disadvantage that it can easily be misunderstood. The cardinal principle is that Paul applies it to God *only* when God is its subject, or the initiator of propitiation. He *chooses* that the cross is a means of propitiation. But without that explanation, *expiation* remains perhaps a safer word. 'Place of meeting' is an even better, popular term, even if it is superficial for those who want to understand more of God's ways in Christ.

The place of meeting as reconciliation

For the modern world Paul's use of the term *reconciliation* takes its place among the other terms as probably having most substance today. Everywhere we see alienation and estrangement, whether between nations or between spouses, or between parents and children. Existentialist atheists such as Sartre and Camus cannot avoid it. In this context reconciliation is the putting right of a relationship of estrangement or hostility. Paul uses this term repeatedly of the cross. But to understand its basis we need to explore Paul's variety of images and analogies more deeply. He asserts that he has been given 'the ministry of reconciliation' (2 Cor. 5.19). 'We entreat you on behalf of Christ, be reconciled to God' (2 Cor. 5.20).

Paul expresses a 'participatory' dimension often in terms of sharing the death and resurrection of Christ. Schweitzer many years ago claimed that Paul and Jesus were at one in saying that 'Everything depends upon the realization of fellowship with Jesus.'[12] Paul speaks of knowing or experiencing 'the fellowship (Greek *koinōnia*) of his (Christ's) sufferings, being conformed to his death' (Phil. 3.10). He declares that Christians are 'fellow heirs with Christ, if we suffer with him' (Rom. 8.17). In baptism we are 'buried with him' (Rom. 6.4). When he says that he carries in his body 'the marks (Greek *stigmata*)

---

[12] Schweitzer, *The Mysticism of Paul the Apostle*, p. 107; cf. p. 121.

of Jesus', Paul refers to the brandings by which a slave was made recognizable as his master's property (Gal. 6.17). Paul has been crucified with Christ, and (he says) 'it is no longer I who live, but it is Christ who lives in me' (Gal. 2.20).

Being in Christ

Another way in which Paul expresses this is 'being in Christ'. Some have distinguished up to five ways in which 'in Christ' is used:[13] (1) it can mean 'because Christ has come' (Rom. 3.24); (2) it can be used as a simple preposition, for example 'boast in Christ' (1 Cor. 1.31); (3) Paul has an instrumental use, for example, 'we beseech you in the Lord Jesus' (1 Thess. 4.1); and (4) he has a representative use, for example, 'as in Adam, so in Christ' (1 Cor. 15.22); and (5) he has a 'mystical' or corporate use, for example, 'I can do all things in him who strengthens me' (Phil. 4.1). All Christians are 'in Christ' primarily as an identity and status, by which 'the Christian lives in a new world, and is a new creature'; but also as a daily *living out* of union in Christ, in sharing in his death and resurrection.[14] The experiences of Christ are re-enacted in the individual and church. The main emphasis falls on the grafting of branches, as it were, into one entity. An ever-closer intertwining follows the initial grafting. Here we speak not only of 'substitution' but of 'identification'.

Nevertheless, if 'being in Christ' constitutes both the basis of Christian existence and a long process of daily experience, how can Paul say that Christians have *already died* with Christ (as the basis of their new creation) and that they *continue to die and be raised* with Christ (as their daily experience)? Robert Tannehill grapples with this question.[15] He divides his book on the subject into two parts. The first addresses being in Christ (or dying with Christ) as the basis of the new life, and considers such passages as Rom. 6.3–6 and 2 Cor. 5.14–17. The second part addresses dying and being raised with Christ (being in Christ) as the structure of the new life. This, in turn,

---

[13] Weiss, *Earliest Christianity*, vol. 2, pp. 468–9.

[14] Alfred Wikenhauser, *Pauline Mysticism: Christ in the Mystical Teaching of St. Paul*, trans. J. Cunningham (Edinburgh: Nelson and Freiburg: Herder, 1960), pp. 93–4; cf. pp. 50–65.

[15] Robert C. Tannehill, *Dying and Rising with Christ: A Study in Pauline Theology* (Berlin: Töpelmann, 1967).

is divided into the experience of ethical action, the experience of suffering, and transformation at Christ's coming.

The ethical implications of dying with Christ or being in Christ are found in Romans 6. Paul exhorts his readers, 'Reckon yourselves to be dead to sin' (Rom. 6.11) not as a mental or private exercise, but as 'living it out'.[16] The indicative, 'you are dead to sin' becomes also the imperative: 'live as those who are dead to sin'. Again, our analogy (p. 12) of being warmed by the fire while pockets of ice remain applies. Christ died 'once for all' (Rom. 6.10). We cannot supplement it; but we can appropriately implement it. The new life is characterized by serving one another (Gal. 5.13–15).

The implications for suffering with Christ occur at 2 Cor. 4.7–14, as in many places. In 2 Corinthians 4.10, Paul speaks of participation or involvement in 'the dying (Greek, *nekrōsis*) of Jesus and his life (Greek, *zōē*)'. In 2 Cor. 13.4 and Phil. 3.10 Paul speaks of sharing in his resurrection power. This is intensely practical. Sharing in the death and resurrection is a means of understanding the experience of our own life. Referring to Christ's death, Paul says that 'we came to the end of our tethers' (J. B. Phillips' paraphrase) or 'we felt that we had received the sentence of death' (NRSV), so that we would rely on 'God who raises the dead' (2 Cor. 1.9). When he beseeches God to remove his 'thorn in the flesh' (or 'a sharp physical pain'), Paul receives the reply, 'My grace is sufficient for you; for my power is made perfect in weakness' (2 Cor. 12.8). This is so that 'the power of Christ may dwell in me' (12.9), namely that power defined by being crucified and raised with Christ (we consider future resurrection in Chapter 16). Meanwhile Paul tells us in Philippians, 'I want to know Christ and the power of his resurrection and the sharing of his sufferings by becoming like him in his death, if somehow I may attain the resurrection from the dead' (Phil. 3.10–11). He adds, 'Not that I have already obtained this' (3.12). Philippians 3.7–16 concerns this *second* sense of being 'in Christ'.

These passages help us to understand one more difficult passage. Paul writes, 'I am now rejoicing in my sufferings for your sake, and in my flesh I am completing what is lacking in Christ's afflictions for

---

[16] Tannehill, *Dying and Rising with Christ*, pp. 77–8. Cf. Kenneth Grayston, *Dying, We Live: A New Enquiry into the Death of Christ in the New Testament* (Oxford and New York: Oxford University Press, 1990), pp. 45–68, 93–110, and 127–30.

the sake of his body, which is the Church' (Col. 1.24). This does not mean that Paul tries to 'add' to Christ's sufferings. Paul would have endorsed the words of the Book of Common Prayer that these are 'full, perfect, and sufficient'. But they remain to be 'completed' not in the sense of their atoning power, but in the sense of their reflecting the life of the Church and its members. Whiteley compares the light of the moon which cannot 'add' to the sun, but reflects it.[17] The total sufficiency and once-for-all-ness of Christ's atonement is not in question. There is an objective 'primary' side, but also a derivative 'secondary' side of involvement.

In the end, however, Paul needs and uses (as do we in the modern world) every possible way of seeking to explain the work of Christ. Whether we use the term *redemption, sacrifice, expiation, propitiation, place of meeting, cancellation of debt,* or *reconciliation,* all are needed. Paul implicitly acknowledges that human description falls short of entirely explaining the work of Christ. But in his gospel, the message of the cross is central, and cannot be compromised. It is 'God's wisdom'.

---

[17] Whiteley, *The Theology of St. Paul*, pp. 148–9; cf. Moule, *The Epistles of Paul the Apostle to the Colossians and to Philemon*, pp. 74–80; Dunn, *The Epistles to the Colossians and to Philemon*, pp. 113–17; and Dunn, *The Theology of Paul the Apostle*, pp. 482–7.

11

Justification and the law

Many think of justification by grace through faith alone as a legalistic way of talking about forgiveness of sins. The term, in fact, is much broader than 'forgiveness', and is a term partly denoting a personal relationship with God, rather than one focused mainly on guilt, and requiring regular renewal. It also signifies, as a verb, 'putting things right' (Hebrew *ts-d-q*, Greek *dikaioō*). Although the noun can mean 'righteousness', another meaning is 'being in a right relationship' (Hebrew noun, *tsedeq*; Greek noun, *dikaiosunē*). One popular evangelist, Tom Rees, used the slogan 'Get right with God' for his campaign held in the Albert Hall, and this is not a bad popularization of 'be justified by faith with God'.

José Porfirio Miranda, a liberation theologian, argues that Paul uses the corporate Greek term *dikaiōma*, to denote God's demand for justice.[1] This implies a social and cosmic 'putting things right' between neighbour and neighbour. Grobel, Bultmann's translator, translates *dikaioō* as 'to rightwise'. It usually describes a once-for-all act, whereas forgiveness is regularly renewed.[2] In 2009, Tom Wright, Bishop of Durham, produced a very important and thorough book on justification by grace through faith.[3] Among many things, he also has shown that justification concerns not only 'us' and human sin, but also the whole God-centred nature of Paul's gospel and the Old Testament covenantal roots and promises. He would not normally regard the Greek word for *righteousness* (*dikaiosunē*) as denoting *justice*, which it may do in earlier classical Greek, but does not in Paul's time.

---

[1] José Porfirio Miranda, *Marx and the Bible: A Critique of the Philosophy of Oppression*, trans. J. Eagleson (London: SCM Press, 1977), pp. 40–3.

[2] Joseph A. Fitzmyer, *Romans: A New Translation with Introduction and Commentary* (Anchor Bible; New York: Doubleday, 1992), p. 392 (on Rom. 5.1).

[3] Tom Wright, *Justification: God's Plan and Paul's Vision* (London: SPCK, 2009).

Many questions, however, surround the concept of *justify* (Greek, *dikaioō*) and its related noun (*dikaiosunē*, often translated as right-eousness). (1) One well-worn question is whether these words are *declarative* concerning the status of the Christian, or *behavioural* concerning the actual state of the Christian. We might put the matter in another way: our status is what we are in God's eyes; our state is what we are in ourselves. Ziesler and others argue that the verb (*dikaioō*) refers primarily to a declaration of status, or counting as righteous in the eyes of God, while the noun (*dikaiosunē*) usually denotes a state of actual righteousness. Or does 'rightwise' mean putting Christians in a right relationship with God and others? (2) A second question concerns the importance of this notion for Paul. Is it, as Luther and Calvin thought, the key to Paul's thought, or is it, as a number of twentieth-century scholars have claimed, a secondary theme? This became a widespread and sometimes heated debate. (3) Other questions concern the nature of faith, and (4) the relation to the law, to the Epistle of James, and to Judaism.

The meaning of *justify* in Paul

Tom Wright, like Alister McGrath, rightly insists that the later historical doctrine of justification by faith developed a meaning which is independent of the richer and wider meaning of the term in Paul and in other biblical writings.[4] Nevertheless, the declarative and behavioural interpretations of justification demand attention. Does the verb mean *to count as* righteous or *to make* righteous? In Käsemann's language, does Paul talk about righteousness of faith, or righteousness of life?[5] Weiss is emphatic, writing that it 'does not say what a man (person) is in himself but it states that he is considered, in the eyes of God . . . right with God'.[6] This accords with the Hebrew of Prov. 17.15, where 'to justify' the wicked (that is, to count them righteous and overlook their wickedness) earns the Lord's disfavour (cf. Exod. 23.7). Tom Wright is no less emphatic about this.

---

[4] Wright, *Justification*, pp. 59–60; cf. Alister McGrath, *Iustitia Dei: A History of the Christian Doctrine of Justification from 1500 to the Present Day* (Cambridge: Cambridge University Press, 1986).

[5] Käsemann, *New Testament Questions of Today*, p. 171.

[6] Weiss, *Earliest Christianity*, vol. 2, p. 499.

On the one hand, he writes, the Hebrew *tsedaqah* (righteousness) 'that lovely word, especially as applied to God himself, is full of mercy and kindness, faithfulness and generosity. Yet, it also refers to the behaviour which is appropriate for God's people.' But on the other hand the word 'denotes *the status that someone has when the court has found in their favour* . . . It does not denote *an action which transforms someone so much as a declaration which grants them a status.*'[7]

Ziesler argues that this has in the past constituted a Protestant–Catholic divide of interpretation. He attempts to pour oil on troubled waters by suggesting that the verb mainly refers to 'counting' righteous, while the noun and adjective usually denote ethical righteousness. He claims, 'By one root, verb, noun, and adjective, Paul can express the whole renewal of man by God – relationally, forensically, and ethically.'[8] He adds, 'We have some sort of reconciliation between Protestant and Catholic traditional exegesis.'[9]

Several classic passages confirm the declarative nuance of the verb. Paul uses 'reckoning as' righteous by faith six times in Romans 4: at 4.3, 5, 6, 9, 11, and 22. Quoting Gen. 15.6, he urges: 'Abraham believed God, and it was reckoned to him as righteousness' (4.3). He comments, 'Now to one who *works*, wages are not "reckoned as" a *gift*, but as something due. But to one who without works trusts him who justifies the ungodly, such faith is "reckoned as" righteousness' (Rom. 4.4–5). 'Reckoning as' (Greek *logizō*) righteous is parallel with 'forgiveness' in 4.6–8. Righteousness was 'reckoned' to Abraham before, not after, he had completed the 'work' of circumcision (Rom. 4.10). Hence he is properly the ancestor of 'all who believe' (4.11, 12). The promise of God was thus through faith, not through the law (4.13, 14), and 4.22 repeats the conclusion, together with 4.23–25.[10]

This chapter of Romans carefully works out of the argument of Gal. 3.1–18, and more loosely Gal. 3.19—5.12. Paul declares there also that the promise of God was appropriated in faith by Abraham before the coming of the law (Gal. 3.1–18). Therefore Abraham's faith was 'reckoned to him as righteousness' (Gal. 3.6, 7). This time Paul

---

[7] Wright, *Justification*, pp. 69 and 70 (both sets of italics are Wright's).

[8] John Ziesler, *The Meaning of Righteousness in Paul: A Linguistic and Theological Enquiry* (Cambridge: Cambridge University Press, 1972), p. 169.

[9] Ziesler, *The Meaning of Righteousness in Paul*, p. 171.

[10] Cf. Cranfield, *The Epistle to the Romans*, vol. 1, pp. 224–52; cf. Fitzmyer, *Romans*, pp. 369–90.

alludes to Gen. 12.3 (Gal. 3.8). Indeed, by the logic of law-related Judaism, the *curse* of the law rests on Christ (Gal. 3.15–18), through whom they may now enjoy the freedom of 'sons' (Gal. 4.1–24).

Ziesler's argument, however, runs parallel to our comments above concerning 'substitution' and 'participation' and 'identification'. To be 'reckoned as' righteous involves ethical *consequences*. As Luther and Calvin recognized, while the righteousness of God is received as a gift of grace, it logically follows that the Christian is committed to righteousness of life. Ziesler is broadly right, but the matter is more complex than perhaps he allows, and we cannot solve everything by distinguishing between noun and verb. Luther came to see that righteousness (noun) came from God as a gift, and that striving to attain it was not a condition of salvation. Justification means 'being in Christ', because Christ's righteousness is first imparted; *then* the Christian lives out being 'in Christ'. Righteousness embraces the ethical.

But there is more to the matter than this. As Wright stresses, justification means being in a right *relation* with God. Older Catholic writers such as F. Prat characterized the declarative inter-pretation as a legal fiction, in which the false becomes true, and the true, false. Even before Vatican II, however, more recent Catholic writers, including especially Hans Küng, agreed with Barth: 'Why does he spare him (the sinner)? Because he has chosen from eternity to take on Himself the death of a sinner.'[11] Küng continues, 'The term "justification" means a declaring just . . . a not imputing . . . (2 Cor. 5.19) . . . not an inner renewal.'[12] This springs from the gracious, per-sonal, God as an act of grace, in which he turns to me, Küng asserts, as a sinner. The God-centred nature of this act makes it intensely personal; it is *God's* being gracious. Paul declares, 'His grace to me was not in vain' (1 Cor. 15.10). This then transforms Christians inwardly. Much Catholic theology, Küng concedes, is historically conditioned into an overstatement. Grace is often 'divided up'. But in the main, an emphasis on grace and a personal relationship remains common to the best in Catholic and Protestant theology.[13]

---

[11] Hans Küng, *Justification: The Doctrine of Karl Barth and a Catholic Reflection*, trans. T. Collins and others (London: Burns & Oates, 1964), p. 152.

[12] Küng, *Justification*, p. 203; again, p. 205 and others.

[13] Küng, *Justification*, pp. 187–98.

Setting things right

Bultmann asserts, following Paul, that as 'rightwised' people, Christians 'have peace with God' (Rom. 5.1, 5.9).[14] This 'righteousness', he says, means the abolition of objective enmity or hostility. In faith the believer turns away from himself or herself to God. Nygren also quotes Paul: 'not having a righteousness of my own, based on law, but that which is through faith in Christ, the righteousness of God' (Phil. 3.9), and declares that 'righteousness is an objective relationship'.[15] It is 'being right with God' resulting from his verdict, and living out subsequently being 'in Christ'. Tom Wright and others see this act of putting things right as an implicate of God's *covenant faithfulness* as formerly portrayed in the Psalms, Isaiah, Daniel 9, and elsewhere in the Old Testament.[16] Strictly speaking, it is also an anticipation in the present of God's verdict which belongs to the judgement day. It is part of what Barrett calls 'setting things and persons right'.[17] Strictly, judgement and justification belong together at the last day (Rom. 2.12–13; Gal. 5.5). Richardson, too, sees this as a pronouncement of the last judgement, brought forward by faith.[18]

This brings us to a major question. How prominent in Paul is justification by grace through faith alone? Martin Luther and John Calvin saw it as a central theme. On Gal. 2.16–17 Luther calls justification the rule of Christianity, whereby sin is forgiven, and our sin is 'laid upon Christ' (Isa. 53.5).[19] Human righteousness, like human wisdom, is 'torn down' by Paul's gospel. The Pietist or 'Left-Wing' Reformers begin, like him, with faith alone, but by imposing legalistic codes of holiness on Christians, they unwittingly become 'teachers of the law', like some of the Galatians.[20] Calvin urged the importance of the theme because 'unless you understand first of all what your position is before God, and what the judgment which he

---

[14] Bultmann, *Theology of the New Testament*, vol. 1, pp. 286 and 319.
[15] Nygren, *Commentary on Romans*, p. 75.
[16] Wright, *Justification*, p. 154 and elsewhere.
[17] Barrett, *The Epistle to the Romans*, p. 73.
[18] Richardson, *Introduction to the Theology of the New Testament*, pp. 338–44.
[19] Martin Luther, *A Commentary on St. Paul's Epistle to the Galatians* (1531), trans. J. I. Packer (London: Clarke, 1953), pp. 136 and 138.
[20] Luther, *Galatians*, p. 142.

passes upon you, you have no foundation on which your salvation can be laid'.[21]

Criticism of Luther's and Calvin's view comes most recently from Stendahl and Sanders, but earlier from Weiss and from Albert Schweitzer. Schweitzer argued, 'By taking the doctrine of righteousness by faith as the starting-point the understanding of the Pauline world of thought was made impossible.'[22] Justification, he argues, was a mere tributary to Paul's theology. Ernst Käsemann rightly insists that Stendahl's criticisms are far from new;[23] and F. C. Baur saw Romans 9—11 as the key climax of the epistle.

The burden of Schweitzer's attack on tradition was first that justification or 'being counted right with God' constituted an affair for the individual, whereas Paul addresses a communal problem. Second, he saw no logical connection between justification with the gift of the Holy Spirit and ethics. Further, this theme is largely restricted to addressing Judaizing Christians; and it isolates the atoning death of Christ from dying and being raised with Christ. Wright, however, comments on the approach shared by Wrede and Schweitzer: 'Wrede, aware of the same phenomena which "the new perspective" [explained below] has highlighted, but without any glimmer of the larger context in which such phenomena could gain their true Pauline force declared "justification by faith" a mere polemical aside.'[24]

In Chapter 9 we noted K. Stendahl's claim that Paul was not anxious, as Luther was, about a guilty conscience. Stendahl therefore argues that the theme of Romans and perhaps Galatians was not justification, but the equal status of Jews and Gentiles before God.[25] Sanders presses Stendahl's critique further, defining Second Temple Judaism as 'covenantal nomism', meaning that the law is not 'worthless' obedience, but a way of responding to God's covenant. He used the phrase 'the new perspective on Paul' to characterize his own

---

[21] John Calvin, *Institutes of the Christian Religion*, 2 vols, trans. J. Beveridge (London: Clarke, 1957), Book III, Chapter 11, Section 1, vol. 2, p. 37.

[22] Schweitzer, *The Mysticism of Paul the Apostle*, p. 220, cf. pp. 205–26.

[23] Ernst Käsemann, *Perspectives on Paul*, trans. Margaret Kohl (London: SCM Press, 1971), p. 61.

[24] Wright, *Justification*, p. 64.

[25] Stendahl, *Paul among Jews and Gentiles* (see p. 75 n. 1 above).

approach.[26] James Dunn and Terence Donaldson have recently defended this approach.[27]

Strong attacks, however, have been made on this 'new perspective'. In 1969 Ernst Käsemann responded to Stendahl's article of 1963, as well as to Baur, Wrede, and Schweitzer, arguing that according to these writers the composition of the Church takes precedence, in effect, as Paul's key theme, and they 'make the divine and the human interchangeable, and would allow the church ultimately to triumph over its Lord'.[28] 'Law' means virtually 'legalism', as understood in the Anglo-American world. One of the most recent systematic attacks on 'the new perspective' of Sanders and Dunn is probably Seyoon Kim's *Paul and the New Perspective*.[29] Here the author looks again at the Judaism out of which Paul was converted, at the claims of Dunn and Donaldson, at justification in 1 Thessalonians, Galatians, 1 and 2 Corinthians, and Romans, and at Paul's use of the Jesus tradition.

It is finally worth noting here that while he sympathizes with the 'new perspective's' emphasis on history and community, Wright argues: (1) that it does not take full account of the seriousness of sin and the human plight according to Paul; (2) that it suggests a careless and eclectic use of the Old Testament by Paul; (3) that it distorts Paul's understanding of divine grace and the covenant; and (4) that it pays insufficient attention to God's constant concern for the world and his covenant people (including both Israel and the Church) and what is entailed in his covenant faithfulness. He argues that justification is an all-embracing issue about God and the gospel, not about mere 'legalism' or the respective status of Jews and Gentiles in the Church.[30] Wright is neither an uncritical advocate nor an

---

[26] E. P. Sanders, *Paul and Palestinian Judaism: A Comparison of Patterns of Religion* (London: SCM Press, 1977), throughout, but especially pp. 419–542; cf. E. P. Sanders, *Paul, the Law and the Jewish People* (Philadelphia: Fortress Press, 1983); and *Paul: A Very Short Introduction* (Oxford: Oxford University Press, 2001).

[27] James D. G. Dunn, *Jesus, Paul and the Law* (Louisville: Westminster John Knox Press, 1990), esp. pp. 89–107 and pp. 183–214; and Dunn, *The Theology of Paul the Apostle*, pp. 346–89.

[28] Käsemann, *Perspectives on Paul*, p. 63; cf. pp. 60–78.

[29] Seyoon Kim, *Paul and the New Perspective: Second Thoughts on the Origin of Paul's Gospel* (Grand Rapids: Eerdmans, 2002), pp. 1–84 and throughout.

[30] Wright, *Justification*, pp. 37–58, 101–14; and on Gal. 3.1—4.11 see pp. 101–18, and on Romans see pp. 153–220; also N. T. Wright, *Paul: Fresh Perspectives* (London: SPCK, 2005), pp. 10–12, 34–8.

unqualified critic of the new perspective, but seeks the deeper roots of the theme in God, his covenant, and the Old Testament. Moreover, as Miranda points out, social dimensions are prominent in the notion of God's 'setting things and people right'. Romans 3 and 4 may have strong applications about Gentile acceptance in the Church, but these chapters also stress human dependence on God. We cannot interpret Romans and Galatians as concerning only the composition of the Church. The nature of the gospel is hardly secondary.

The law and faith

The debate between James Dunn and Seyoon Kim partly depends on the nature of 'the works of the law' on which Christians no longer place reliance. Dunn follows 'the new perspective' in limiting these to the particular laws which characterize Jewish identity, or which mark out Israel's 'set-apartness' to God in contrast to the Gentile nations. Kim argues that Paul refers more widely to human obedience as such. It is not mainly a matter of staying in the (old) covenant. Dunn and Kim both offer detailed exegesis in support of their respective views, and Dunn acknowledges that broader legal codes may sometimes be the object of reference. But Kim explicitly attacks Dunn's interpretation. Kim argues, 'Only with the understanding that by "works of the law" Paul means the good (meritorious) works of keeping the law in general can we also account for his . . . polemical treatments of the problem of the law in Gal. 3—4 and Rom. 7—8.'[31] 'Works of the law' do not mean only what is distinctive to the covenant, which includes keeping the Sabbath, circumcision, and cultic and dietary law. Kim examines 1 Thessalonians, Galatians 1 and 2 and 3.10–14, 2 Corinthians 5, Romans 11, and Paul's use of the Jesus-tradition to support his case. Wright concludes, 'There are two interlocking reasons why "works of the law cannot justify". First, God has redefined his people through the faithfulness of the Messiah . . . Second "works of the law" will never justify because what the law does is to reveal sin.'[32]

The faith to which Paul refers in this context is the saving faith given to all Christians. It is not the special gift to which Paul refers

---

[31] Kim, *Paul and the New Perspective*, p. 70; cf. pp. 60–75 and throughout.
[32] Wright, *Justification*, p. 97.

when he discusses 'gifts of the Spirit' (1 Cor. 12.8–10), for these are given to some, but not necessarily to all. The statement in the Epistle of James, 'A person is justified by works and not by faith alone' (James 2.24) does not contradict Paul, but corrects an abuse of Paul. For some devalued obedience, action, and law as a guide, on the basis of Paul's emphatic statements. Matthew and James show that these are still relevant to Christians, for faith as mere intellectual assent falls short of trust and appropriation. If God's verdict of justification is properly future, to appropriate it in the present is precisely what Paul means by 'faith' in the divine promise. For 'we walk by faith, not by sight' (2 Cor. 5.7).

12

Why the Church?

It is easy to forget that the rise of individualism is only since the eighteenth-century Enlightenment. The notion of the self-sufficient autonomous individual arose only then. Immanuel Kant the philosopher (1724–1804) defined the Enlightenment as human liberation from secondhand authorities to think for oneself. Such thinkers as Voltaire (1694–1788) in France and Samuel Reimarus (1694–1768) in Germany encouraged such thought, and individual rights became the focus of the French Revolution and the American Declaration of Independence.

The Church as communal

The Bible does show a strong concern for the individual, especially for example in Deuteronomy, but it views everything from within the framework of the nation, family, tribe, or wider community, rather than from the viewpoint of the individual alone. Society consists of more than a collection of individuals. Parents and teachers shape us; so does the place of our nation within the world; and the Church and local churches shape Christians. Both sides belong to the wholeness of biblical thought. Perhaps 'postmodernity' restores some of the balance on behalf of the community today (discussed in Chapter 17). Human beings were never intended to live as lone individuals (Gen. 2.18; cf. 1.28; 2.19–24).

As a good Jew, Paul inherited the Old Testament emphasis on community, on solidarity within the community, and on the status of Israel as the people of God. The narrative of Achan in Josh. 7.1–26 provides a classic example of corporate solidarity. The chapter begins, 'Israel broke faith' (Josh. 7.1), but it turns out that one individual within the community had broken faith with God's command, namely Achan. It placed the whole nation in jeopardy until Achan was identified, and took responsibility. To modern readers this account may seem unfair, until we recall that in sport it is not 'unfair' for a whole team to be credited with a goal or victory won by one player, or penalized for their failure, or an 'own-goal'. Paul expresses the principle in theological terms: 'If the many died through one man's trespass, much more surely have the grace of God and the free gift . . . of the one man, Jesus Christ, abounded for the many' (Rom. 5.15; cf. 5.16–21). We all gain some advantage or disadvantage from parents, family, friends, or teachers. Yet the individual can also shape his or her environment, and can rise above his or her upbringing, usually with support from others.

Paul sees all individual Christians as part of the people of God. The Church has not *replaced* Israel, for it still embraces Jews and Gentiles. But by being 'in Christ' the Christian community has become the true Israel. It is the 'remnant' of Israel, 'chosen by grace' (Rom. 9.5). It consists of 'the children of promise', who are spiritual descendants of Abraham and Isaac (9.8–13). Israel was the 'firstfruits'; but Christian Gentiles are now 'grafted in' to the 'olive tree' of Israel (11.13–24). The word 'church' occurs seldom in Romans (apart from the greetings of Romans 16), but it is constantly presupposed; Rom. 8.28–39, for example, constantly uses the plural: 'If God is for us, who is against us?' (8.31); 'Who will separate us from the love of Christ?' (8.35). The letter would be read aloud to the whole congregation, not at first passed round to individuals.

The theme of the true people of God and the status of being descendants of Abraham occurs also in Galatians. Paul declares, 'Those who believe are the descendants of Abraham' (Gal. 3.7); 'The promises were made to Abraham and to his offspring' (3.16); 'In Christ Jesus you are all children of God through faith' (3.26). The whole argument from Gal. 3.6 to 4.7 expounds the theme of the people of God in Christ as children of Abraham.

The phrase 'people of God' means especially the assembly of those who belong to God in a special way. In 1 and 2 Corinthians, Philippians, and most epistles, Paul uses the word 'church' (Greek, *ekklēsia*). This does not mean 'those called out' (Greek, *ek-kaleō*) from the world, but is a normal Greek word for 'assembly'. An assembly hardly exists when it is not actually meeting. The emphasis lies on meeting together. The phrase 'absent church members' would have puzzled the world of Paul's day as (except for those ill) virtually a contradiction in terms. The use of the word 'church' comes from early

Christians even before the epistles were written, but it soon replaced such primitive terms as the 'brothers' (and 'sisters') (Acts 1.15), the 'disciples' (Acts 6.1), the 'fellowship' (Acts 2.42), the 'Way' (Acts 9.2) and even 'Christians' (Acts 11.26).[1] In the Septuagint, 'church' regularly translates the Hebrew *qāhāl*, which also means 'assembly', occasionally *synagōgē*. 'Church of God' appears as *qᵉʰal Yahweh* in the Hebrew Bible (Num. 16.3; 1 Chron. 28.8) and in the Dead Sea Scrolls of Qumran (1QM 4.10; CD 7.17; 11.22).

The body of Christ

Paul also calls the Church *the body of Christ*. Like the word 'church', the image of the body also occurs in Graeco-Roman literature. But it is more likely that the term originated for Paul from his experience on the road to Damascus. As J. A. T. Robinson long ago pointed out, it would have come as a startling shock that his aim, as he thought, of stamping out a dangerous heretical sect of Judaism was redescribed by the Lord as 'Why are you persecuting *me*?' (Acts 9.4; 22.7; 26.15). Paul uses the term 'body of Christ' in 1 Cor. 12.14–26, in Rom. 12.4–5, and elsewhere. Robinson rightly claims that, for Paul, being 'members of the body' (1 Cor. 12.12, 14, 20, 22, 27) does not mean *members* 'in a fully metaphorical way, like being "members of a golf club" or "members of the A. A"'. It denotes being Christ's limbs. But we may question his identification of membership of the Church with necessarily being part of *Christ*. Whiteley rightly urges, 'The subject has been both complicated and illuminated by J. A. T. Robinson.'[2] The term expresses the solidarity of Christians with Christ and with one another.

The analogy implies still more than this. It implies both unity and diversity, and diversity in harmony. Ernest Best, Dale Martin, and Margaret Mitchell expound this two-way principle.[3] The 'weak' or vulnerable must not be made to feel that because they are not like

---

[1] Fitzmyer, *First Corinthians*, pp. 551–2.

[2] J. A. T. Robinson, *The Body: A Study in Pauline Theology* (London: SCM Press, 1952), pp. 55–8; Whiteley, *The Theology of St. Paul*, p. 192.

[3] This is worked out in detail by Ernest Best, *One Body in Christ* (London: SPCK, 1955), esp. pp. 74–114; Dale B. Martin, *The Corinthian Body* (New Haven: Yale University Press, 1995), pp. 3–61 and 94–103; and Margaret Mitchell, *Paul and the Rhetoric of Reconciliation* (Louisville: Westminster John Knox Press, 1991), pp. 158–60.

the so-called strong, they are not fully part of the body. Paul writes, 'If the foot should say, "Because I am not a hand, I do not belong to the body", that would not make it any less part of the body' (1 Cor. 12.15). No one should try to tear away limbs of Christ. Similarly no limb can claim to represent 'the whole Christ'. Moltmann argues that not only the 'weak' are needed, but also the disabled. Paul argues that all Christians need one another. The Holy Spirit's gifts are never given in their fullness all to one person, but are distributed throughout the whole community for the good of all (1 Cor. 12.7, 27–30).

Parallels with the 'body' metaphor to denote a community occur in Plato, Livy, Cicero, Epictetus, and Plutarch, and are common in the Graeco-Roman world. Livy the Roman historian recounts the analogy used in Menenius Agrippa's address to the rebel workers who wanted to take action against their employers.[4] Paul turns the analogy upside-down, to urge the self-styled elite or 'strong' that the 'weak' are needed, and stand in solidarity with them. Thus he writes, 'The eye cannot say to the hand, "I have no need of you"' (1 Cor. 12.21); 'The members (or limbs) we think less honourable we clothe with greater honour . . . If one member suffers, all suffer with it' (12.23, 26); 'If the whole body were an eye, where would the hearing be?' (12.17); 'If it were a single member (or limb) where would the body be?' (12.19). To suggest that there are parallels in the Graeco-Roman world does not mean that Paul borrowed directly from these classical authors; this analogy was probably familiar both to Paul and to many of his readers. Another possible source is that of the terracotta models of body-parts, still preserved in the museum at Corinth today, relating to 'cures' by the pagan god Asklepios, the Greek god of medicine.

Gifts of the Holy Spirit and consecration of a temple

Paul uses a third image, namely that of a community equipped by the gifts of the Holy Spirit. These gifts are distributed throughout the body 'as God has chosen', or 'as the Spirit chooses' (1 Cor. 12.11). *Varieties* of gifts come from the one God and from the one Holy Spirit

---

[4] Livy, *Ab Urbe Condita* 2.32; cf. Cicero, *De Officiis* 1.35.

(12.4). They are given to one and to another (12.8–10). Paul writes, 'Are all apostles? Are all prophets? Are all teachers? . . . Do all speak in tongues?' (12.27–30). Paul introduces his didactic poem on love to show that these gifts cannot be competitive or self-glorifying. To flaunt one's gifts is to show insensitivity; they serve the whole.

A fourth piece of imagery concerns the Church as *God's Temple* (1 Cor. 3.16–17). To modern ears this may sound like the identification of a church with a place of worship or building. In Paul, 'church' (*ekklēsia*) does not denote a building; church is anywhere where those 'in Christ' assemble together. The image of the Temple denotes God's or Christ's presence, indwelling a gathering which is holy, and meets for worship. *Holy* in this context means set apart for God. One writer after an exhaustive study rightly asserts, 'Temple imagery serves to underpin the holiness and unity of the . . . community, and to demarcate its boundaries . . .'[5] In 1 Cor. 3.16 Paul writes, 'You are God's temple and God's Spirit dwells in you.' He refers to the gathering of Christians. But in 1 Cor. 6.19 the words 'Your body is a temple of the Holy Spirit' is more individualistic. More typically 2 Cor. 6.16 speaks of God's dwelling among his people, and states, 'We are the temple of the living God.' Paul writes that he is a libation poured out 'over the sacrifice of your faith' (Phil. 2.17).

Paul inherits much of this thinking from the Old Testament and from contemporary Judaism. *Jubilees* compares the erection of the Temple with creation (*Jubilees* 1.27–28) and with the vision of the new creation at the end-time. The Temple Scroll of the Qumran community concerns God's presence in the Temple (11QT[a] 29.7; 45.12–14; 46.3, 4). This must not be profaned or defiled. Qumran, or the community of the Dead Sea Scrolls, builds on the post-exilic hope of the restoration of the Temple in Jerusalem, as the gathering of God's holy people at the last times (1QS 8.6–7; 4Q 174). The Temple becomes a metaphor for the community of God's people (1QS 8.5–6; 9.6).[6] In Greek thought the image or statue of the pagan deity in his or her temple was thought to represent the person and presence of the deity. But Paul is influenced more powerfully by the Old Testament: 'The Lord is in his holy temple' (Ps. 11.4); 'Your holy

---

[5] Hogeterp, *Paul and God's Temple*, p. 358, cf. pp. 271–386.
[6] Further expounded in Hogeterp, *Paul and God's Temple*, pp. 93–114.

temple have they defiled' (Ps. 79.1); 'I saw the Lord . . . high and lofty, and the hem of his robe filled the temple' (Isa. 6.1); 'a voice from the temple' (Isa. 66.6).

The Church as local and universal

Many disagree about whether Paul conceived of a 'universal' church. Paul certainly speaks of 'churches' as local congregations. He speaks of 'all the churches of the Gentiles' (Rom. 16.4); 'the churches of God greet you' (Rom. 16.16); 'in every church' (1 Cor. 4.17); 'the churches' (1 Cor. 11.16; 16.19); 'messengers of the churches' (2 Cor. 8.23); 'other churches' (2 Cor. 12.13); 'churches of Galatia' (Gal. 1.2); and 'church of the Thessalonians' (1 Thess. 1.1). Dunn stresses the plurality of local churches in Paul.[7] But even Dunn recognizes that 'It is only later that *ekklēsia* is used in Pauline letters with a more universal reference.'[8] It is striking that Paul regularly refers to 'churches' in his earlier letters (Thessalonians, Galatians, 1 and 2 Corinthians and Romans) but often to 'the Church' in his later letters, Colossians and especially Ephesians, and (if they are Pauline) 1 and 2 Timothy and Titus (Eph. 1.22; 3.10, 21; 5.23–29, 32; Col. 1.18, 24; cf. 1 Tim. 3.15).

Pannenberg insists that although the concept of the local church is basic to the Reformation as well as to Paul, the proclamation of the pure gospel in a variety of places implies 'the universal unity of the church across the ages'.[9] The notion of the Church as the body of Christ and the one Bread in the Eucharist, he urges, demands a more universal concept of the Church. Both aspects appear in Paul. But the Roman Catholic tradition (including Pope Benedict) insists that Christ can be met *only* in the one universal church. Pannenberg concedes that the term 'local church' is ambiguous today, referring either to a local congregation, or to a diocese or province.[10] Although there are also other factors which may point to a post-Pauline date of Colossians, Ephesians, and the Pastoral Epistles (the collective

---

7 Dunn, *The Theology of Paul the Apostle*, pp. 537–43.

8 Dunn, *The Theology of Paul the Apostle*, p. 541.

9 Pannenberg, *Systematic Theology*, vol. 3, p. 101.

10 Pannenberg, *Systematic Theology*, vol. 3, p. 109.

name given to 1 Timothy, 2 Timothy, and Titus), the notion that Paul seldom spoke of 'the Church' becomes a circular argument. Might not Paul have come to see that 'the churches' in their doctrine, in the Communion or Eucharist, and in worship, imply the universal Church? A later development in Paul seems reasonable.

On this basis it is legitimate to consider Colossians and Ephesians. Even if Paul's authorship is rejected, these epistles are regarded as reflecting what Paul taught.[11] In Colossians Paul urges Christ's supreme power over all cosmic forces, including angels and structural powers on earth (Col. 1.15–17). He is head of the body, or of his Church (1.18). The Church is already raised with Christ (2.12; 3.1). The Church, however, is still growing (Col. 1.10) and 'grows with a growth that is from God' (2.19). Much in Colossians is universal, cosmic, or world-wide.

Ephesians 1.3–23 expounds the conception of the Church in accordance with God's purpose (1.11), and as an inheritance over whom Christ is Head (1.11, 22). Chapter 2 might be called the construction of the Church as it is renewed from death to life (2.1–6). God has broken down the wall that divides Jew from Gentile, to make in Christ 'one new humanity' (Eph. 2.13–17). The Church has become the true Israel; who are 'no longer strangers and aliens but . . . citizens with the saints and also members of the household of God, built upon the foundation of the apostles and prophets, with Christ Jesus himself as the cornerstone' (Eph. 2.19–20). As in earlier epistles, the Church is 'a holy temple . . . a dwelling place for God' (2.21–22). Chapter 3 continues this theme with reference to the very constitution of the Church. It exists 'for the sake of Gentiles' (3.1) or to include Gentiles (3.6), but 'fellow-heirs' (i.e. Jews and Gentiles) are united as God's one people. God has revealed that 'through the Church' God's wisdom and purpose may be known (Eph. 3.10). Chapter 4 takes up the distribution of different gifts familiar in 1 Cor. 12.4–31. But in 4.8 these gifts come from Christ rather than from the Spirit, and Ephesians contains a rare reference in Paul to the ascension (Eph. 4.8). Ephesians 4.17—6.20 mainly concerns the conduct of the Church. In Eph. 5.25–27 the Church is *the bride of Christ*, cleansed

---

[11] E. Schweizer, *Church Order in the New Testament*, trans. F. Clarke (London: SCM Press, 1961), pp. 105–10.

and holy. This offers another image of the universal Church (cf. Rev. 21.9; 22.13).

The epistles of 1 and 2 Timothy and Titus especially concern the organization of the Church and the stabilization and regulation of its ministry. Schnackenburg argues that if these letters are by Paul, they reveal another side of his thought, but one which fits the account of the Acts of the Apostles.[12] It is conceivable that after a period of imprisonment Paul may have reflected on the next step for the organization and regulation of his missionary churches. Many sociologists argue that after an initial stage of creative vision, a concern for infrastructure may follow later. An increasing concern for supporting machinery occurs in Ephesians and in the Pastorals. The Church is mentioned explicitly only in 1 Tim. 3.5, 15; 5.16; where it is the 'house of God' and 'the pillar and ground of truth'. The house of God is the temple of 1QS 5.5 and 8.5–9, and of 1 Cor. 3.16, 17; 6.19; 2 Cor. 6.26; Eph. 2.21. But in the Pastorals it is a more complete structure, with ecclesial officers, as discussed next in Chapter 13. The people of God need officers in charge, just as a family or any household needs management and agreed disciplines (1 Tim. 3.5). Paul speaks of a bishop or overseer and of deacons (1 Tim. 3.4, 12). The community of the Church shares in right belief (1 Tim. 1.19; 2.7; 4.1, 3, 6; Titus 1.13–14; 2 Tim. 2.10, 15).

Paul never loses the corporate vision of the Old Testament. As Thornton wrote, 'The hope of Israel went down into the grave . . . When the Messiah was in the tomb, Israel was in the tomb . . . so also finally . . . when Christ rose, the Church rose from the dead.'[13] The Church inherits a common life, shares together what it is to be 'in Christ', shares together the Holy Spirit, shares God's love and Christ's victory, participating in his resurrection and his life. The post-Pauline creedal formula that the Church is one, holy, universal and apostolic is implied in Paul's earlier writings and becomes explicit in his later ones.[14] The Church is to express a 'messianic way of life',

---

[12] Cf. Rudolf Schnackenburg, *The Church in the New Testament*, trans. W. J. O'Hare (Freiburg: Herder, 1965), pp. 94–102.

[13] Thornton, *The Common Life in the Body of Christ*, p. 282.

[14] Anthony C. Thiselton, *The Hermeneutics of Doctrine* (Grand Rapids and Cambridge: Eerdmans, 2007), pp. 479–508.

lived 'in the power of the Spirit'.[15] It is the 'servant' Church, existing for the sake of God, the gospel, and the world, not as an institutional end in itself. God chose the Church before all time 'to be holy and blameless . . . to the praise of his glorious grace' (Eph. 1.4, 6).

[15] Jürgen Moltmann, *The Church in the Power of the Spirit: A Contribution to Messianic Ecclesiology*, trans. Margaret Kohl (London: SCM Press, 1977), p. 317.

13

The ministry of the word

Collaborative service

Although 1 Timothy and Titus give us an exposition of the qualifications required for ministry, and discuss its nature, Anthony
Hanson rightly observes that we can best understand Paul's view of
the ministry by looking at how ministry was actually carried out.
Systematic treatises on the ministry do not exist (except perhaps in
1 Timothy and Titus).[1] Hanson grounds ministry in the mission of
the remnant of Israel and the Church as the true Israel, to the world
and for the glory of God (Isa. 8.16–20; 42.1–6, 19; 43.8, 10, 12, 20–21;
cf. *1 Enoch* 38.5; 91.12; 95.3; 98.12). This finds expression in Paul's
language about Hagar and Sarah as respectively the slave and free
woman (Gal. 4.22–24, 28), and his argument in Rom. 9.6–9 that
not all Israel is the true Israel, or 'Abraham's descendants' (cf. 9.24).
In 2 Corinthians this becomes central for the ministry as sharing
authentically in Christ's death and resurrection, as we shall see.

Ministry for Paul remains ideally a corporate or communal enterprise. We have already seen that in his missionary travels and in
his pastoral follow-up, he worked with colleagues or 'co-workers',
who included Barnabas, Silvanus (Silas), Apollos, Timothy, Titus,
Epaphras, Aquila and Priscilla, Junia, Phoebe and others. Often 'we'
in his letters refers to Paul and his co-workers (1 Cor. 4.10; 2 Cor.
4.7–18; 5.11—6.10; Gal. 1.18, 19; 1 Thess. 1.2–9). But sometimes
an 'epistolary *we*' occurs, as in 'We write', meaning 'I write' (1 Thess.
2.17—3.2).

In 1 Cor. 3.5–15 Paul sees ministers as those engaged in working
together for a common goal, but as often performing different tasks
to reach that goal. The Corinthians in one sense overvalue ministers
because they rally behind particular personalities or local celebrities

---

[1] Anthony T. Hanson, *The Pioneer Ministry* (London: SCM Press, 1961), p. 46.

as a vehicle for a power-struggle (Greek, *schismata*). The slogans, 'I am for Peter', or 'I am a follower of Apollos', do not refer to theological 'parties', but to personality cults (1 Cor. 1.10–12).[2] Therefore Paul uses the neuter, asking, 'What is Apollos? What is Paul? Servants through whom you came to believe, as the Lord assigned to each' (3.5).

From another point of view the Corinthians undervalue the ministry. Paul declared, 'I planted, Apollos watered, but God gave the growth' (3.6). By 'selecting' their favoured celebrities, they 'cheat themselves' out of resources which God has provided (3.18–23). Paul insists, '*All* things are yours, whether Paul or Apollos or Cephas . . .' (3.21–22). If, as Paul says, they are God's field (3.9), they need a plurality of ministers who 'plant' and 'water'. To neglect uncongenial ministers cheats them out of something that they need. Similarly, as God's building, they need one to lay the foundation, and another to build on it. Paul is like an architect or 'master-builder'; others on this project assume various subordinate roles (3.10–12). In 4.1–5 ministers are 'servants of Christ, and stewards of God's mysteries' (4.1). The key requirement is faithfulness, but only the judgement day, the last day, will disclose the quality of their work. Therefore, he says, 'Do not pronounce judgement before the time, before the Lord comes' (4.5).

In 1 Cor. 4.8–13 ministers and apostles share in the dying and rising of Christ, as do all genuine Christians. Thus Paul writes, 'We are weak, but you are strong. You are held in honour, but we are in disrepute' (4.10). We are 'what people scrape off their shoes' (4.13).[3] However, 1 Cor. 12.28–30 speaks of apostles, prophets, teachers, those who work miracles, healers, and those who speak in tongues, as those who exercise varied ministerial gifts. On the other hand, there is not yet a clear line between possible 'office-holders' and those who have ministerial gifts. As we have earlier suggested (p. 63), it is likely that 'prophets' means here those who preach the gospel with pastoral application, in contrast to those who teach. Paul does appear to rank the first three, although he may be simply listing 'gifts of the Spirit'; first (Greek, *prōton*) apostles; second (Greek, *deuteron*)

---

[2] L. L. Welborn, 'Discord in Corinth', in *Politics and Rhetoric in the Corinthian Epistles* (Macon, GA: Mercer University Press, 1987), pp. 1–42. Cf. Thiselton, *The First Epistle to the Corinthians*, pp. 111–33; Fitzmyer, *First Corinthians*, pp. 136–45.

[3] Welborn, *Paul the Fool of Christ*, pp. 165–8, 248–53.

prophets or prophetic preachers; third (Greek, *triton*) teachers; then (Greek, *epeita*) the rest.[4] Barrett observes, 'This threefold ministry of the word is, according to Paul, the primary ministry. By it the church is founded and built up . . . Other activities . . . occupy only a secondary place.'[5] The church does not 'raise up' apostles, but responds to the apostolic witness. Throughout 1 Corinthians 12—14 'what edifies' or builds up the church as a whole is in view, and service to God and to the Church remains central. Some writers interpret this passage in a more egalitarian way, but Fitzmyer insists that the numbers indicate 'an order of importance'.[6]

Romans 12.4–8 also uses the metaphor of the body, and stresses the variety of ministries that relate to a range of gifts. These are 'gifts that differ', and include prophetic speech, service, teaching, exhortation, giving and leading. Service or ministry translates the Greek word *diakonia*. If this relates to the work of a deacon, the most recent research suggests that a deacon is a deputy or assistant to an apostle, with their main job being mission rather than administering funds or food to the poor. Collins speaks of the 'mediating' role of *diakonia* and *diakonos*.[7] In 1 Corinthians 12 Paul's rhetorical question, 'Are all apostles?' indicates that most are not apostles.

Ministry in 2 Corinthians

In 2 Corinthians 1.3–9 Paul explains that the experience of 'coming to the end of our tether' (1.9, Phillips) was a participation in the dying and rising of Christ common to all genuine Christians, but also an act of solidarity with those who suffer, and to bring them comfort (1.9). Paul further explains, 'I do not mean to imply that we lord it over your faith; rather, we are workers with you for your joy, because you stand firm in the faith' (2 Cor. 1.24). He proclaims Christ with integrity, not with ambiguity; along with Silvanus and Timothy who do likewise (2 Cor. 1.18–20). If he did change his travel plans, it was

---

[4] See Thiselton, *The First Epistle to the Corinthians*, pp. 1013–24.
[5] C. K. Barrett, *A Commentary on the First Epistle to the Corinthians*, 2nd edn (London: A. & C. Black, 1971), p. 295.
[6] Fitzmyer, *First Corinthians*, p. 482.
[7] J. N. Collins, *Diakonia: Re-interpreting the Ancient Sources* (Oxford and New York: Oxford University Press, 1990), esp. pp. 227–44.

to spare them pain (2.1–4). He writes, 'For we are the aroma of Christ among those who are being saved . . . not peddlers of God's word like so many' (2.15, 17). Paul does not need, though, to commend himself, because the Corinthian Christians are testimony to his effective work with Timothy and Silvanus (3.1–3). Their ministry brings life and glory through the Holy Spirit, which unlike the ministry of Moses retains permanence, namely 'the glory of the Lord' which transforms its hearers 'from one degree of glory to another' (2 Cor. 3.7–18, especially v. 18). The edification and transformation of the church is proof of Paul's genuine apostleship. The minister declares the glory of God, fully revealed in Jesus Christ.

In 2 Cor. 4.2 the ministry is 'an open statement of the truth'. It is veiled or unclear only to those whom the god of the world has blinded (4.4). Often today we hear anecdotal sermons about the preacher and his or her experiences. But Paul asserts, 'We do not proclaim ourselves; we proclaim Jesus Christ as Lord, and ourselves as your slaves for Jesus' sake' (4.5). Paul refers to the revelation which came at his call, when God shone his 'light' which was perceived in the face of Jesus Christ (4.6). Apostles and other ministers have the 'treasure' of the gospel in clay jars. Many understand this as a container for safe keeping. But jars of baked clay may mean more; they are breakable, fragile, and expendable. Paul compares the priceless nature of the gospel with the fragile nature of the human beings through whom it is proclaimed.[8] The power of the gospel to change lives therefore comes not from weak ministers, but from God. Some ministers, like clay jars, may seem unattractive and vulnerable, but this does not cause Paul to lose heart. For the transforming power of the gospel comes from God.

Hanson comments that the last clause of 2 Cor. 4.15 'reminds us that even the salvation of the Church is not the final objective: greater than all is the glory of God'.[9] This verse reads: 'Everything is for your sake, and so that grace may increase . . . to the glory of God' (4.15). Paul continues, 'So we do not lose heart' (4.16). He quotes Ps. 116.10 (LXX), which accepts the experience of affliction. Yet he knows that the ministry proclaims a God who is eternal (4.18). For

---

[8] Harris, *The Second Epistle to the Corinthians*, pp. 339–41.
[9] Hanson, *The Pioneer Ministry*, p. 76.

all that, like all Christians, they 'walk by faith, not by sight' (5.7), ministers are urged on by the love of Christ (5.14).

Paul therefore concludes this section, 'So we are ambassadors for Christ, since God is making his appeal through us; we entreat you, on behalf of Christ, be reconciled to God' (2 Cor. 5.20). Even though there are 'afflictions, hardships, calamities, beatings, imprisonments, riots, labours, sleepless nights, hunger' (6.4–5), the dying and rising with Christ involves both these hardships and 'holiness of spirit, genuine love, truthful speech, and the power of God' (6.6, 7). Ministers and apostles are 'as sorrowful, yet always rejoicing; as poor, yet making many rich' (6.10). They must practise speaking frankly (6.11). This lives out precisely the ministry of Christ (Matt. 21.42; Mark 12.10–11; Luke 20.17). It is for this reason that Hanson describes ministers, in Paul's view, as the nucleus of the Church, or as 'the pioneer church'.[10]

Ephesians, ministry of women, and 1 Timothy and Titus

Ephesians concerns the Church in many ways, but contains less about ministry as such. Ephesians 4.11–12 repeats the point about a diversity of ministries, but ministers also respond to gifts given by the ascended Christ. Paul (or his disciple) writes, 'He gave gifts . . . that some would be apostles, some prophets (or preachers), some evangelists, some pastoral teachers, to equip the saints for the work of ministry, for building up the body of Christ.' Again the writer enjoins 'speaking the truth in love' (Eph. 4.15), and shaping the conduct of the Church (Eph. 5.8—6.9).

Paul gives a prominent place to the ministry of women.[11] Junia, we recall Epp arguing, was a woman apostle (Rom. 16.7); Phoebe was a deacon and patron of the church in Cenchreae. Priscilla and Aquila had leading roles in three (or at least two) churches, at Rome, Corinth, and Ephesus (Rom. 16.3; 1 Cor. 16.19; 2 Tim. 4.19; and Acts 18.2). Not least, Priscilla instructed the learned Apollos. Paul commends Mary, Tryphaena, Tryphosa, and Persis, for their leadership

---

[10] Hanson, *The Pioneer Ministry*, p. 87.
[11] Dunn, *The Theology of Paul the Apostle*, pp. 586–93; Ben Witherington, *Women in the Earliest Churches* (Cambridge: Cambridge University Press, 1988); and Epp, *Junia*.

(Rom. 16.6, 12). He commends the church in Corinth for following the tradition that women can lead in prayer in public worship, and can preach or 'prophesy' and tell forth the gospel (1 Cor. 11.5). An injunction to silence on the part of women, we noted, applied to the special case of evaluating prophecy (14.33–36). Admittedly, if Paul wrote it, 1 Tim. 2.12–14 remains a difficult passage. Some argue that 2.12 is limited in time and place to ancient Ephesus, and some argue that it applies only 'currently' or 'for the present'.[12] The author's awareness of the other material already cited would make him cautious in implying that this is a universal principle.

Formal qualifications for ministry are offered in 1 Timothy 3. Paul (or the writer) considers overseers or bishops (1 Tim. 3.1–7) and deacons (1 Tim. 3.8–13). The Epistle to Titus has a related passage (Titus 1.5–9). The office of overseer or of bishop (Greek, *episkopē*) is worthy to be doubly honoured (1 Tim. 5.17). But he must be 'above reproach, married only once, temperate, sensible, respectable, hospitable, (and) an apt teacher, not violent but gentle . . . not a lover of money. He must manage his own household well . . . not be a recent convert . . . well thought-of by outsiders' (1 Tim. 3.2–7). Opponents forbade any marriage (4.3); the writer affirms it, but forbids promiscuity. The Greek *nēphelios* means 'clear-minded'. The Church Fathers were at one with these epistles in insisting on the role of bishops as teachers. The Greek word *didaktikos* means 'skilled in teaching'. The problem in Ephesus included false teaching. *Epieikēs* means 'gracious'. If the Church is the household of God, experience in managing a 'household' well (it probably included both children and servants or slaves) points to proven management skills.

Deacons are required to show largely overlapping qualities (1 Tim. 3.8–13). As we have noted, Collins argued that deacons in the New Testament were not primarily administrators of funds for the poor or social workers, but deputies or assistants of bishops or senior ministers in the corporate ministry of mission. Clement and Polycarp confirm this (*1 Clem.* 42; Polycarp, *Ep. Phil.* 5). Mounce has a comparative table of qualities required respectively for 'overseers' or bishops, 'elders', and deacons, on the basis of 1 Tim. 3.1–13 and

---

[12] William D. Mounce, *Pastoral Epistles* (Nashville: Nelson, 2000), pp. 117–49; cf. Witherington, *Women in the Earliest Churches*, p. 122.

Titus 1.5–9, with a further comparison with 1 Tim. 5.17–23.[13] All three orders are to be above reproach (*anegklētos*, blameless, they cannot be accused of anything); all three are to be committed to one woman; all three are not to be greedy for money or gain; all are to have managed their household well.

In addition, a deacon should be dignified (nowadays we might speak of *gravitas*), tested, of clear conscience, not a gossip, and well-grounded in the faith. Elders are also to be disciplined people (Greek, *egkratēs*), able to exhort with wholesome teaching, not arrogant, stewards of God, just, holy, and holding firmly to the faithful word. To what extent bishops or overseers (Greek, *episkopoi*) overlap with elders (Greek, *presbyteros*) forms a long-standing controversy, and much depends on whether we think that bishops or overseers continue the distinctive apostolic task, which seems to have been trans-local.

Apostles once again

For Paul's concept of 'apostle', we must turn to the 'major' epistles, namely, Romans, 1 and 2 Corinthians, and Galatians. In one sense to be an apostle is an unrepeatable office, since an apostle is witness to the resurrection of Christ (1 Cor. 9.1; 15.8, 9). (In terms of being a witness to the resurrection, it has been pointed out that Mary Magdalene is uniquely the first witness (John 20.1–18; cf. Matt. 28.5–10; Luke 24.10).) In Eph. 2.20 apostles belong to the foundation of the Church. But in another sense the apostles are not confined to the Twelve in Paul, and Crafton has convincingly argued that as witnesses to the cross and to the resurrection they function as transparent windows through which we see the person and work of Christ.[14] Many from Chrysostom onwards argue that Paul uses the term with great humility, not to bid for domination or power, but to point away from himself to Christ. To make a third point, apostles and bishops are guardians of the faith, as well as witnesses to Christ. The task of an apostle is to live out the death and resurrection of Christ, and thereby to witness to Christ in word and in life (2 Cor. 1.5–11).

---

[13] Mounce, *Pastoral Epistles*, pp. 155–66, esp. 156–8.
[14] Crafton, *The Agency of the Apostle*, pp. 53–103.

14

Baptism and the Lord's Supper or Eucharist

Paul includes a significant body of teaching about the two Dominical sacraments, baptism and the Lord's Supper or Eucharist. The word 'sacrament' does not occur in the New Testament, but Paul's language about baptism and the Lord's Supper implies outward signs of invisible grace. In the Catechism of the Book of Common Prayer (1662) a sacrament is defined as 'an outward and visible sign of an inward and spiritual grace ... ordained by Christ himself, whereby we receive the same, and a pledge to assure us thereof'. Similarly Article XXV writes of sacraments as 'witnesses and effectual signs of grace' which 'confirm our faith'. Paul uses the terms *Lord's Supper* (1 Cor. 11.20, 25), *Communion*, or sharing in common (1 Cor. 10.16), and *Eucharist*, or giving of thanks (1 Cor. 11.24). The term 'sacrament' is also used today more broadly to denote any 'outward form' which represents a spiritual reality, but Paul neither denies nor uses this term in this broader sense. The Catholic Church lists seven, following the Council of Trent.

Baptism as allegiance to Christ

The most important Pauline references to baptism occur in Gal. 3.27; Rom. 6.3–4; 1 Cor. 1.13; 12.13; and Col. 2.12; although many include 1 Cor. 6.11, this remains controversial. In epistles of which many doubt the authorship of Paul, Eph. 5.26 and Titus 3.5 deserve attention. Rudolf Schnackenburg has produced a masterly book called *Baptism in the Thought of St. Paul*, in which he classifies Paul's texts into (a) those which speak of baptism as 'assignment to Christ and incorporation in Christ'; (b) those which see baptism as 'salvation-event with Christ' (*sun Christō*); and (c) a rare group which sees baptism as washing or a bath.[1] This is the work of a Roman Catholic scholar, translated by a leading Baptist, so it has ecumenical appeal.

Schnackenburg ascribes assignment to Christ and incorporation in Christ to 1 Cor. 1.13; Rom. 6.3; and Gal. 3.27. Paul's denial that anyone in Corinth was baptized in his name implies that people were baptized in the name of Christ (1 Cor. 1.13, 15). The Corinthian church gave allegiance to 'personalities' or celebrities, to Peter, to Apollos, to 'Christ', and to Paul (unless, as some have argued, these were hypothetical names to protect leaders in Corinth). These are 'splits' (Greek, *schismata*), not theological parties, for Paul criticizes the 'Paul' group as much as any other. The 'Christ' group may have been those who rejected any human leader. Christ, Paul argues, cannot be divided or apportioned out, as if he were the monopoly of some group. Paul borrows the political language of those who made a bid for power.[2] But 'Paul' was not crucified for them. They belong exclusively to Christ, in whose name they were baptized. Schnackenburg comments, 'The formula expresses a binding to Christ.'[3]

Galatians 3.27 and Rom. 6.3 both use (Greek) *baptizein eis Christon*, 'baptized in (or into) Christ'. But the preposition 'in' has a different nuance in each of the two passages. Gal. 3.27b is said to describe a relation to Christ of being or identity. Schnackenburg calls it a 'mystical' immersion into Christ. But he doubts whether the preposition carries this sense in the first part of the verse. The Greek *eis* denotes not only 'into', but 'with a view to' or (with a participle) 'in the direction of' or even simply 'in'. It denotes 'a sign of adherence' in the context of baptism, especially in the parallel 'baptized into Moses', which means 'adhere to him as leader'. It signifies 'the direction of faith', but not any 'mystical movement'.[4] In Galatians Paul speaks of 'putting on' Christ, like a garment. The same metaphor is used in Rom. 6.3. Some, including A. Oepke, dissent from that view. But the 'putting on' of clothing seems to support Schnackenburg's interpretation. The baptized are clothed with Christ. He is not in these passages a 'sphere' into which we are plunged, but Christ as a person.

---

[1] Rudolf Schnackenburg, *Baptism in the Thought of St. Paul*, trans. G. R. Beasley-Murray (Oxford: Blackwell, 1964), pp. 3, 18, and 30.

[2] Welborn, *Politics and Rhetoric in the Corinthian Epistles*, pp. 1–42.

[3] Schnackenburg, *Baptism in the Thought of St. Paul*, p. 20.

[4] Schnackenburg, *Baptism in the Thought of St. Paul*, pp. 22–3.

Dunn has carefully corrected false interpretations of 1 Cor. 12.13 (baptized in the one Spirit), although he also follows Schnackenburg. Baptism here, he insists, does not refer to some subsequent experience after becoming a Christian, but to the single event of becoming a Christian, in a united body of Christ. It may well be that today many Christians, especially those in the Pentecostal Church, undergo a genuine experience which they often call 'baptism in the Holy Spirit'. This was an essential mark of Pentecostal discipleship for Charles Parham and William Seymour, the founders of Pentecostalism. The genuineness of the experience is not in question, but whether the phrase is used in accordance with Paul in 1 Cor. 12.13 is seriously open to doubt. Dunn writes, 'As the one passage which speaks explicitly of baptism in the Spirit, 1 Cor. 12.13 is crucial for the Pentecostal'; but, he comments, 'Once the initiatory and incorporative significance of the metaphor is grasped, the Pentecostal arguments fall to the ground . . . The reception of the Spirit is the beginning of the Christian life (3.3–5).'[5] Schnackenburg observes, 'The operation of the *Pneuma* (Spirit) is part of the operation of the *Kyrios* (Lord) . . . All have been incorporated through the one Spirit into a single Body.'[6]

Baptism in Christ's death and resurrection

A second set of passages point to baptism as a 'salvation event' with Christ (Schnackenburg's term). The *locus classicus* is Rom. 6.1–11. From Rom. 1.18 to 5.21 Paul has been describing salvation in Christ. Christ is the last or new Adam. If all is by grace, however, shall Christians remain in sin? In 6.2 Paul declares that Christians have died to sin. Romans 6.4a states, 'We have been buried with him in (Greek, *eis*) his death.' The sphere of power from which Christians have been delivered is sin. But: 'all we who were baptized to Christ Jesus were baptized to his *death*' (6.3). Behind 6.3–4 stands the earliest *kērygma*, or proclamation (cf. 1 Cor. 15.3, 4). The phrase 'buried with' presupposes Paul's own extension of the *kērygma*. 'Being in Christ', as we saw in Chapter 10, carries Christlike and ethical consequences. Life then follows this death. Paul writes, 'If we have been

---

[5] Dunn, *Baptism in the Holy Spirit*, pp. 107–17 and 127–31, esp. 108.

[6] Schnackenburg, *Baptism in the Thought of St. Paul*, pp. 27 and 28.

united with him in a death like his, we shall certainly be united with him in a resurrection like his' (Rom. 6.5); 'Whoever has died is freed from sin' (6.7); 'You must consider yourselves dead to sin and alive to God in Christ Jesus' (6.11). In 5.19, Cranfield comments, 'God in Christ identified Himself with sinners'; in 6.3, he concludes, 'the relationship to Christ with which baptism has to do includes, in particular, a relationship to His death'.[7] Colossians 2.12 also speaks of being 'buried with him in baptism' and therefore of sharing with Christ in the resurrection.

Cranfield, Schnackenburg, and Günter Wagner reject the theory that Paul was influenced by the pagan mystery religions, with their notion of a god who died and rose again.[8] These mystery cults saw an initiation ceremony or rite as accomplishing union with the dying-and-rising god. But baptism in Paul related to the historical Jesus Christ, and the historical events of his death and resurrection. It is not a myth. Further, Wagner mentions the difficulty of dating the mystery religions prior to Paul. He appealed to what the church in Rome knew already. Paul depends on the Old Testament and its imagery of promise, and the representative and eschatological character of Christ's work. More recently still Tom Holland stresses the role of the Old Testament, including the new Exodus theme and the journey to the promised land, and the corporate or communal character of Rom. 6.1–11; Gal. 3.26–29; and Eph. 5.27.[9] The mystery-religions theory has become outdated and is false.

This view is confirmed by the special use of the Greek word *sumphutoi* (planted together, growing together, or grafted) in Rom. 6.5. *Grafting* means sharing a common life, but also growing ever more inextricably intertwined and inseparable as time moves on. Thus baptism is primarily an initiatory event, but also marks the beginning of a long process.

The third group of passages concerns baptism as washing or cleansing. Today this is probably the most widespread popular view of baptism, but it is rare in Paul. Many writers assume that 1 Cor.

---

[7] Cranfield, *The Epistle to the Romans*, vol. 1, pp. 291 and 301.

[8] Cranfield, *The Epistle to the Romans*, vol. 1, p. 302; Schnackenburg, *Baptism in the Thought of St. Paul*, pp. 12–15, 44–7, 50–5, 139–49; Günter Wagner, *Pauline Baptism and the Pagan Mysteries*, trans. J. P. Smith (Edinburgh: Oliver & Boyd, 1967), throughout, esp. pp. 276–94.

[9] Holland, *Contours of Pauline Theology*, pp. 141–54.

6.11 necessarily refers to baptism, perhaps as a 'baptismal bath', and many assume this without argument. Yet the argument is circular. It is assumed that becoming a Christian is always experienced literally at baptism, rather than that baptism is the outward sign of becoming a Christian. Normally, but not necessarily, the two coincide. James Dunn is again careful and helpful here. He regularly speaks of a conversion–initiation experience, which allows for a coming to faith which may be separated in time from the rite of baptism, although theologically and ideally they belong together. Hence Paul states about the new life, 'You were washed, you were sanctified, you were justified in the name of the Lord Jesus Christ' (1 Cor. 6.11). This may or may not imply the actual moment of baptism. Although many writers refer to this as a 'baptismal aorist', this is an assumption, no more, based on an ideal situation. 'Washed' may refer to forgiveness and cleansing, which is bound up with becoming a Christian.[10]

If we cannot be certain about 1 Cor. 6.11, this leaves us to rely at best on 'Deutero-Pauline', or isolated very late Pauline, references to baptism as washing, whether or not other parts of the New Testament may suggest the idea. Although Eph. 5.26 speaks of 'cleansing with the washing of water', this is 'by the word', and baptism is not explicitly mentioned. The same may be said of Titus 3.5, although the connection with baptism is stronger. It does not mention baptism explicitly, but speaks of 'the water of rebirth and renewal by the Holy Spirit'. In other references Paul prefers to speak of resurrection rather than of rebirth.

There is a further reason why baptism is more primarily connected with 'dying' to the old life and with sharing in the death and resurrection of Christ. Rightly, C. F. D. Moule and Alan Richardson insist that it is like pleading guilty in advance before the last judgement. It is, they rightly say, a once-for-all acceptance (Greek, *ephapax*) of what happened once-for-all in history, namely the death of Christ.[11]

We should be cautious in assuming that Paul taught either infant baptism or the baptism of believers only. The arguments on both sides

---

[10] Dunn, *Baptism in the Holy Spirit*, pp. 120–3.
[11] C. F. D. Moule, 'The Judgment Theme in the Sacraments', in W. D. Davies and D. Daube (eds), *The Background of the New Testament and its Eschatology: Studies in Honour of C. H. Dodd* (Cambridge: Cambridge University Press, 1956), pp. 464–81; cf. Richardson, *Introduction to the Theology of the New Testament*, pp. 341–4.

have regularly been rehearsed by many writers, especially J. Jeremias and K. Aland.[12] Oscar Cullmann insists that Paul sees baptism as a pledge of initiating grace, not primarily as a symbol of public confession of faith, and this would strengthen the case for infant baptism.[13] Many also argue that it is a covenant pledge of assurance, parallel to circumcision in the Old Testament. We must be cautious about historical anachronism, however. In a first-generation church, it is as much an assumption to believe that infants of Christians would be excluded from the covenant, as to assume that 'households' did or did not include infants, as well as slaves (1 Cor. 1.16).

The Lord's Supper or Eucharist

The Lord's Supper, Holy Communion, or the Eucharist, equally firmly grounds the Christian's and the Church's experience in the death and resurrection of Christ. In 1 Cor. 11.17–34 we have what may be the earliest written account of the events of the Last Supper and the institution and the theology of the Lord's Supper. The 'remembrance' (in a sense to be discussed) of Christ's death is fundamental to the meaning of the rite: 'For as often as you eat this bread and drink the cup, you proclaim the Lord's death until he comes' (1 Cor. 11.26). In the liturgy of the word the speaker or speakers proclaim the gospel; in the liturgy of the Communion, *every* member of the Church, as it were, has the opportunity to proclaim the gospel, and their acceptance of it *publicly*.

One controversy to consider initially is the unlikely hypothesis of Hans Lietzmann. From 1926 to 1979 successive editions of his book *Mass and Lord's Supper* have appeared. Lietzmann advocated an influential theory that two different 'primitive types' of the Lord's Supper existed. The Roman liturgy allegedly derived from the 'Pauline type', which emphasized 'proclaiming the Lord's death' in

---

[12] J. Jeremias, *Infant Baptism in the First Four Centuries*, trans. David Cairns (London: SCM Press, 1960); and *The Origins of Infant Baptism: A Reply to Kurt Aland*, trans. D. M. Burton (London: SCM Press, 1963); and Kurt Aland, *Did the Early Church Baptize Infants*, trans. G. R. Beasley-Murray (London: SCM Press, 1962). Cf. Pierre Marcel, *The Biblical Doctrine of Infant Baptism: Sacrament of the Covenant of Grace*, trans. Philip Hughes (London: Clarke, 1953).

[13] Oscar Cullmann, *Baptism in the New Testament*, trans. J. K. S. Reid (London: SCM Press, 1950).

solemnity, while the alleged 'Jerusalem type' differed from Paul, to reflect a more joyous mood of celebrating the presence of the risen Christ in a fellowship meal (Acts 2.46).[14] This was reflected in early Egyptian or Alexandrian liturgies. The origins of the latter supposedly lay in the common fellowship meal or *chaburah*. In English-speaking circles A. J. B. Higgins and Dom Gregory Dix promoted a modified version of this theory, arguing for the 'real presence' of Christ, and more. Ernst Lohmeyer identified the Jerusalem type with a Galilean type.

The death-blow to Lietzmann's hypothesis, however, came with the more careful work of Joachim Jeremias and many others. Jeremias argues that the role of the *chaburah*, or fellowship meal, was not as Lietzmann claimed for it, and that every religious meal had 'religious solemnity' in first-century Judaism. Lietzmann gave us 'an *ad hoc* conjecture for which there is absolutely no evidence'.[15] While I. Howard Marshall and C. F. D. Moule corroborate these criticisms, many, including J. Jeremias, F. J. Leenhardt, and also I. H. Marshall, emphasize instead the *Passover framework* of Paul's understanding and that of the whole Church, of the Lord's Supper.

The Passover and 'remembrance of me'

The Passover provides the key to interpreting 'This is my body that is [given] for you. Do this in remembrance (Greek, *anamnēsis*) of me' (1 Cor. 11.24) and 'The cup is the new covenant in my blood. Do this, as often as you drink it, in remembrance of me' (11.25). Paul quotes an apostolic tradition that came from Jesus. However we date the Passover (the first three Gospels and John appear to have different datings, although 'solutions' to the chronological differences abound), Jesus and the disciples celebrated 'their' Passover at the Last Supper (just as some have 'their' Christmas on a day which does not coincide with 25 December (cf. Matt. 26.17–19; Mark 14.12–16; Luke 22.1–13). The narrative of the Passover (Exod. 12.1–51) takes the form of a dramatic narrative which finds its way into the Jewish

---

[14] Hans Lietzmann, *Mass and Lord's Supper: A Study in the History of the Liturgy*, with Introductions and Notes by R. D. Richardson (Leiden: Brill, 1979), esp. pp. 172–86.
[15] Joachim Jeremias, *The Eucharistic Words of Jesus*, trans. Norman Perrin (London: SCM Press, 1966), p. 30; cf. pp. 16–36 and 108–25.

Haggadah and *Sēder* (or *tsēder*) liturgy. After the grace or thanks-giving, which entails blessing God (Matt. 26.26; Mark 14.22), Cecil Roth records the words, 'This is the bread of affliction that our fore-fathers ate in the land of Egypt.'[16] To the amazement of the disciples Jesus changed 'bread of affliction' to 'my body'.

Participants in the Passover meal were 'there', with the gener-ation who came out of Egypt; Christian participants were 'there' at the cross, reliving a past event as if it were a present event. Hence 'remembrance' is a dramatic making-present; it is more 'objective' than merely mental recollection, but not repeated re-enactment. It is accurately reflected in the Black Spiritual, 'Were you "there" when they crucified my Lord?' Taking and eating is the activity of a par-ticipant, who is not a mere spectator. It is to say: 'Christ died; and died for me'; and 'I am part of it.' But the event which is dramatically 'remembered' remains once-for-all (Greek, *ephapax*). It is an 'effect-ive sign', which gives the assurance of solidarity with Christ and with Christ's people, in his death and resurrection.

Other themes in 1 Cor. 11.17–34 mainly arise from the local situ-ation at Corinth, although they can also be applied today. Although some dissent from this interpretation, it seems likely that wealthy householders in Corinth were adhering to Roman dining customs, as evidenced by Tacitus and others. It was customary to give the pri-vileged position of reclining on couches to favoured guests, who were invited into the *triclinium*, or best reception room. They might be friends of the host, or people of wealth and high status. The more anonymous guests would be left to crowd into the *atrium*, or lounge-hall, where they probably remained standing. First-class food and wine were served in the *triclinium*; while inferior food and wine were provided for those in the *atrium*. Hence the whole meal became class-ridden and divisive. Some ate and drank to excess, while others remained hungry (1 Cor. 11.21).

---

[16] Cecil Roth, *The Haggadah: New Edition with Notes* (London: Soncino, 1934 and 1959), p. 8; cf. Jeremias, *The Eucharistic Words of Jesus*, pp. 49–54; Ottfried Hofius, 'The Lord's Supper and the Lord's Supper Tradition', in Ben Meyer (ed.), *One Loaf, One Cup: Ecumenical Studies of 1 Cor. 11: 17–34* (Macon, GA: Mercer University Press, 1993), pp. 75–115; and F. J. Leenhardt, 'This is My Body', in O. Cullmann and F. J. Leenhardt, *Essays on the Lord's Supper*, trans. J. G. Davies (London: Lutterworth Press, 1958), pp. 39–40.

Paul says that to arrange the Lord's Supper along such lines does more harm than good (11.17). It leads to divisions, whereas there should be one common fellowship or sharing (11.18). It may be better, he tells the Corinthians, to invite guests to dine at a different time from that of solemnly 'remembering' the Lord's death (11.20–22, 23–34). To participate in the Lord's Supper is a serious act, and calls for self-examination (11.27–32). Not 'discerning the body' (11.29) may mean the body of the Church, or perhaps the body of Christ represented by the bread. An insincere participation in the Lord's Supper can invite 'judgement against oneself' (11.29), for in effect the false witness incurs the guilt of perjury, and may cause, or cease to delay, death.[17]

However, Paul's main points are independent of a local situation. The Lord's Supper, like baptism, ensures that all Christian experience is anchored in the cross, or in the death and resurrection of Jesus Christ. It allows the Church, both corporately and individually, to 'relive' the event of the cross, and to become intimately involved in it. To understand what Paul says we need to pay attention to the Passover framework. This helps with the meaning of 'This is my body', and 'Do this in remembrance of me.' Here Paul is at one with what the apostles transmitted. The narrative and its meaning is the earliest tradition of the post-Easter Church, and the legacy of Jesus. In moments of doubt, to see, to touch, to share, and to eat and to drink constitute an assurance, a pledge, a promise, and an 'effective sign' of covenant grace.

---

[17] Cf. Thiselton, *The First Epistle to the Corinthians*, pp. 848–99 for the whole passage.

15

Paul's ethics and views on Christian lifestyle

Paul did not simply communicate the gospel in the sense of calling people to Christian faith. He was equally concerned with the *formation* of Christians and of the Christian community. He writes, 'I first announced the gospel . . . I am in pain of childbirth until Christ is formed in you' (Gal. 4.12, 13, 19). We saw in Chapter 8 (p. 70) Käsemann's correct notion that the gift of the 'body is that piece of the world which we are', which makes Christian discipleship *visible, communicable,* and *credible* in the public world. The body and the world form the theatre of redemption on display. While Luke urges that what people do with their money shows the genuineness of their discipleship, Paul urges that how people conduct themselves 'in the body' shows the genuineness of their confession of Christ as Lord. He writes, 'Present your bodies as a living sacrifice' (Rom. 12.1); and, 'The body is meant . . . for the Lord, and the Lord for the body' (1 Cor. 6.13).

The body, apocalyptic, and Christ

Paul was faced with a multiplicity of day-to-day problems and questions which he addressed. These included relations between Jewish Christians and Gentile Christians; relations between men and women; problems about sex and marriage; eating meat formerly dedicated to pagan deities; different kinds of immorality; greedy, grasping, or manipulative behaviour; attitudes of the rich and the poor; and stability and order in church life; and other questions. But unlike the Stoics, he did not produce a free-floating or self-contained system of ethical rules. Brian Rosner writes, 'Doctrine and ethics are intimately related in Paul's letters.'[1] Richard Hays asserts, 'His ethical teachings are rooted in his theological thought.'[2]

Hays points out that Paul's moral vision finds roots in his background in apocalyptic or eschatology. This gives prominent place to new creation (2 Cor. 5.14–18), and to the continuance of this world-order alongside the in-breaking of the new age and new creation. This at times leaves room for some ambiguity in life. In accordance with the promise of Isa. 65.17–19, Paul looks forward to the new creation, which embodies the whole created order (Rom. 8.18–25). But the old world-order persists, and Christians face sufferings and death in the present, because 'hope that is seen is not hope, for who hopes for what he sees?' (Rom. 8.24–25). We tried to capture this double perspective in Chapter 2, on new creation.

Some claim that an apocalyptic perspective makes ethical teaching difficult. But it can be shown that some of Paul's most important ethical statements or injunctions come precisely in apocalyptic contexts. The discussion about 'no longer living for oneself' comes in the context of new creation in 2 Cor. 5.14–18. The same occurs in 1 Cor. 10.11, where Paul speaks of 'us on whom the ends of the ages have come'. As well as 1 and 2 Corinthians, this connection between ethics and apocalyptic occurs in Rom. 8.18–25. It is certainly the case where Paul discusses eschatological expectation in 1 Thess. 4.13–18. He offers strong statements about conduct. Perhaps this causes surprise only because the grammar of what 'expect' means is often wrongly thought of as implying a particular mental state. Wittgenstein urged that to expect means to conduct one's actions in an appropriate way. We look at this in further detail in the next chapter, on eschatology.

The way of the cross also provides a theological root for Paul's ethics. The death and resurrection of Jesus Christ are pivotal for bringing

---

[1] Brian S. Rosner, 'Paul's Ethics', in James D. G. Dunn (ed.), *The Cambridge Companion to Paul* (Cambridge: Cambridge University Press, 2003), p. 212; cf. pp. 212–23. Cf. Brian S. Rosner, *Paul, Scripture and Ethics: A Study of 1 Corinthians* (Leiden: Brill, 1994). pp. 5–7.

[2] Richard B. Hays, *The Moral Vision of the New Testament: A Contemporary Introduction to New Testament Ethics* (New York: Harper One, 1996), p. 18.

forward the new age and new creation. Paul urges, 'Bear one another's burdens, and in this way you will fulfil the law of *Christ*' (Gal. 6.2). He also declares, 'We who are powerful ought to bear the weaknesses of the powerless, and not to please ourselves. Each of us must please our neighbour . . . For *Christ* did not please himself . . . Welcome one another, therefore, as Christ has welcomed you' (Rom. 15.1–3, 7). The best-known passage illustrating this point is probably Phil. 2.3–11: 'Do nothing from selfish ambition or conceit, but in humility regard others as better than yourselves. Let each of you look not to your own interests, but to the interests of others. Let the same mind be in you that was in *Christ Jesus*, who though he was in the form of God, did not regard equality with God as something to be exploited, but emptied himself, taking the form of a slave . . . and became obedient to the point of death, even death on a cross. Therefore God also highly exalted him . . .' Sometimes this theme is called 'Adam in reverse', since 'Adam' followed the opposite path. Stephen Fowl observes, 'Christ's obedience unto death, is the ultimate testimony to his appearance as a servant. That this death took place on the cross emphasized the extent of his humiliation.'[3]

Dodd and Moule concede that the *content* of Paul's ethics often overlaps with the ethics of the best of the Hellenistic world. But whereas Seneca and other Stoics promote a free-standing or self-contained ethical system, Paul distinctively stresses a new *motivation* for ethical conduct. Material in 1 Thess. 4.1–9 and 5.14–18 may be shared both by 1 Pet. 1.13–22 and Heb. 13.1–3, and also by some Hellenistic and Jewish writers. But in Paul such bodily conduct is a response to God's generous grace in Christ.[4] It is possible that sometimes this ethical material becomes abstracted into the form of an early Christian catechism, pointing the way to what is expected of a new Christian. This point was made especially by E. G. Selwyn on 1 Peter and more

---

[3] Fowl, *The Story of Christ in the Ethics of Paul*, pp. 63–4.

[4] Charles H. Dodd, *Gospel and Law* (Cambridge: Cambridge University Press, 1951), pp. 10–21; and Charles F. D. Moule, 'Obligation in the Ethics of Paul', in W. R. Farmer, C. F. D. Moule, and R. R. Niebuhr (eds), *Christian History and Interpretation: Essays in Honour of John Knox* (Cambridge: Cambridge University Press, 1967), pp. 389–406.

broadly by Philip Carrington, although 'lists' of virtues and vices also feature prominently in Judaism, as O. L. Yarbrough notes.[5]

Even if they are drawn from common catechetical material, Paul nevertheless interprets the material with a strong doctrinal foundation. The ethical injunctions of Romans 12—15 follow the theological teaching of Romans 1—11. The ethics of Galatians 4.12—6.18 follow Galatians 1.1—4.11. In 1 and 2 Corinthians, Philippians, and 1 and 2 Thessalonians the doctrinal and ethical are intertwined. Colossians 3 and 4 (on ethics) follows Colossians 1 and 2. Ephesians 4—6 (largely on conduct) follows Ephesians 1—3 (largely on theology). Even where there are lists or 'catalogues' of virtues and vices (Rom. 1.29–31; 1 Cor. 6.9–11) it is a mistake to assume that Paul borrows them wholesale from Hellenistic ethics. They can be found in the first place in Jewish sources (*1 Enoch* 10.20; 91.6–7; *Jubilees* 7.20–21; and 1QS 4.9–11 at Qumran, among the Dead Sea Scrolls). But Paul firmly puts them to theological *use* in his argument, whatever their ultimate origin. All these virtues are 'how we ought to walk and please God' (1 Thess. 4.1). Paul often uses the practical metaphor of the Christian 'walk' (Greek, *peripatō*: Rom. 6.4; 8.4; 13.13; 14.15; 1 Cor. 7.17; 2 Cor. 4.2; 10.2, 3; Gal. 5.16; Phil. 3.17; Col. 4.5; 1 Thess. 4.1, 12; 2 Thess. 3.11; cf. Eph. 2.2; 4.1, 17; 5.2, 3). His discourse on love in 1 Corinthians 13 finds parallels in content in Rom. 12.9–20; 13.8–10; and 15.1–7.

The role of love

Paul aims to present every person 'mature in Christ' (Col. 2.28), and to encourage people to live 'in a manner worthy of the gospel' (Phil. 1.27). Victor Furnish rightly comments that Paul's teaching on

---

[5] Philip Carrington, *The Primitive Christian Catechism* (Cambridge: Cambridge University Press, 1940); and E. G. Selwyn, *The First Epistle of St. Peter*, 2nd edn (London: Macmillan, 1947); cf. O. L. Yarbrough, *Not Like the Gentiles: Marriage Rules in the Letters of Paul* (SBLDS 80; Atlanta: Scholars Press, 1985), pp. 8–26; Siegfried Wibbing, *Die Tugend und Lasterkataloge im Neuen Testament und ihre Traditions geschichte unter besonderer Berücksichtigung der Qumran-Texte* (Berlin: Töpelmann, 1959), esp. pp. 14–76; and Victor P. Furnish, *Theology and Ethics in Paul* (Nashville and New York: Abingdon, 1968), pp. 81–91.

love is 'vitally related' to what he says about justification by faith: 'Thereby one's whole life is radically re-orientated from sin to righteousness, as he is freed from bondage to himself.'[6] Spicq has no doubt that 1 Corinthians came from Paul's pen, and provides a response to grace. He also recognizes that it forms a close link with putting spiritual gifts in their proper place.[7] He and others observe that far from being an abstract meditation on love, in spite of its style, its specific themes reflect the life of the church in Corinth. Love is not 'puffed up' (Greek, *ou phusioutai*, 1 Cor. 13.4) reflects 'knowledge (*gnōsis*) puffs up' (8.1, again, Greek, *phusioi*). 'Tongues of angels' (13.1) reflects 'tongues' in 14.1–25. 'Love is not envious or boastful or arrogant' (13.4) reflects 'Where there is jealousy and quarrelling, are you not of the flesh?' (3.3; cf. 5.2). 'Love is not rude. It does not insist on its own way' (13.4) reflects, 'Each goes ahead with his or her own meal' (1 Cor. 11.21–22), and 'Let there be two or at most three' (14.27–33). 'Love never ends' (13.8) reflects, 'The dead will be raised imperishable' (1 Cor. 15.52; cf. 15.34–49, 58).

Paul's Greek uses dynamic verbs. These are better translated, as we have in part noted (p. 7), 'Love waits patiently; love shows kindness. Love does not burn with envy; does not brag – is not inflated with its own importance. Love does not behave with ill-mannered impropriety; is not preoccupied with the interests of the self; does not become exasperated into pique; does not keep a reckoning up of evil. Love does not take pleasure at wrongdoing, but joyfully celebrates the truth. It never tires of support, never loses faith, never exhausts hope, never gives up.'[8]

Paul also treats love as a theme in Rom. 12.9–21. Roman Christians are to let their love, Cranfield observes, be 'the real thing, genuine and not counterfeit. Paul twice uses this word (Greek, *anupokritos*) with reference to *agapē* (here and in 2 Cor. 6.6), suggesting that he [Paul] was aware of the danger . . . of self-deceit.'[9] Paul also urges *philadelphia*, an intimate affection and tenderness found

---

[6] Victor P. Furnish, *The Love Command in the New Testament* (London: SCM Press, 1973), p. 92.

[7] C. Spicq, *Agapē in the New Testament*, trans. Sr Marie Aquinas McNamara, 3 vols (London: Herder, 1963–6), vol. 2, pp. 139–41; cf. 139–81.

[8] Thiselton, *First Epistle to the Corinthians*, p. 1026; defended on pp. 1026–60; cf. Thiselton, *First Corinthians*, pp. 217–21.

[9] Cranfield, *The Epistle to the Romans*, vol. 2, pp. 630–1.

between members of a family (12.10). Christians must surpass one another in showing honour and respect to one another, as if to Christ. All this takes place with and in the Spirit's fervour (12.11), rather than as the listless performance of a routine virtue. Romans 13.8–10 resumes the notion of love as a debt: 'Owe no one anything, except to love one another; for the one who loves another has fulfilled the law' (13.8). Romans 15.1–7 appeals to the example and character of Christ, for the 'strong' to bear with the failings of 'the weak' (15.1, 3). 'Weak' may include Jewish converts to the Christian faith, or Christians who still observe some of the Jewish dietary laws. But in 1 Corinthians Paul has used the term to denote those who may feel insecure and vulnerable. At all events, Jewish Christians and Gentile Christians are to 'welcome one another, therefore, just as Christ has welcomed you (Rom. 15.7).

Ideas shared with Jews and Hellenists

The concrete outworking of love in a variety of different situations gives a distinctive character to the common material allegedly borrowed from Hellenistic and Jewish sources. These are not merely 'personal' matters, but also community or interpersonal matters. Further, they are a response to grace (1 Cor. 4.7) and to the character of Christ, of whom Christians are now a part (Rom. 15.1–7; Phil. 2.3–11). Given this difference of motivation, some common material occurs, as we might expect. This concerns: (1) humility and patience; (2) family relations or 'household codes'; (3) the state and good citizenship; and (4) the general stability and well-being of society. Two more 'virtues' overlap with those of Jewish synagogues: (5) relations within the congregation, including respect for elders; and (6) concern for 'outsiders' and the world.

Even some of these 'virtues' have a distinctive turn in Paul. His teaching on sexual intimacy in marriage has an unexpectedly creative application, as we have seen. Virtually all writers in Paul's day thought that the sexual act served for reproduction and the one-sided pleasure of men. Paul regards long-term abstinence as depriving both men and women of their legitimate rights, implying a two-sided pleasure in this intimacy (1 Cor. 7.3–7). This forms a breakthrough, far ahead of the rest of the ancient world. He also denies the force of what surely must have been a slogan used often in Corinth: 'It is well for a man not to touch a woman' (1 Cor. 7.2). There are no inverted commas in Greek, so we cannot be certain of this; but otherwise Paul seems to contradict himself. Moreover his possible acceptance of slavery (1 Cor. 7.21–24; Philem. 11–16) is not only due to the times, or to supposed hierarchical paternalism, but because, as we saw in Chapter 5, slavery in the right conditions could promote security, reputation, and a career. A good 'lord' could prosper the career and standing of a slave more than could be gained as a free person.

The law

Paul's ethics are not lawless or 'antinomian'. The Christian has become free from the law as a means of justification. Obeying the law does not win God's favour. This would make nonsense of grace. But *Torah*, or law, also expresses the will of God for the blessing and well-being of humankind. In this sense the law functioned as a kind of tutor (Greek, *paidogōgos*) in charge, until Christ came (Gal. 3.24). Yet without Christ, it may also have the unintended effect of multiplying law-breaking (Rom. 5.20). Those who rely on it for salvation remain under a curse (Gal. 3.10). But the law, Paul argues, is in itself 'holy, just, and good' (Rom. 7.12–13). Paul describes Christian conduct, not as obeying the law as such, but as responding to, and showing, 'the law of the Spirit'. Thus Whiteley rightly distinguishes between three different senses of 'law' in Paul: (1) the law, or *Torah*, is the declared will of God, especially in Scripture; (2) the law can be misused as an instrument of justification by Christians; (3) it may also mean 'principle', or process of cause and effect.[10] In the first sense, Paul's ethics will not conflict with, or set aside, the law. Paul writes, 'He who loves . . . has fulfilled the law' (Rom. 13.8; cf. 13.10).

Paul also conveys a sense of urgency for Christians. But he also recognizes that sometimes ambiguity arises where the coming of the new creation overlaps with the continuance of the old. J. Paul Sampley, as well as Furnish, Dunn, and others, calls attention to 'the two horizons of Paul's thought world' in his book *Walking between*

---

[10] Whiteley, *The Theology of St. Paul*, pp. 76–86.

the Times.[11] Christians have been brought from death to life (Rom. 6.13), and this implies an ethic of 'no longer'. But Christians still look forward in hope to the resurrection (Rom. 6.4–5), and so 'two ages' coexist. There is urgency about the coming of the new: 'Salvation is now nearer to us than when we first believed; the night is far gone, the day is near' (Rom. 13.11, 12). The law of cause and effect imprisons humankind in part bondage to sin; but the Spirit of life brings a new 'law' orientated to the future. Christians, according to Paul, should appropriate and bring forward what God will destine them to be. Meanwhile some 'grey areas' of ethics arise from the ambiguities of an overlapping situation. Business contacts, for example, may be facilitated by the 'strong' who wish to eat meat sacrificed to idols. They argue that 'an idol has no real existence' (1 Cor. 8.1–6). But because of the scruples of the insecure and vulnerable, 'if food is a cause of (my brother's) falling, I will never eat meat' (8.13). Yet if the weak are absent, dining in the temple precincts provided a useful meeting place for contacts, even if the food had been dedicated to non-existent deities.

Identity of the Christian Church

Much of Paul's concern for appropriate behaviour concerns the very identity, cohesion, stability, and unity of the Church. Hays points out that the community, the cross, and the new creation provide key focal images, which Paul shares with other writers in the New Testament. Hays writes, 'The primary sphere of moral concern is not the character of the individual but the corporate obedience of the church' (Rom. 12.1–2).[12] This brings us to the special problem of the later Pauline epistles, especially Ephesians. These may be from Paul's pen, or they may be what Hays calls 'developments of the Pauline tradition'. Possibly open arrest or semi-confinement in Rome offered to Paul time for reflection, which may have enabled him to think about the

---

[11] J. Paul Sampley, *Walking between the Times: Paul's Moral Reasoning* (Minneapolis: Fortress Press, 1991), pp. 7–24 and throughout; cf. Furnish, *Theology and Ethics in Paul*, pp. 115–34; and Dunn, *The Theology of Paul the Apostle*, pp. 680–706.

[12] Hays, *The Moral Vision of the New Testament*, p. 196.

stability and order of the Church. At all events, in these epistles we see that God 'has broken down the dividing wall, that is, the hostility between us' (Jewish and Gentile Christians), and has created one undivided body 'through the cross' (Eph. 2.14–16). Ephesians sets forth God's glorious purpose for the Church. After showing its conception and construction in Ephesians 1—3, Paul urges appropriate conduct in Ephesians 4—6.

The so-called household codes appear in Col. 3.18—4.1 and Titus 2.1–10. The term 'household' is applied to the church in 1 Tim. 3.14–15. As we saw in Chapter 13, 1 Tim. 3.2, 3 and Titus 1.3–9 set out qualifications of an overseer, including the capacity to teach ably and to guard the apostolic tradition. Ethical qualities remain important, but the emphasis has moved from the new creation to the social cohesion of the Church.[13] Yet concern for good citizenship and for peace in the world remains in earlier epistles and in 'Deutero-Pauline' epistles (Rom. 13.1–7; 1 Tim. 2.1–6). The Pastoral Epistles also stress future hope or eschatology (1 Tim. 4.1–5; 2 Tim. 3.1–5; Titus 2.12–14). Within this frame Christians must be 'zealous for good deeds' (Titus 2.14), not be quarrelsome, but patient (2 Tim. 3.24), and avoid greed and love of money (1 Tim. 6.10). The later epistles do not entirely abandon the vision of the earlier writings. Many sociologists agree that an initial vision is likely to develop in due time into concerns about infrastructure and implementation of the vision by good order and management.

---

[13] Hays, *The Moral Vision of the New Testament*, p. 71.

16

Cosmic and human destiny and the present: resurrection, judgement, and the *Parousia*

Popular misunderstandings

Paul's teaching about the 'last things' differs from how it is often popularly presented. First, Paul is less interested in individual destiny, or survival of death, and 'heaven', than in the three great corporate and cosmic events of the resurrection, the last judgement, and the *Parousia* of Christ. Second, these are not events of the remote future, so much as future events which profoundly shape attitudes in the present. These events are not like a terminus on an underground map, which states, 'You are here', at an intermediate station, to count how many you have yet to go. They are not part of a chronological time-chart.

Some writers used to think that Paul moved away from interest in the last things, or eschatology, and presented a different picture in the epistles from 2 Corinthians onwards, unlike earlier ones. We shall challenge this older view. Further, Paul has nothing to do with secular progressivism, that is, he does not believe that the innate forces of human progress alone will generate the hoped-for tomorrows. Here again he is like the apocalyptists. His epistles are full of hope in God for the future.

To imagine that Paul's emphasis lies on individual human survival is to narrow his vision of the End. He does include this, but always as part of his bigger picture. Jürgen Moltmann points out that the future cosmic End neither *enters* time, nor is isolated *outside* time, but changes the very *conditions* of time.[1] In Isaiah we read, 'Do not

---

[1] Jürgen Moltmann, *The Coming of God: Christian Eschatology*, trans. Margaret Kohl (London: SCM Press, 1996), p. 26; cf. J. A. T. Robinson, *In the End, God . . .* (London: Clarke, 1950), esp. p. 11.

remember the former things . . . I am about to do a new thing' (Isa. 43.18–19). Paul appropriates this. The 'new' comes as radically different, like the act of creation; it is no less radical than the miracle of existence (Rom. 4.17). God is faithful to his creation, and brings about a new state that has never been. It is the restoration (*apokatastasis*) of all things, when God will become 'all in all' (1 Cor. 15.28). The whole cosmos, or universe, will undergo transformation.

These future events have profound implications for the present (1 Cor. 15.58; Phil. 3.20—4.1; 1 Thess. 5.2–11). Some years ago Rudolf Bultmann tried to make us see 'the point' of much language about the last things by interpreting these as 'myths' which ultimately conveyed language about the present. For example, language about the last judgement did not promote a view of what would happen in the remote future, but called us to present accountability or responsibility. Believers, he said, will not actually 'meet the Lord in the air', or see the Lord descend from heaven with the sound of a trumpet (1 Thess. 4.16, 17; cf. 4.15—5.11). This 'myth' belongs to apocalyptic. It should be interpreted in a practical way, or 'existentially'.[2] Bultmann may be half right, for this language always carries practical consequences for life now. But why is this language *either* to promote present attitudes *or* be about events in the future? If, as Bultmann claims, there is no last judgement, the call to accountability becomes virtually a bluff. I have argued elsewhere that Bultmann's programme of 'demythologizing' is inconsistent and self-defeating, even if it conveys elements of truth.[3] As John Macquarrie observes, how could it make sense to speak of being raised with Christ, if Christ was not actually raised?[4]

Although strong in the earlier epistles, Paul's emphasis on future expectation is alleged to disappear in those letters which were written from 2 Corinthians onwards. Three theorists, among others, are well

---

[2] Rudolf Bultmann, 'Jesus Christ and Mythology', in Hans-Werner Bartsch (ed.), *Kerygma and Myth*, 2 vols, trans. R. H. Fuller, vol. 1 (London: SCM Press, 1964), pp. 1–44; also Rudolf Bultmann, *New Testament Mythology and Other Basic Writings Selected and Edited by Schabert Ogden* (Philadelphia: Fortress Press, 1984), pp. 1–44.

[3] Anthony C. Thiselton, *The Two Horizons: New Testament Hermeneutics and Philosophical Description* (Grand Rapids: Eerdmans and Exeter: Paternoster Press, 1980), pp. 205–92.

[4] John Macquarrie, 'Philosophy and Theology in Bultmann's Thought', in Charles W. Kegley (ed.), *The Theology of Rudolf Bultmann* (London: SCM Press, 1966), p. 141.

known for holding this dubious view, although all write in the first half of the twentieth century. In 1913 R. H. Charles tried to distinguish between four stages of hope in Paul: (1) apocalyptic material in 1 and 2 Thessalonians; (2) the future perspective in 1 Corinthians (1 Cor. 4.5; 11.26; 15.51; 16.22); (3) 2 Corinthians and Romans, both of which focus on 'inner transformation'; and (4) Philippians, Colossians, and Ephesians, which largely concern the cosmic Christ.

Charles is broadly followed by C. H. Dodd and W. L. Knox. Dodd speaks of 'realized eschatology' to denote events once future, but that have entered the present in Christ and W. L. Knox believes that according to Acts 17.32–33 Paul's speech about the resurrection was a 'failure', and that he progressively adapted his message to the expectations of the Hellenistic world, away from the last things.[5] Most scholars today reject this view.

John Lowe replied to all three writers shortly after this time. He showed in an incisive article that the earliest epistles of Paul were written at least 12 years after his call, when he was already a mature thinker, and that he faced 'Hellenism' in the early days of mission. More especially, not all of the early letters are orientated to the future, especially Galatians, while Romans and Philippians, among the later letters, speak of the future (Rom. 8.18–25; 13.11–14; Phil. 3.11–16, 20–21). He rejects a 'linear' development in Paul.[6] Nowadays many scholars speak of the 'bipolarity', or double emphasis, on both the present and the future, in Paul.[7] Moreover, Moltmann declares, 'From first to last . . . Christianity is eschatology, is hope . . . Presumption is a premature self-willed anticipation of the fulfilment of what we hope for from God. Despair is the premature, arbitrary anticipation of the non-fulfilment of what we hope for from God.'[8] Both suggest un-Pauline forms of hopelessness.

A further misunderstanding is to confuse Paul's ground of hope with secular progressivism. We shall see more of this in our next

---

[5] Wilfred L. Knox, *St. Paul and the Church of the Gentiles* (Cambridge: Cambridge University Press, 1939), p. 1 and throughout.

[6] John Lowe, 'An Examination of Attempts to Detect Developments in St. Paul's Theology', *Journal of Theological Studies* 42 (1941), pp. 127–42.

[7] Cf. for example, Oscar Cullmann, *Christ and Time*, 2nd edn, trans. F. V. Filson (London: SCM Press, 1962).

[8] Jürgen Moltmann, *Theology of Hope*, trans. J. W. Leitch (London: SCM Press, 1967), pp. 16 and 23.

chapter, in connection with the postmodernity of Richard Rorty. Hope does not lie in the abilities of humankind, even in their religious searching or achievements. Hope, as the apocalyptists believed, becomes focused in God alone, and his transforming, creative action. The Holy Spirit, Moltmann urges, is the well of life.

Further misunderstandings have distorted an accurate assessment of the living Paul on the matter of the resurrection, last judgement, and the *Parousia* of Christ. First, *expectation is not a mental state*. It is not a matter of chronological calculation or of projecting our imagination into the future. The later thought of the philosopher Ludwig Wittgenstein makes this clear. Expectation, he urges, consists of *appropriate conduct or behaviour in a given situation*. If I 'expect' someone to come to tea at four o'clock, he argues, to 'expect' is to put out cups, saucers, and plates, to buy cake, and perhaps to tidy the room and to begin boiling the kettle.[9] It is not to imagine a guest's arrival. Paul does not make a 'mistake' when he says '*We* who are alive and remain' (1 Thess. 4.15), because this expresses solidarity with those who are expectant.[10] Neither Paul nor Jesus, as Caird rightly argues, made a 'mistake'. Putting out the crockery says nothing about the visitor being early or late; but shows the currency of what it means to 'expect'.[11] In the case of the Thessalonian Christians, they must seek holiness and work hard. While 2 Cor. 5.8 suggests that Paul simply does not know whether the *Parousia* will occur during his lifetime, 1 Thess. 5.10 also expresses open-minded doubt about 'whether we are awake or asleep'. Whichever is the case, Paul says, 'We shall live with him.'

A second misunderstanding is about the nature of time. Will the resurrection, judgement, and *Parousia* either continue time, or usher in a state of timelessness, or something else? These events will trans-

---

[9] Ludwig Wittgenstein, *Philosophical Investigations*, IIx, pp. 191–2; I §§572–86 and *Zettel* (German and English, Oxford, Blackwell, 1967), §§67 and 71–7.

[10] Thiselton, *The Hermeneutics of Doctrine*, pp. 546–52. Cf. Arthur L. Moore, *The Parousia in the New Testament* (NovTSup 13; Leiden: Brill, 1966), pp. 108–10; and A. L. Moore, *1 and 2 Thessalonians* (New Century Bible; London: Nelson, 1969), pp. 70–1; Earl J. Richard, *First and Second Thessalonians* (Collegeville, MN: Liturgical Press, 2007), pp. 241–2.

[11] George B. Caird, *The Language and Imagery of the Bible* (London: Duckworth, 1980), pp. 243–71.

form time from time-as-we-know-it, into *God's* time. Divine time allows for purposive change in the living God and in post-mortal resurrection existence, and does not deny that the transformation of the world will be decisive. Once again, Moltmann sheds light on the situation. The future is not a mere extension of the past, for it is *new* creation. It not only subsumes creation within it, but also transforms it. The transformation of the world involves *transformation*, not abolition, of time.[12]

Participant and observer viewpoints

The so-called 'sleep of the soul' appears to be drawn from the notion of an interval between death and the general resurrection of the dead (1 Cor. 15.51–54). This may appear to conflict with immediate entry into the presence of Christ (Phil. 1.23, 24). Some, like Knox, see this as a contradiction. But the philosopher Gilbert Ryle and others have shown that paradoxes (not contradictions) arise because of a clash between an *observer* (or ontological) point of view (1 Corinthians 15) and a *participant* (or existential) point of view (Phil. 1.23, 24).[13] We may compare a parent's saying, 'As soon as you fall asleep, Christmas will be here.' This is an existential, experience-based, or participant view. But creeping upstairs late in the night with an armful of presents is the observer or ontological view. Both are true, each from a different perspective, and there is no real conflict. In experience Christians enter at once into Christ's presence; in reality, unbeknown to them, they wait until we all appear together.

Credibility of the resurrection

Paul discusses the resurrection primarily in 1 Corinthians 15. Hans Conzelmann sees this as a separate treatise.[14] There were probably several reasons why 'some' had ceased to regard the resurrection as

---

[12] Moltmann, *The Coming of God*, pp. 22–9.

[13] Gilbert Ryle, 'Achilles and the Tortoise' (1954), in *Dilemmas* (Cambridge: Cambridge University Press, 1966), pp. 36–53. See also Moltmann, *The Coming of God*, pp. 101–10.

[14] Hans Conzelmann, *1 Corinthians: A Commentary*, trans. J. W. Leitch (Philadelphia: Fortress Press, 1975), p. 249.

central or even credible. Some had typical Greek doubts imagining a 'bodily' resurrection. The tradition from at least the time of Plato believed that the body was a tomb, and belonged to the contingent or imperfect realm of physical objects, in contrast to the soul or spirit, which was perfect, immortal, and eternal. Others believed that the resurrection was inner and spiritual and had already taken place. They were already 'raised with Christ', whose resurrection had taken place (cf. 1 Cor. 4.8–13; 2 Tim. 2.18). Still others, a third group, had simply been seduced by the materialist view that life after death was impossible. Luther, Mitchell, and Eriksson convincingly argue that each of these groups plays a part among the doubters.[15] Above all, Luther and Barth urge, some at Corinth failed to see that belief in resurrection was a matter of faith in, and knowledge of, God (1 Cor. 15.34). Resurrection lay beyond human competence and power. Immortality for Plato and many other Greeks was an innate capacity of the human soul. But, as Gaston Deluz succinctly expresses it, 'They confused this pagan doctrine of immortality with Christian teaching on the resurrection.'[16]

Using patterns of Graeco-Roman rhetoric, Paul begins the chapter with a *narratio* or 'statement' in 1 Cor. 15.1–11, which recounts the resurrection of Christ as an established apostolic tradition, and provides a foundation for the rest of the argument. The first part of the *narratio* (15.1–7) establishes the bodily resurrection of Christ, as handed down by witnesses. The second part (15.8–11) states the reality of God's creative, sovereign, grace, alongside the reality of Christ's resurrection.

Several factors are important for the subsequent argument. First, this established tradition is not Paul's invention, but was handed on to him by common apostolic testimony as a 'given'. Second, it embodies a scriptural principle. Primitive teaching always saw the event as 'according to the Scriptures' (cf. Luke 24.25–27, 44–46). Paul does not narrow his focus to a particular passage (such as Hos. 6.2), but looks to the wider notion of God's vindication of his Servant (Isa.

---

[15] Martin Luther, *Luther's Works*, vol. 28: *Commentaries on 1 Corinthians 7 and 15* (St Louis: Concordia, 1973), pp. 63–75; cf. Barth, *The Resurrection of the Dead*, p. 18.

[16] Gaston Deluz, *A Companion to 1 Corinthians*, trans. Grace Watt (London: Darton, Longman & Todd, 1963), p. 225.

53.11–12; cf. Deut. 18.15–18; Ps. 22.8–28; Lam. 3.19–33).[17] Third, the burial of Christ (1 Cor. 15.4) shows that this constituted a genuine death, as well as resurrection. The theory of a 'swoon' and resuscitation cannot account for a two- or three-day burial. Fourth, Christ was raised (passive) by God. This enables Paul to say, 'He who raised Christ from the dead will give life to your mortal bodies also.'[18] Dahl rightly comments that in Paul and elsewhere God is virtually always the subject in language about the resurrection of Christ (Acts 3.15; 4.10; 5.30; 10.40; Rom. 4.21; 8.11; 10.9; 1 Cor. 6.14; 15.15; 2 Cor. 4.14; Gal. 1.1; Col. 2.12; 1 Thess. 1.10 and elsewhere).

Fifth, and finally, in what sense is the resurrection of Christ *'bodily'*? We shall examine the bodiliness of the resurrection when we consider 1 Cor. 15.42–44. But, for the record, a number of scholars argue that 'he appeared' (Greek, *ōphthē*) says only that a theophany occurred, without specifying whether this was 'bodily'. Willi Marxsen is a leading exponent of this view.[19] But the logic of parts of 1 Corinthians 15 seem to demand continuity between Christ's resurrection and the resurrection of the dead, and the latter is, in some sense, 'bodily'. At all events, W. Künneth, Wolfhart Pannenberg, and N. T. Wright (and Thiselton) convincingly defend a 'bodily' view, and in our opinion are much more convincing than Marxsen.[20]

From his 'statement', or *narratio*, in 1 Cor. 15.1–11, Paul moves on to present what in Graeco-Roman rhetoric would constitute a *refutatio*. This is a negative argument concerning the consequences of denying the resurrection in principle (15.12–19). There would be no future life (15.12–14). But this makes nonsense of all that Christ has done and the apostles are exposed as liars (15.15–16). Further, there is no release from sin (15.17); and dead believers are lost (15.18, 19). To complement this *refutatio*, Paul then produces a

---

[17] Cf. Barrett, *The First Epistle to the Corinthians*, pp. 338–9; and C. H. Dodd, *According to the Scriptures* (London: Nisbet, 1952), e.g. p. 127.

[18] See M. E. Dahl, *The Resurrection of the Body* (London: SCM Press, 1962), pp. 96–100.

[19] Willi Marxsen, *The Resurrection of Jesus of Nazareth*, trans. Margaret Kohl (Philadelphia: Fortress Press, 1970).

[20] W. Künneth, *The Theology of the Resurrection*, trans. J. W. Leitch (London: SCM Press, 1965); and Pannenberg, *Systematic Theology*, vol. 2, pp. 343–72; and vol. 3, pp. 375–80 and 555–646. Cf. Thiselton, *The First Epistle to the Corinthians*, pp. 1169–1213 and 1257–1313; Wright, *The Resurrection of the Son of God*, pp. 5–10 and 317–25.

confirmatio in 15.20–34. This first *confirmatio* begins, 'But in reality Christ has been raised.' Now his resurrection is presented as the 'firstfruits' (Greek, *aparchē*), which is like in kind to the resurrection of Christians 'in Christ'. The firstfruits also gave a pledge and assurance of a full harvest. God has made a promise, but its fulfilment will occur in God's time and in God's ordered way. Christ is presented as the last Adam (15.22). Christ is king for the period of the Messianic reign, after which he hands the kingdom back to God, who will be all in all (15.24–28).

This 'apocalyptic drama' serves to underline the timeliness and orderliness of God's purposes: first Christ is raised; then those who are Christ's (15.23). Death remains 'the last enemy' to be destroyed (15.26). In 15.29–34, Paul turns from the majestic contemplation of God, to resume his expansion of the consequences of denying the resurrection. Otherwise, he asks, why 'be baptized for the dead'? This notorious verse has numerous interpretations. In my larger commentary on the Greek text, I have noted 23. But I have argued for the view that 15.29 alludes to those who have come to faith and been baptized for the sake of (Greek, *huper*) the dying testimony of Christians who died before Paul's time of writing.[21] Perhaps their confident radiance in the face of death was the persuasive factor. So-called vicarious baptism does not appear elsewhere in Paul, and suggests an un-Pauline, later, and extreme 'sacramentalism'. Paul also alludes to the pointlessness of his own ministry and suffering, if such a denial were to be valid (15.30–33).

Paul now moves to a second *refutatio* and second *confirmatio* in 1 Cor. 15.35–58. How can the resurrection, he asks on behalf of the doubters, be conceivable or credible? The second *refutatio* (15.35–49) begins with an *exclamatio*. It is not his or the reader's job to try to imagine the resurrection. *Everything hinges on what kind of God they believe in.* 'Some have no knowledge of God' constitutes the transitional verse (15.34). '*God* gives it a body as he has chosen' (15.38). That is why Luther calls the linchpin of the argument 'in brief, that God is *God*'.[22] Karl Barth likewise singles out 'knowledge of God' as the key to believing in the resurrection.[23] Belief rests not on whether

---

[21] Thiselton, *The First Epistle to the Corinthians*, pp. 1240–9.

[22] Luther, *Luther's Works*, vol. 28, pp. 94–5.

[23] Barth, *The Resurrection of the Dead*, pp. 18 and 139, and 189–91.

we can conceive of the resurrection, but on whether God, the Creator of all, can create and transform new creation and resurrection of the 'body'. Paul now offers analogies from creation to show that God has set in motion death, new life, and continuity of existence. He has already created different kinds of 'body'. Each kind of 'body' is appropriate to its environment, whether we think of animals for the ground, of fish for the sea, of birds for the air, or of stars for space (15.38–41).

The 'spiritual body'

Paul declares that with the resurrection of the dead, 'What is sown is perishable; it is raised imperishable. It is sown in dishonour; it is raised in glory. It is sown in weakness; it is raised in power. It is sown a physical body; it is raised a spiritual body' (1 Cor. 15.42–44). This needs clarification. (1) There is contrast or discontinuity: 'You do not sow the body which is to be' (v. 37). (2) There is transformation and creativity: 'It is raised in glory' (v. 43). (3) There is continuity of identity: 'What is sown . . . is raised.' 'Body', we saw from Käsemann (p. 70), makes possible recognition of, and communication with, others. The term 'spiritual' is not a denial of 'bodiliness'. It is not even an oxymoron, as Fitzmyer seems to claim (though in the end, he stresses the work of the Spirit).[24] The adjective 'spiritual' (Greek, *pneumatikos*) means regularly in Paul, and certainly in 1 Corinthians, 'shaped in accordance with the Holy Spirit'. Here it means that the Holy Spirit will animate or control it. I have long argued this, and recently N. T. Wright has corroborated it. He writes, 'They will have a *sōma pneumatikon*, a body animated by, enlivened by, the Spirit of the true God, exactly as Paul has said in several other passages' (Rom. 8.9–11; cf. Ezek. 36.27; 37.9–10).[25]

Further, the contrast 'perishable' and 'imperishable' denotes not a static contrast between the mortal and immortal, but one between a life that stagnates into death, and a life that is rejuvenated with increasing 'power'. This life takes the form, as it were, of an increasing crescendo, as it moves from glory to glory, to match the dynamic nature of the living God. The Greek *en aphtharsia* is a reversal of the

---

[24] Fitzmyer, *First Corinthians*, p. 596.
[25] Wright, *The Resurrection of the Son of God*, p. 354. Cf. Thiselton, *The First Epistle to the Corinthians*, pp. 1271–81.

Hebrew *hebel*, meaning evanescent, fruitless, decaying.[26] It is *life on the move*, and increasing in quality.

This is further corroborated by Paul's closing section (1 Cor. 15.45–58). The last Adam became a life-giving Spirit (v. 45). Christians will bear 'the image' of the Man from heaven (v. 49). Christ alone bears the true image of God. Thus Christians will be like Christ in form and in character, fully to bear the image that God intended. Hence flesh and blood *can* now approach the immediate presence of the holy God (vv. 50–51). Paul is interested in whether sinful humanity can approach a holy God, not in whether a quasi-physical 'body' can enter a spaceless heaven. In both respects, Paul writes, 'We shall all be changed' (v. 51). This will happen in the blink of an eye, when the victorious note will be sounded. The metaphor is as when a trumpet wakes a sleeping army (v. 52). Then 'death is swallowed up in victory . . . God . . . gives us the victory through our Lord Jesus Christ' (vv. 53–57).

Other passages in Paul are almost an anticlimax, but they corroborate what he says in 1 Corinthians 15. Romans 4.25 affirms the resurrection of Christ, probably from a tradition earlier than Paul's letters; 6.4, 9 and 7.4 also refer to Christ's resurrection; 8.11 affirms that the Holy Spirit, who raised Christ from the dead, will also raise Christians from the dead. In 2 Corinthians 1.9, Paul speaks of resurrection as a principle of God's acting, but 4.14 alludes both to Christ and to Christians. The resurrection of Christ also occurs in Gal. 1.1; Eph. 1.20; Col. 2.12; and 1 Thess. 1.10. The resurrection of Christ (Greek, *anastasis*) receives mention in Rom. 1.4; but Rom. 6.5, 8; and perhaps Phil. 3.10, also link the future resurrection of believers with that of Christ.

The last judgement

Between half a dozen and a dozen passages in Paul refer to future judgement. Paul writes, 'God will judge the secrets of humankind' (Rom. 2.16); 'God will judge the world' (Rom. 3.6); he warns his readers that they cannot 'escape the judgement of God' (Rom. 2.2, 3); who

---

[26] Cf. Brown, *Hebrew and English Lexicon*, pp. 210–11.

has given 'evidence of the righteous judgement of God' (2 Thess. 1.5); he writes, 'We shall stand before the judgement seat of Christ' (Rom. 14.10); and most famously, 'We must all appear before the judgement seat of Christ' (2 Cor. 5.10). But although he inherits this doctrine from the Old Testament and from Judaism, there are fewer direct references than we might expect (Deut. 32.35; Pss. 2.37; 15.13; Isa. 2.4; 3.13–14; 10.20–23; Jer. 11.20; *1 Enoch* 47.3; 91.12–17; 2 Esdras 12.32, 34; *Jubilees* 1.29; 23.27–31). In mediaeval art often Christ is seen as Judge, as in 2 Thess. 2.1–12.

We understand perhaps a little of judgement when we note that often victims of oppression or violence nurture hope for a final judgement. They have longed for public vindication of their faithfulness and plight. Hence judgement is sometimes seen in Paul and elsewhere in the New Testament as 'putting things right' (Greek, *apokatastasis pantōn*, the restoration of all things, cf. Acts 3.21). God will at the end 'gather up all things in Christ' (Eph. 1.10; Col. 1.20). Judgement as vindication provides one theme. Another is putting an end to illusion, delusion, seductive disguise, and falsehood. A definitive verdict will put an end to self-deception and uncertainty. Moreover God's final verdict cannot be challenged or overturned. Faith will be eclipsed by sight, and reality finally disclosed. A third theme is the public demonstration of the 'grammar' of evil. It is not as if a celestial headmaster will read out pass-or-fail marks. The consequences of evil purposes and acts will become clear to all. Good and evil will no longer be disguised by ambiguity or secrecy.

In one sense people judge themselves. But the consequences will become public. That explains why the image of the lawcourt has currency. But just as the 'judgement' on respectively sloppy or conscientious piano practice results in disappointing or uplifting piano performance, public recognition will occur of where evil beginnings have led. All the same, Christians remain unimpeachable at the last day (1 Cor. 1.8), so Christ, not deeds, has the final word.

Yet this does not entirely exclude the traditional idea of the last judgement. It does not suggest an eternal dualism of God and evil, but it also retains the idea of 'death' (Rom. 2.2, 12, 16; 1 Cor. 15.22; 2 Cor. 5.10; 1 Thess. 5.3). This is not fully explicit, for Paul is writing to Christians. But just as through Christ's resurrection 'life' increases and moves to ever richer quality under the influence of the Holy Spirit, there is a hint that evil may reach a condition where, deprived of the animating Spirit of God, there may be wasting away into self-destruction and death (2 Thess. 2.8). Paul does not dwell on this, or explicate its details. Like so much else, he leaves the matter in the hands of God, who is gracious, righteous, and loving. Contrary to popular expectation, Paul remains less harsh than some other parts of the New Testament (Matt. 5.29; 23.31; Mark 9.43; 2 Pet. 2.4). He does not even speak of 'hell', but occasionally of 'destruction'.

The *Parousia*

Paul speaks of signs and accompaniments of the *Parousia*. But often he speaks of it simply as an end-event. In 1 Thess. 2.19 he writes, 'For what is our hope or joy or crown of boasting before our Lord Jesus Christ at his coming (*Parousia*)? Is it not you?' In 1 Thess. 3.13 he declares: 'that you may be blameless before our God . . . at the *Parousia* of the Lord Jesus with all his saints' (cf. 5.23); and 1 Cor. 1.8 repeats this: 'He will strengthen you to the end, so that you may be blameless (or unimpeachable) on the day of our Lord Jesus Christ.'

In 1 Thess. 4.14–18 Paul hastens to assure his readers that 'Those who are alive, who are left until the *Parousia* of our Lord, will by no means precede those who have died' (4.15; cf. 1 Thess. 5.23; 2 Thess. 2.1, 8, 9). The *Parousia* will, as the Church believes, take the form of a dramatic cosmic event, but Christians who have already died will not (emphatic form) miss anything. They, too, will be raised to join the celebration of meeting Christ. The two epistles to the Thessalonians have the fullest details about Christ's destroying 'the man of lawlessness', when delusion will come to an end, at Christ's coming and presence (2 Thess. 2.7–12). God's dispersed people will be gathered together (1 Thess. 4.12–18; 2 Thess. 2.1). References to the metaphor of the last trumpet call, and the conjunction of the resurrection and the *Parousia*, occur in 1 Cor. 15.51–52, 55 and 1 Thess. 4.16–17. In 1 Cor. 15.23 he writes, 'then at his *Parousia* those who belong to Christ'. The 'coming' of Christ occurs elsewhere in the New Testament, especially in those passages generally called 'apocalyptic' (Matt. 24.37–39; 2 Pet. 1.16; 3.4, 12).

Sometimes Paul also uses the Greek word *epiphaneia*, which denotes 'appearing' or 'revelation' (2 Thess. 2.8; cf. 1 Tim. 6.14; 2 Tim. 1.10; Titus 2.13). Jouette Bassler correctly comments, 'The Parousia is described with traditional apocalyptic imagery, yet Paul's use of that imagery is remarkably restrained (cf. Mark 13; 2 Thess. 1.7–10; and of course Revelation). He does not comment on the status of the dead before their resurrection, except to refer to them as 'asleep' (1 Thess. 4.13–15; 5.10) . . . This was a common metaphor for death.'[27] His focus, Bassler argues, is that all Christian believers will experience these events together, when they cross the boundaries of death. But in trying to make this language fit together, we should not forget the difference between the perspectives of *observer* and *participant*, which we earlier discussed. We need to recall also *the 'grammar' of expectation*. Above all, the last events constitute *a creative act of God*, as sovereign, righteous, and gracious.

---

[27] Jouette M. Bassler, *Navigating Paul: An Introduction to Key Theological Concepts* (Louisville and London: Westminster John Knox Press, 2007), p. 90.

17

Paul and postmodernity

Is postmodernism confined to our era?

It may seem surprising to leap across the centuries to write about Paul and postmodernism. Is not postmodernism a twentieth- and twenty-first-century phenomenon only, and irrelevant to Paul? If we confine postmodernism to a particular era, this is true. But, as we shall see, many rightly regard it as a *mood*, not an era.

To try to define postmodernism is notoriously difficult. Short definitions are bound to be selective and over-general. Its many versions all oppose the tendency in modernity to generalize and to abstract. It regards many, if not most, of the traditional distinctions and alternatives of modern culture, philosophy, and even logic, as unreal or illusory ones, based on mere human convention, rather than on truth. Thus it opposes the view that science constitutes a universally valid model for all knowledge. Indeed it usually opposes any narrative that seeks to legitimize all knowledge, whether this be Marxism, Darwinism, Freudianism, or any other major 'ism'. Postmodern thought largely believes that every conceptual scheme, or way of seeing the world, is for the most part the product only of race, class, gender, and history.

Is Paul sufficiently self-critical to appreciate some of the issues involved in postmodernism? Hegel and Strauss restricted the critical concept (*Begriff*) to philosophy, but argued that religious thinkers used only representations (*Vorstellungen*) or myth, in the sense of ideas expressed as narrative. Further, we may also distinguish between postmodernism and postmodernity, although so many use the terms interchangeably that it is now impossible to put the clock back. We may examine five issues when discussing Paul in relation to post-modernism.

(1) Many rightly claim that postmodernism constitutes a *mood*. Thomas Docherty argues that some see it as a *period*, but more see it

as a *mood*.[1] Richard Roberts comments, 'Pre-modernity, modernity, and postmodernity co-exist . . . Postmodernity does not exist as an epoch . . . Pre-modern, modern, and postmodern coexist within individual communities and within countries . . .'[2] Postmodernism's *pluralism*; multiple value-systems; emphasis upon *rhetoric* rather than truth; concern about *perception* rather than reality; its regard for the *local* and rejection of the universal; and its social *construction*, rather than acceptance of what is given; all these characteristics of postmodernism remind us of the mood at Corinth, with which Paul had to contend.[3]

(2) If it is seen as a reaction against modernity, this seems to distance postmodernity from Paul. Richard Bernstein defines it as 'a rage against humanism and the Enlightenment legacy'.[4] But many issues that it represents and raises are perennial. It rejects modernity's *individualism*, its confidence in the power of *reason*, and its general optimism about *human progress*. Norman Denzin ascribes to it the belief that the self no longer controls its destiny, hence 'anger, alienation, anxiety . . . racism and sexism' characterize it.[5] Jean-François Lyotard suggests the most famous simplified definition (to which we shall later return), namely as '*incredulity towards metanarratives*'; that is, 'narratives' of world-processes or events such as those of Darwin, Freud, and Marx, which have the effect of legitimizing and promoting deeply held attitudes towards life and related value-systems.[6] It looks back to Friedrich Nietzsche (1844–1900), who wrote *The Antichrist* (1895), and who saw philosophy and religion as 'fictions'

---

[1] Thomas Docherty, 'Postmodernist Theory', in Richard Kearney (ed.), *Twentieth-Century Philosophy* (London: Routledge, 1994), p. 476.

[2] Richard Roberts, 'A Postmodern Church?', in D. F. Ford and D. L. Stamps (eds), *Essentials of Christian Community: Essays for Daniel W. Hardy* (Edinburgh: T. & T. Clark, 1996), pp. 182 and 189; cf. 179–95.

[3] Cf. Thiselton, *First Corinthians*, pp. 12–17, 40–3, 50, and 74–6, for fuller details.

[4] Richard Bernstein (ed.), *Habermas and Modernity* (Cambridge: Polity Press, 1985), pp. 1–34.

[5] Norman Denzin, *Images of Postmodern Society* (London: Sage, 1991), p. vii.

[6] Jean-François Lyotard, *The Postmodern Condition: A Report on Knowledge*, trans. Geoff Bennington and Brian Massumi (Manchester: Manchester University Press and Minneapolis: University of Minnesota Press, 1984), p. xxiv (my italics).

and 'lies', and believed that *'nothing is "given"*, except our desires and passions'.[7]

The mood of modernity, by contrast, stems from Immanuel Kant and the thinkers of the 'Enlightenment', and perhaps from Descartes' rationalism and Locke's empiricism. Kant defined the Enlightenment as humankind's freedom from dependence on second-hand authorities and traditions, freedom to use the power of reason for oneself, an optimistic view of human progress. In England this was especially characterized by the deist thinkers, and in Germany such thinkers as Samuel Reimarus and G. E. Lessing.

Paul builds on the tradition of the Old Testament and the pre-Pauline apostolic teaching or tradition. *This is a 'given'*, and in this sense he would have been critical of 'modernity', with its hostility to authority and tradition, and its individual 'autonomy'. But he would have been no less critical of postmodernism, with its pluriformity and relativism. Paul encourages the use of reason and the mind (as we saw in Chapter 8). He rejects the notion that the self can fully develop without interaction with the community. All humankind is *relational*. We saw this in Paul's view of the Church. Moreover, like many postmodern writers, he rejects the 'myths' of the control of the universe by 'powers', including the imperial power of Rome, at least for Christians. These 'powers' were the equivalent in the ancient world of 'legitimizing' forces with grand narratives. Today we see them differently but as in principle the same, in the claims of Darwin, Marx, Freud, and science or technology, to offer a universal world-view or grand narrative, which assimilates others. Paul no longer felt 'anger, alienation, anxiety', or 'racism and sexism', when he urged that in the Church, 'There is no longer Jew or Gentile, there is no longer slave or free, there is no longer male and female: for all of you are one in Christ Jesus' (Gal. 3.28).

(3) How critical is Paul's self-awareness? He is well aware of self-deception (1 Cor. 4.1–5). Paul uses sophisticated concepts and Graeco-Roman rhetoric impressively. He uses antithesis, analogy, *confirmatio*, *refutatio*, metonymy, and many forms used by Cicero or Quintilian, as well as deliberative, forensic, epideictic rhetoric,

---

[7] Friedrich Nietzsche, *Beyond Good and Evil*, trans. R. J. Hollingdale (London: Penguin, 1973 and 1990), sect. 36 (my italics).

and so on.[8] The notion that he has no self-conscious critical awareness of how he is using language simply does not stand up. This is
confirmed by his very different style from Corinthian provincial
rhetoric.[9] Granted that Paul was not a philosopher, he was aware of
popular philosophical thought. Several centuries before him Zeno
and others were formulating a number of complex paradoxes; Paul
(or if not Paul, the writer to Titus) would probably have been aware
of some, and deliberately played upon them.[10] Many, I have argued,
have misunderstood Titus 1.13 because they lack this philosophical
and critical awareness today.

(4) American postmodernism is irredeemably pragmatic. If, as its
leading exponent, Richard Rorty, believes, the only criterion of truth
is what conforms to the interests and values of a given community,
how can Scripture or some other source be capable of reforming or
correcting it? Luther insists that the Bible addresses us as 'our adver-
sary'. As I have written elsewhere, Bonhoeffer writes, 'If it is I who
say where God will be, I will always find there a God who in some
way corresponds to me, is agreeable to me . . . But if it is God who
says where He will be, then that will truly be a place which at first
is not agreeable to me . . . That place is the cross of Christ . . . This
does not correspond to our nature at all.'[11] This lack of critical consciousness is the greatest defect of American postmodernism, and
conflicts with Paul.

(5) David Lyon rightly contrasts *postmodernity* and *postmodernism*.
In postmoderni*sm*, he argues, the emphasis becomes placed on
the cultural and *philosophical*. In postmoderni*ty* it is placed on the

---

[8] Mitchell, *Paul and the Rhetoric of Reconciliation*, esp. pp. 20–64; and Stanley E. Porter
and T. H. Olbricht (eds), *Rhetoric and the New Testament* (Sheffield: Sheffield
Academic Press, 1993), pp. 429–42.

[9] Stephen M. Pogoloff, *Logos and Sophia: the Rhetorical Situation of 1 Corinthians*
(Atlanta: Scholars Press, 1992).

[10] Anthony C. Thiselton, 'The Logical Role of the Liar Paradox in Titus 1: 12, 13: A Dissent
from the Commentaries in the Light of Philosophical and Logical Analysis', *Biblical
Interpretation* 2 (1994), pp. 207–23; reprinted in Anthony C. Thiselton, *Thiselton on
Hermeneutics: The Collected Works of Anthony C. Thiselton with New Essays* (Aldershot:
Ashgate and Grand Rapids: Eerdmans, 2006), pp. 217–28.

[11] Dietrich Bonhoeffer, *Meditating on the Word* (Cambridge, MA: Cowley, 1986), pp. 44–5;
quoted in full in Thiselton, *Thiselton on Hermeneutics*, p. 73.

social.[12] Postmodern*ism* reacts against 'foundationalism', or against traditional theories of knowledge. It reacts against the Enlightenment. Postmodern*ity*, by contrast, stresses a virtual and *constructed* reality, in which much has been created by the media. In consumerist terms, young people often want what has been advocated in the media by celebrities. The market is no longer controlled by genuine needs. An element of *fantasy* begins to control people's lives. Graham Ward suggests only a slightly different contrast.[13]

We may imagine that the era of Paul was free from mass media. But Corinth was dominated by rhetoricians, who often conveyed *perceptions*, rather than reality. Paul fought against this, urging that truth and reality should control life, while many at Corinth preferred to invite perceptions and 'recognition'. Illusion marked the ancient world no less than it does today.

The contrast between modernity and postmodernism is useful and justifiable. But so many use the two terms without distinction that it has become too late to try to rescue the difference between the two terms. At least they call attention to two different aspects of postmodernism. It is too easy to generalize about postmodernism in its various forms, and no *general* definition is possible. We shall therefore consider some specific leading writers, and then compare Paul's relevant themes.

Michel Foucault

One major exponent of postmodernism is Michel Foucault (1926–84). Among his most prominent and distinctive themes is the relation between claims to truth and disguised power. Much of his work concerns the role of psychiatrists and the phenomenon of 'madness', as well as hospitals, clinics, prisons, the armed forces, and various bureaucratic regimes. He argues that madness is not a 'given', but that the concept is built up as a construction from age to age, in which the 'power' is held by the psychiatrist. To deviate from norms set by psychiatrists and accepted by the public is to be regarded as mad. Enormous power belongs to the medical guild, which defines

---

[12] David Lyon, *Postmodernity* (Buckingham: Open University Press, 1994), pp. 6–7.
[13] Graham Ward (ed.), *Postmodern God: A Theological Reader* (Oxford: Blackwell, 1997), p. xxiv.

'truth' for the public. On the surface we see 'the smile in the white coat', but it conceals power.

Foucault also targets the regimes of prisons, and the surveillance of police. No knowledge or *truth* exists, he claims, outside the networks of *power* relations. Regimes of power exist in 'penal colonies, disciplinary battalions, prisons, hospitals, almshouses'.[14] Anonymous power is 'everywhere and always alert . . . it functions largely in silence'.[15]

Antoinette Wire accuses Paul of using a rhetoric of power to establish what he regards as 'the structure of reality'.[16] This includes passages about fatherhood: 'Though you have many caretakers in Christ, you do not have many fathers, for it was I who became your father in Christ Jesus through the gospel. So I plead with you, be imitators of me' (1 Cor. 4.15–16). Elizabeth A. Castelli makes a similar assessment of this passage, though more tentatively.[17] Fathers in Paul's day, she argues, had absolute power over their children. The word 'father' had authoritarian overtones. Imitation (Greek, *mimēsis*) has no boundaries. It imposes a uniform structure on a diverse, pluralist community. Paul uses a manipulative rhetorical strategy, even if he sometimes disguises it as self-effacement. Paul writes thus to the church at Thessalonica, 'We dealt with each one of you like a father with his children' (1 Thess. 2.11).

Far from seeking power, however, Paul writes, 'Our appeal does not spring from deceit or trickery' (1 Thess. 2.3). He was prepared to suffer 'shameful treatment' for the gospel in spite of 'great opposition' (1 Thess. 2.2). He did not seek their approval by flattery (1 Thess. 2.5, 6), but was 'gentle . . . like a nurse tenderly caring for her own children' (2.7). The feminine 'nurse' shows the Cynic philosopher's overtones of being straightforward, as we note below, as well as care.

---

[14] Michel Foucault, *Discipline and Punish*, trans. A. Sheridan (New York: Pantheon and London: Allen Lane, 1977), p. 300; cf. Michel Foucault, *Madness and Civilizations*, trans. P. Howard (New York: Pantheon, 1965); and Michel Foucault, *The Order of Things*, trans. A. Sheridan (New York: Random House, 1970).

[15] Foucault, *Discipline and Punish*, pp. 176–7.

[16] Antoinette Clark Wire, *The Corinthian Women Prophets: A Reconstruction through Paul's Rhetoric* (Minneapolis: Fortress Press, 1990), pp. 35–6.

[17] Elizabeth A. Castelli, *Imitating Paul: A Discussion of Power* (Louisville: Westminster John Knox Press, 1991), pp. 97–115.

This mood characterizes Paul's approach in 1 Corinthians. He does not defend the so-called Paul group as a power base (1 Cor. 1.12) or seek allegiance to himself (1.14–16). He refuses to enter the expected game of applause-seeking orators, even if this church would respect him more for doing so (1 Cor. 2.1–5; 9.12–23).[18] Although many despised manual labour, Paul forgoes the right to maintenance and professional status, lest he should be beholden to the wealthy to shape his agenda (9.12–18).

Paul frequently speaks of entering the presence of God, and of being judged by God, and only Nietzsche's wholesale cynicism about theism would understand this appeal as merely manipulative rhetoric. Admittedly some so-called religious people *do* use appeals to God or to the Bible as a means of bullying people into doing what they want. They use supposed truth as an instrument of disguised power. But Paul constantly adopts the role of a despised servant, often to great personal cost. Only a paid-up cynic could ascribe to Paul a manipulative ambition to gain power.

It is impossible to ascribe to Jesus a desire for power. Not only did he teach humility and selflessness, he chose to live without a secure home (Matt. 6.25–34; 8.20; cf. 10.39; Luke 9.58), and suffered and died the death of torment on the cross (Mark 15.25–37). Yet Paul consistently appeals to following this example, as one who is 'in Christ'.

Roland Barthes

Roland Barthes (1915–80) became a major figure in French structuralism and subsequently in post-structuralism. In 1964 he published his *Elements of Semiology* (English 1968).[19] We agree that the use of language should not always be taken at its face value. Following closely the linguistician Ferdinand de Saussure's distinction between a potential reservoir of language (*la langue*), and the chosen act of using speech (*la parole*), Barthes shows that furniture-language, or

---

[18] Andrew D. Clarke, *Secular and Christian Leadership in Corinth* (Leiden, New York, and Cologne: Brill, 1993), throughout; and Pogoloff, *Logos and Sophia*, throughout, but see pp. 188–9.

[19] Roland Barthes, *Elements of Semiology*, trans. A. Cavers and C. Smith (New York: Hill & Wang, 1968).

clothes-language, may depend less on convenience, or on the 'natural' demands of the weather, as on social aspirations to class or social role. But Barthes' essay 'From Work to Text' moves away from the author to an autonomous and authorless 'text' (1971). He rejects the authority of the author.

Paul's writings differ on at least two major grounds. First, Paul rejects using language as a disguise. In 1 Cor. 2.1–5 he disclaims anything other than a straight proclamation of the cross. He rejects 'plausible words of wisdom', which might distract from the work of the Holy Spirit (2.4, 5). In 2 Cor. 3.12—4.6 he chooses to speak frankly and boldly (3.12), and 'refuse to practise cunning or to falsify God's word; but by the open statement of the truth we commend ourselves to the conscience of everyone in the sight of God' (4.2). 'The god of this world', not Paul, creates disguises (4.4).

Paul reflects the same concern in 1 Thessalonians; he writes, 'Our appeal does not spring from deceit . . . or trickery . . . We speak not to please mortals, but to please God, who tests our hearts' (1 Thess. 2.3, 4). Paul did not use flattery or pretext (2.5, 6). As Malherbe, Paddison, and many now urge, Paul's speaking and acting gently 'like a nurse' (1 Thess. 2.7) reflects also the Cynic background, where Dio Chrysostom (AD 40–120) sets out the qualities of a true philosopher, in contrast to those of charlatans or masqueraders.[20]

The second parting of the ways lies in Barthes' attempt to abstract the author from the text. Many, notably Robert Funk, argue that Paul's letters function in place of his apostolic presence.[21] Paul often uses the word 'proclaim' (Greek verb, *kērussein*). Hence, Beaudean writes, 'The work of the herald (Greek, *kērux*) was to speak on behalf of a recognised authority . . . It is God who sends the preacher of the gospel (Rom. 10.14–17).'[22] Preaching rests on divine authority.

[20] A. J. Malherbe, '"Gentle as a Nurse": The Cynic Background to 1 Thess. ii', *Novum Testamentum* 12 (1970), pp. 203–17; and Angus Paddison, *Theological Hermeneutics and 1 Thessalonians* (SNTSMS 133; Cambridge: Cambridge University Press, 2005), pp. 6–7 and 62–4.

[21] Robert Funk, *Parables and Presence: Forms of the New Testament Tradition* (Philadelphia: Fortress Press, 1982), pp. 81–102.

[22] John W. Beaudean, *Paul's Theology and Preaching* (Macon, GA: Mercer University Press, 1988), p. 193; cf. Duane Litfin, *St. Paul's Theology of Proclamation: 1 Corinthians 4 and Greco-Roman Rhetoric* (SNTSMS 79; Cambridge: Cambridge University Press, 1994).

Jacques Derrida

Probably no other philosopher in Europe has become more notorious, controversial, or given rise to such misunderstanding, as Jacques Derrida (1930–2004). He rejects ontology, or a philosophy of 'being'. Being is on the move, and attempts to make it static are mistaken. Paul might have been sympathetic with this, for he would agree that to try to capture the living God under some static conceptualization is to reduce him. In Exod. 3.14, the Septuagint translation, 'I am', may better be rendered by the Hebrew 'I will be'.

Derrida addressed the question of 'deconstruction' in 1967, in *Of Grammatology*.[23] He insists that it constitutes a positive task. Its goal is not to destroy texts, but to discern a second meaning beyond the first. In this sense allegorical interpretation of the Bible is relevant. Derrida, like Paul Ricoeur, seeks a 'supplement' in reading the text. Like Barthes, Derrida tends to reject 'the intention of the author'. On the other hand, in his 'Afterword' to *Limited Inc.*, Derrida insists that deconstruction does not undermine the stability of the text.[24] It rests on discernment. It is debatable whether Paul really uses allegory (a parallelism of *ideas*), rather than typology (a parallelism of *events* or *persons*) in Gal. 3.15–16; 4.22–31. But Paul is prepared to see a 'second' meaning in these texts.

Derrida, however, follows Barthes in insisting on 'the death of the author', and in his 'White Mythology' and elsewhere attacks not only ontology, but also metaphysics. Much philosophy, he argues, seems to present literal meanings, but really relies on metaphors. He claims, 'The metaphor is no longer noticed, and it is taken for the proper meaning . . . It [philosophy] could perceive its metaphysics only around a blind spot or central deafness.'[25]

Paul advocates discernment, and recognizes the deceitfulness of the human heart (1 Cor. 4.1–5; cf. 3.18). But too much iconoclasm and 'deferment' of meaning would undermine the establishment of any

[23] Jacques Derrida, *Of Grammatology*, trans. G. C. Spivak (Baltimore: Johns Hopkins University Press, 1975 (1967)).
[24] Jacques Derrida, *Limited Inc.*, trans. J. Mehlmann and S. Weber (Evanston: Northwestern University Press, 1988), p. 143.
[25] Jacques Derrida, 'White Mythology: Metaphor in the Text of Philosophy', in J. Derrida, *Margins of Philosophy*, trans. Alan Bass (New York and London: Harvester Wheatsheaf, 1982), pp. 211 and 228, cf. 207–71.

transmitted pre-Pauline or Pauline tradition. But, as Anders Eriksson and others have shown, Paul uses common apostolic tradition as a shared presupposition on which to lace his arguments (1 Cor. 11.23–25; 15.3–7; Rom. 4.25). Paul also advocates discrimination on the basis of a mind renewed by the Holy Spirit, and he holds an epistemology of the cross.

Jean-François Lyotard

Jean-François Lyotard (1924–98) tries to capture the varied themes of postmodernism by offering a simple definition. He defines it as 'incredulity towards metanarratives'.[26] By 'metanarratives' he means those grand narratives of the history of the world which serve to give legitimacy to attitudes and actions. In modernity, we see the grand narratives of scientific progress; a technological world-view; the Marxist analysis of history in terms of economic production and class; the Darwinian narrative of progress by natural selection; and Freud's account of a self as driven by unconscious forces of desire. Consumerism perhaps provides another 'legitimating' narrative of humankind's 'advance', through money, ownership, technology, and power.

Paul has a 'grand narrative' of promise and fulfilment in the history of Israel and of Christ (Romans 9—11). Lyotard does not explicitly discuss the biblical narrative. Richard Bauckham argues that the Bible presents a series of 'little narratives' involving in-dividuals or groups, rather than a grand narrative.[27] On the basis of Bauckham's argument, the Bible escapes the criticism of Lyotard. But this counter-argument is only half right. Bauckham is right to stress the contingency of biblical material. But the 'little narratives' are not an *alternative* to grand narrative. This seems to elevate human experience. Paul writes of Israel's world-history in Romans 9—11, and sees Christ's redemption as cosmic in scope and as a fulfilment of God's purposes in history-as-a-whole (Gal. 4.3–4). Pannenberg rightly observes, 'This universality of theology is unavoidably bound

---

[26] Lyotard, *The Postmodern Condition*, p. xxiv.

[27] Richard J. Bauckham, *Bible and Mission: Christian Witnesses in a Postmodern World* (Grand Rapids: Baker Academic and Carlisle: Paternoster Press, 2003), pp. 87–93.

up with the fact that it speaks of *God* . . . It belongs to the task of theology to understand *all* being in relation to God.'[28]

Lyotard points out that grand narratives or metanarratives compete with each other. Here he appeals to 'incommensurability' as a term borrowed from the philosophy of science. He insists that no final court of appeal exists which can arbitrate between them. Paul agrees that shifting horizons of understanding may make the cross appear either 'foolish' or 'wise' (1 Cor. 1.18–25). Alexandra Brown observes, 'From the conventional perspective of the old world it (the cross) is the symbol of suffering, weakness, folly, and death.'[29] But the new creation calls for a renewed mind, and reasonable judgement. In Paul, André Munzinger writes, we neglect 'the call for believers to examine themselves, in order to retrieve the focal point of their faith, and . . . ethical conduct' (1 Cor. 10.12; 11.27–32; 14.37–38; 2 Cor. 13.5; Gal. 6.4).[30]

In Lyotard, however, 'incommensurable' belief systems lead to a pluralism that cannot be resolved. He explicitly terms this 'paganism'. Pagan religions are necessarily polytheistic and pluralist. Lyotard defends 'paganism' as a necessary implicate of incommensurability. Grand narratives cannot decide which systems are right.

This gives rise to the claim that two or more parties only *appear* to reach consensus. Agreement emerges not through rational negotiation, but through *force*. Lyotard sees the spectre of political or imperial power. The more powerful party has subtly imposed its rules of discourse. The stronger party imposes 'the language-game', or what is possible within the rules of language. This will win the supposed debate. Lyotard describes this as the '*differend*'. To see that dominant arguments depend on power, not on reason, is to gain a measure of emancipation from their tyranny.[31]

To infer that the vulnerable, often persecuted, Pauline communities were so powerful that they could impose rules of language onto those who could not be persuaded to come to faith defies credibility. Paul does concede that 'our message of the gospel came to you not

[28] Wolfhart Pannenberg, *Basic Questions in Theology*, 3 vols, vol. 1, trans. G. H. Kehm (London: SCM Press, 1970), p. 1 (my italics).

[29] Brown, *The Cross and Human Transformation*, p. 14.

[30] Munzinger, *Discerning the Spirits*, p. 36; cf. p. 59, and pp. 75–98.

[31] Jean-François Lyotard, *The Differend*, trans. G. van den Abbeele (Manchester: Manchester University Press, 1990).

in word only, but also in power and in the Holy Spirit with full conviction' (1 Thess. 1.5). But this has nothing to do with force; for it results in the hearers becoming 'imitators . . . of the Lord' (1.6). Paul renounced violence.

Paul acknowledges that people often choose the 'pluralism' of Lyotard's 'paganism'. He recognizes that 'grand narratives' (such as the growing and established power of Rome and Caesar) should not control personal allegiance and ways of life. But he also appeals to the Old Testament and apostolic tradition as part of God's definitive purpose for the world. He sees faith as arising from rational judgement, especially for the renewed mind. It does not derive from force. As George Lindbeck rightly argues, in harmony with Paul, Christians insert their lives into the larger biblical narrative, to give them meaning.[32]

Rorty and Fish, and Paul

Richard Rorty (1931–2007) and Stanley Fish (b. 1938) represent American neo-pragmatism with a postmodern turn. Like Lyotard, Rorty expounds a pluralist account of the later Wittgenstein, which remains open to doubt, but he also draws on Martin Heidegger. Most of all he draws on American pragmatism and progressivism. Progress toward the American dream under liberal democracy becomes a legitimizing myth for much in American politics. The sociologist Pauline M. Rosenau rightly distinguishes between American and French or European postmodernism, characterizing that of America as relatively 'affirmative', and European writers as 'sceptical'. The distinction is true, but I dissent from her in regarding the American version as more positive, and the European as more dangerous and seductive. European postmodernism warns us against seeing power-bids as truth in religion, and views science and all human metanarratives as seductive, whereas American postmodernism rests on the myth of secular progress, and an absence of self-criticism.[33]

---

[32] George Lindbeck, *The Nature of Doctrine: Religion and Doctrine in a Postliberal Age* (London: SPCK, 1984), p. 118.

[33] Pauline M. Rosenau, *Post-modernism and the Social Sciences* (Princeton, NJ: Princeton University Press, 1992); Thiselton, *Thiselton on Hermeneutics*, pp. 586–690; and Thiselton, *New Horizons in Hermeneutics* (Grand Rapids: Zondervan and London: HarperCollins, 1992), pp. 529–57.

Rorty was profoundly influenced by the pragmatists William James and John Dewey, and also by W. V. O. Quine, D. Donaldson, and Wilfred Sellars. In his earlier book *Philosophy and the Mirror of Nature* (1979) he spoke of 'hermeneutics' only as a way of *coping*. In his later book *Contingency, Irony and Solidarity* (1989) he claimed that truth cannot exist, as if it were independent of the human mind. He attacks metaphysics, which he associates with the era before Nietzsche. Supposed *knowledge* is only a matter of social practice. This derives from the consensus of a particular community. Many accuse him of relativism, but he prefers to substitute 'cultural politics' for traditional philosophy.

In his book *Objectivity, Relativism and Truth* (1991) Rorty attacks a 'representational' view of language, and rejects the basic distinction between appearance and reality. 'Knowledge' is merely 'conservatism'. He draws on William James' dictum that *truth* is *what is 'good' in the way of belief*.[34] Rorty's debt to Dewey is explicit in *Truth and Progress* (1998). Truth is not a 'goal of enquiry', but what proves itself to be *useful* to a given community. Rorty calls it an 'ethnocentric' community.[35] The baggage of traditional philosophy invites 'rubbish-disposal'. As I comment elsewhere, this is like A. J. Ayer's sweeping comments about the supposed 'non-sense' status of religious and ethical language. This, too, seduced the public, but only for a time.[36]

Pragmatism, or the doctrine that truth is what is *useful for 'progress'*, is deeply embedded in the American tradition, as Robert Corrington, Roger Lundin, and S. Bercovitch have reminded us.[37] History will show that this presents a variable criterion, depending on where one is situated in history. Islam, for example, might have appeared more 'true' than Christianity at a point in the Middle Ages. Ralph Waldo Emerson equated truth with 'what is beneficial to us', and called his party 'the party of the future', while he called his

---

[34] Richard Rorty, *Objectivity, Relativism and Truth: Philosophical Papers, Volume 1* (Cambridge: Cambridge University Press, 1991), pp. 113–25, esp. 126–8, 129–50, and 192–4 (my italics).

[35] Richard Rorty, *Truth and Progress: Philosophical Papers, Volume 3* (Cambridge: Cambridge University Press, 1998), pp. 670; cf. 1–15, 19–42, and 153–65.

[36] Thiselton, *Thiselton on Hermeneutics*, pp. 591–2 and 797.

[37] Robert S. Corrington, *The Community of Interpreters: On the Hermeneutics of Nature and the Bible in the American Philosophical Tradition* (Macon, GA: Mercer University Press, 1987); cf. Thiselton, *Thiselton on Hermeneutics*, pp. 589–92.

opponents 'the party of the past'. Progressivism is facile and over-optimistic. History proves it to be false, and it remains trapped within its limited historical horizon. It represents human non-theistic *hubris*.

Moreover, if a community accepts as true only what is congenial to it, and fosters its supposed progress, it has no means of criticizing its own values. For it has already defined as *false* anything that might undermine it. This also runs counter to all that Luther and Bonhoeffer said about the Bible.

Stanley Fish presses this criterion just as forcefully, but in the context of literature. Meaning is always the reader's response to the text; it is in no sense 'given'. But how can this transform any reader?[38] The Bible ceases to be transformative, but can only accord with the reader's expectations. This is not only a contradiction of Luther and Bonhoeffer; it ignores Hans Robert Jauss's emphasis on 'provocation' in reception theory.

Few have articulated the problem better than John Moores. He declares, '*Paul* . . . does not think (as some modern upholders of the importance of reception factor do) that the identity of the message . . . is in any sense determined by what it means for those at the receiving end. For him it is rather *their* identity than that of the message which is determined by their response. To subject him to the criteria of present-day reception or reader-response theory would be to turn *his* ideas on the subject upside down.'[39] Paul says to the Galatians that to proclaim 'a different gospel' is to invite God's curse (Gal. 1.6–9). His gospel is by revelation and by apostolic tradition, not human construction (Gal. 1.11–23).

Human 'progress' is not inevitable, apart from divine grace. Such an impression remains at odds, for example, with Rom. 1.18—3.20. Further, 1 Cor. 4.6–13 and 2 Cor. 1.9 do not see 'success' as the criterion of truth, but the reverse. The Corinthians, not Paul, prized 'success', and saw everything from within the horizons of their own local community (1 Cor. 1.2; 3.18–21).

---

[38] Stanley Fish, *Doing What Comes Naturally: Change, Rhetoric, and the Practice of Theory in Literary and Legal Studies* (Oxford: Clarendon Press, 1989), pp. 1–33.

[39] John D. Moores, *Wrestling with Rationality in Paul: Romans 1—8 in a New Perspective* (SNTSMS 82; Cambridge: Cambridge University Press, 1995), pp. 133–4 (my italics).

Paul faced pluralism, sophistic rhetoric, an emphasis on *perception* or recognition of status, a cult of celebrities, and a socially constructed 'world' through rhetoric. This is 'postmodern', and yet it also reflects many elements in our own present culture. Paul might have shared with Rorty his reservations about purely human 'knowledge' of *truth*. He would have repudiated the legitimizing 'grand narratives' of Marxism, Freudianism, Darwinism, and Materialism; but also the myth of human progress without grace. The economic crisis at the time of writing may even suggest that Consumerist 'grand narratives' carry the seeds of their own destruction. The heart can easily be deceived (1 Cor. 4.1–5). Paul's message is 'to turn from idols (of human construction) to the *living God*' (1 Thess. 1.9). The 'wisdom' of the cross will outlive postmodernism in all its forms, and Paul's voice will continue to live.

Bibliography

Aland, Kurt, *Did the Early Church Baptize Infants*, trans. G. R. Beasley-Murray (London: SCM Press, 1962)

Austin, John L., *How to Do Things with Words* (Oxford: Clarendon Press, 1962)

Banks, Robert, *Paul's Idea of Community*, 2nd edn (Peabody: Hendrickson, 1994)

Barr, James, 'Abba Isn't Daddy', *Journal of Theological Studies* 39 (1988), pp. 28–47

Barr, James, *The Semantics of Biblical Language* (Oxford: Oxford University Press, 1961)

Barrett, C. K., *A Commentary on the Epistle to the Romans* (London: A. & C. Black, 1962)

Barrett, C. K., *A Commentary on the First Epistle to the Corinthians*, 2nd edn (London: A. & C. Black, 1971)

Barth, Karl, *The Resurrection of the Dead*, trans. H. J. Stenning (London: Hodder & Stoughton, 1933)

Barthes, Roland, *Elements of Semiology*, trans. A. Cavers and C. Smith (New York: Hill & Wang, 1968)

Bassler, Jouette M., *Navigating Paul: An Introduction to Key Theological Concepts* (Louisville and London: Westminster John Knox Press, 2007)

Bauckham, Richard J., *Bible and Mission: Christian Witnesses in a Postmodern World* (Grand Rapids: Baker Academic and Carlisle: Paternoster Press, 2003)

Bauckham, Richard J., *Jesus and the Eyewitnesses: The Gospels as Eyewitness Testimony* (Grand Rapids/Cambridge: Eerdmans, 2006)

Beaudean, John W., *Paul's Theology and Preaching* (Macon, GA: Mercer University Press, 1988)

Beker, J. Christiaan, *Paul's Apocalyptic Gospel: The Coming Triumph of God* (Philadelphia: Fortress Press, 1982)

Beker, J. Christiaan, *Paul the Apostle: The Triumph of God in Life and Thought* (Edinburgh: T. & T. Clark, 1980)

Bell, Richard H., *Provoked to Jealousy: The Origin and Purpose of the Jealousy Motive in Romans 9—11* (WUNT 2.63; Tübingen: Mohr, 1994)

Bell, Richard H., *The Irrevocable Call of God* (WUNT 2.184; Tübingen: Mohr, 2005).

Bernstein, Richard (ed.), *Habermas and Modernity* (Cambridge: Polity Press, 1985)

Best, Ernest, *A Commentary on the First and Second Epistles to the Thessalonians* (London: A. & C. Black, 1972)

Best, Ernest, *One Body in Christ* (London: SPCK, 1955)

Bonhoeffer, Dietrich, *Meditating on the Word* (Cambridge, MA: Cowley, 1986)

Bornkamm, Günther, 'Faith and Reason in Paul', in *Early Christian Experience*, trans. P. L. Hammer (London: SCM Press, 1969), pp. 29–46

Bousset, Wilhelm, *Kyrios Christos: A History of the Belief in Christ from the Beginnings of Christianity to Irenaeus*, trans. John Seely, 5th edn (Nashville: Abingdon, 1970)

Brown, Alexandra R., *The Cross and Human Transformation: Paul's Apocalyptic Word in 1 Corinthians* (Minneapolis: Fortress Press, 1989)

Brown, Francis (ed.), a revision of F. Brown, S. R. Driver, and C. A. Briggs (eds), *Hebrew and English Lexicon* (Lafayette, IN: Associated Publishers, 1988)

Bruce, F. F., *Paul: The Apostle of the Free Spirit* (Exeter: Paternoster Press, 1977)

Bruce, F. F., *The Epistle to the Galatians: A Commentary on the Greek Text* (NIGTC; Grand Rapids: Eerdmans and Exeter: Paternoster Press, 1982)

Bultmann, Rudolf, 'Jesus Christ and Mythology', in Hans-Werner Bartsch (ed.), *Kerygma and Myth*, 2 vols, trans. R. H. Fuller, vol. 1 (London: SCM Press, 1964), pp. 1–44; alternatively Rudolf Bultmann, *New Testament Mythology and Other Basic Writings Selected and Edited by Schabert Ogden* (Philadelphia: Fortress Press, 1984), pp. 1–44

Bultmann, Rudolf, *Theology of the New Testament*, trans. K. Grobel, 2 vols (London: SCM Press, 1952 and 1955)

Caird, George B., *The Language and Imagery of the Bible* (London: Duckworth, 1980)

Calvin, John, *Institutes of the Christian Religion*, trans. J. Beveridge, 2 vols (London: Clarke, 1957)

Carrington, Philip, *The Primitive Christian Catechism* (Cambridge: Cambridge University Press, 1940)

Castelli, Elizabeth A., *Imitating Paul: A Discussion of Power* (Louisville: Westminster John Knox Press, 1991)

Cerfaux, L., *The Church in the Theology of Paul*, trans. G. Webb and A. Walker (New York: Herder & Herder, 1959)

Chadwick, Henry, 'St. Paul and Philo of Alexandria', *Bulletin of the John Rylands Library* 48 (1966), pp. 286–307

Chilton, Bruce, *Rabbi Paul: An Intellectual Biography* (New York and London: Doubleday, 2004)

Clarke, Andrew D., *Secular and Christian Leadership in Corinth* (Leiden, New York and Cologne: Brill, 1993)

Collins, John N., *Diakonia: Re-interpreting the Ancient Sources* (Oxford and New York: Oxford University Press, 1990)

Conzelmann, Hans, *1 Corinthians: A Commentary*, trans. J. W. Leitch (Philadelphia: Fortress Press, 1975)

Coombs, L. A. H., *The Metaphor of Slavery in the Writings of the Early Church* (Sheffield: Sheffield Academic Press, 1998)

Corrington, Robert S., *The Community of Interpreters: On the Hermeneutics of Nature and the Bible in the American Philosophical Tradition* (Macon, GA: Mercer University Press, 1987)

Crafton, Jeffrey A., *The Agency of the Apostle: A Dramatistic Analysis of Paul's Response to Conflict in 2 Corinthians* (JSNTSup 51; Sheffield: Sheffield Academic Press, 1991)

Cranfield, C. E. B., *A Critical and Exegetical Commentary on the Epistle to the Romans*, 2 vols (International Critical Commentary; Edinburgh: T. & T. Clark, 1975, 1979)

Crossan, John Dominic, *The Historical Jesus: The Life of a Mediterranean Jewish Peasant* (San Francisco: Harper, 1991)

Cullmann, Oscar, *Baptism in the New Testament*, trans. J. K. S. Reid (London: SCM Press, 1950)

Cullmann, Oscar, *Christ and Time*, trans. F. V. Filson, 2nd edn (London: SCM Press, 1962)

Cullmann, Oscar, *The Christology of the New Testament*, trans. J. G. Guthrie and C. A. M. Hall (London: SCM Press, 1963)

Dahl, M. E., *The Resurrection of the Body* (London: SCM Press, 1962)

Danker, W. F. (ed.), *Greek–English Lexicon of the New Testament*, based on Walter Bauer, W. F. Arndt and F. W. Gingrich's *Lexicon*, 3rd edn (Chicago: University of Chicago Press, 2000)

Davies, W. D., *Paul and Rabbinic Judaism: Some Rabbinic Elements in Pauline Theology* (London: SPCK, 1958)

Deissmann, Adolf, *Light from the Ancient East: The New Testament Illustrated by Recently Discovered Texts from the Graeco-Roman World*, trans. L. R. M. Strachan (London: Hodder & Stoughton, 1927)

Deluz, Gaston, *A Companion to 1 Corinthians*, trans. Grace Watt (London: Darton, Longman & Todd, 1963)

Denzin, Norman, *Images of Postmodern Society* (London: Sage, 1991)

Derrida, Jacques, *Limited Inc.*, trans. J. Mehlmann and S. Weber (Evanston: Northwestern University Press, 1988)

Derrida, Jacques, *Of Grammatology*, trans. G. C. Spivak (Baltimore: Johns Hopkins University Press, 1975 (French, 1967))

Derrida, Jacques, 'White Mythology: Metaphor in the Text of Philosophy', in J. Derrida, *Margins of Philosophy*, trans. Alan Bass (New York and London: Harvester Wheatsheaf, 1982), pp. 207–71

Docherty, Thomas, 'Postmodernist Theory', in Richard Kearney (ed.), *Twentieth-Century Philosophy* (London: Routledge, 1994)

Dodd, Charles H., *According to the Scriptures* (London: Nisbet, 1952)

Dodd, Charles H., *Gospel and Law* (Cambridge: Cambridge University Press, 1951)

Dodd, Charles H., *The Apostolic Preaching and its Developments* (London: Hodder & Stoughton, 1936)

Dunn, James D. G., *Baptism in the Holy Spirit* (London: SCM Press, 1970)

Dunn, James D. G., *Christianity in the Making*, vol. 1: *The Remembered Jesus* (Grand Rapids and Cambridge: Eerdmans, 2003)

Dunn, James D. G., *Jesus, Paul and the Law* (Louisville: Westminster John Knox Press, 1990)

Dunn, James D. G., *Romans 1—8* (Dallas, TX: Word Books, 1988)

Dunn, James D. G., *Romans 9—16* (Dallas, TX: Word Books, 1988)

Dunn, James D. G., *The Epistles to the Colossians and to Philemon: A Commentary on the Greek Text* (Grand Rapids: Eerdmans and Carlisle: Paternoster Press, 1996)

Dunn, James D. G., *The Theology of Paul the Apostle* (London: T. & T. Clark, 1998)

Eckstein, H.-J., *Der Begriff Syneidēsis bei Paulus* (Tübingen: Mohr, 1983)

Epp, Eldon Jay, *Junia: The First Woman Apostle* (Minneapolis: Fortress Press, 2005)

Eriksson, Anders, *Traditions as Rhetorical Proof: Pauline Argumentation in 1 Corinthians* (Stockholm: Almqvist & Wiksell, 1998)

Fish, Stanley, *Doing What Comes Naturally: Change, Rhetoric, and the Practice of Theory in Literary and Legal Studies* (Oxford: Clarendon Press, 1989)

Fitzmyer, Joseph A., *First Corinthians: A New Translation with Introduction and Commentary* (Anchor Yale Bible 32; New Haven and London: Yale University Press, 2008)

Fitzmyer, Joseph A., *Romans: A New Translation with Introduction and Commentary* (Anchor Bible; New York: Doubleday, 1992)

Foucault, Michel, *Discipline and Punish*, trans. A. Sheridan (New York: Pantheon and London: Allen Lane, 1977)

Foucault, Michel, *Madness and Civilizations*, trans. P. Howard (New York: Pantheon, 1965)

Foucault, Michel, *The Order of Things*, trans. A. Sheridan (New York: Random House, 1970)

Fowl, Stephen E., *The Story of Christ in the Ethics of Paul* (JSNTSup 36; Sheffield: Sheffield Academic Press, 1990)

Funk, Robert, *Parables and Presence: Forms of the New Testament Tradition* (Philadelphia: Fortress Press, 1982)

Furnish, Victor P., *The Love Command in the New Testament* (London: SCM Press, 1973)

Furnish, Victor P., *Theology and Ethics in Paul* (Nashville and New York, Abingdon, 1968)

Gale, Herbert M., *The Use of Analogy in the Letters of Paul* (Philadelphia: Westminster Press, 1964)

Gillespie, Thomas W., *The First Theologians: A Study in Early Christian Prophecy* (Grand Rapids: Eerdmans, 1994)

Gooch, Peter D., 'Conscience in 1 Corinthians 8 and 10', *New Testament Studies* 33 (1987), pp. 244–54

Grayston, Kenneth, *Dying, We Live: A New Enquiry into the Death of Christ in the New Testament* (Oxford and New York: Oxford University Press, 1990)

Grenz, Stanley J., *The Social God and the Relational Self: A Trinitarian Theology of the Imago Dei* (Louisville: Westminster John Knox Press, 2001)

Grillmeier, A., *Christ in Christian Tradition: From the Apostolic Age to Chalcedon*, trans. J. Bowden (London: Mowbray, 1965)

Hall, David R., *The Unity of the Corinthian Correspondence* (London and New York: T. & T. Clark International, 2003)

Hamilton, Neill Q., *The Holy Spirit and Eschatology in Paul* (Edinburgh: Oliver & Boyd, 1957)

Hanson, Anthony T., *The Pioneer Ministry* (London: SCM Press, 1961)

Harris, Murray J., *The Second Epistle to the Corinthians: A Commentary on the Greek Text* (NIGTC; Grand Rapids: Eerdmans, 2005)

Hawthorne, Gerald F., *Philippians* (Waco, TX: Word Books, 1983)

Haykin, Michael A. G., *The Spirit of God: The Exegesis of 1 and 2 Corinthians in the Pneumatomachian Controversy of the Fourth Century* (VCSup 27; Leiden and New York: Brill, 1994)

Hays, Richard B., *The Moral Vision of the New Testament: A Contemporary Introduction to New Testament Ethics* (New York: Harper One, 1996)

Hock, Ronald F., *The Social Context of Paul's Ministry: Tentmaking and Apostleship* (Philadelphia: Fortress Press, 1980)

Hofius, Ottfried, 'The Lord's Supper and the Lord's Supper Tradition', in Ben Meyer (ed.), *One Loaf, One Cup: Ecumenical Studies of 1 Cor. 11: 17–34* (Macon, GA: Mercer University Press, 1993), pp. 75–115

Hogeterp, Albert L. P., *Paul and God's Temple* (Leuven, Paris and Dudley, MA: Peters, 2006)

Holland, Tom, *Contours of Pauline Theology: A Radical New Survey of Influences on Paul's Biblical Writings* (Fearn, Rosshire: Mentor, 2004)

Hurtado, Larry W., *Lord Jesus Christ: Devotion to Jesus in Earliest Christianity* (Grand Rapids and Cambridge: Eerdmans, 2003)

Hurtado, Larry W., *One God, One Lord: Early Christian Devotion and Ancient Jewish Monotheism* (London: SCM Press, 1988)

Jeremias, Joachim, 'Abba', in J. Jeremias, *The Central Message of the New Testament* (London: SCM Press, 1965), pp. 9–30

Jeremias, Joachim, *Infant Baptism in the First Four Centuries*, trans. David Cairns (London: SCM Press, 1960)

Jeremias, Joachim, *The Central Message of the New Testament* (London: SCM Press, 1965)

Jeremias, Joachim, *The Eucharistic Words of Jesus*, trans. Norman Perrin (London: SCM Press, 1966)

Jeremias, Joachim, 'The Key to Pauline Theology', *Expository Times* 76 (1964), pp. 27–30

Jeremias, Joachim, *The Origins of Infant Baptism: A Reply to Kurt Aland*, trans. D. M. Burton (London: SCM Press, 1963)

Jeremias, Joachim, *The Parables of Jesus*, trans. S. H. Hooke, rev. edn (London: SCM Press, 1963)

Jewett, Robert, *Paul's Anthropological Terms: A Study of Their Use in Conflict Settings* (Leiden: Brill, 1971)

Jüngel, Eberhard, *God as the Mystery of the World*, trans. D. L. Guder (Edinburgh: T. & T. Clark, 1983)

Käsemann, Ernst, *New Testament Questions of Today*, trans. W. J. Montague (London: SCM Press, 1969)

Käsemann, Ernst, *Perspectives on Paul*, trans. Margaret Kohl (London: SCM Press, 1971)

Kim, Seyoon, *Paul and the New Perspective: Second Thoughts on the Origin of Paul's Gospel* (Grand Rapids: Eerdmans, 2002)

Knox, Wilfred L., *St. Paul and the Church of the Gentiles* (Cambridge: Cambridge University Press, 1939)

Koch, Klaus, *The Rediscovery of Apocalyptic: A Polemical Work on a Neglected Area of Biblical Studies and its Damaging Effects*, trans. Margaret Kohl (London: SCM Press, 1972)

Kramer, Werner, *Christ, Lord, Son of God*, trans. Brian Hardy (London: SCM Press, 1966)

Küng, Hans, *Justification: The Doctrine of Karl Barth and a Catholic Reflection*, trans. T. Collins and others (London: Burns & Oates, 1964)

Künneth, W., *The Theology of the Resurrection*, trans. J. W. Leitch (London: SCM Press, 1965)

Leenhardt, F. J., 'This is My Body', in O. Cullmann and F. J. Leenhardt, *Essays on the Lord's Supper*, trans. J. G. Davies (London: Lutterworth Press, 1958)

Lietzmann, Hans, *Mass and Lord's Supper: A Study in the History of the Liturgy* (with Introductions and Notes by R. D. Richardson (Leiden: Brill, 1979)

Lindbeck, George, *The Nature of Doctrine: Religion and Doctrine in a Postliberal Age* (London: SPCK, 1984)

Litfin, Duane, *St. Paul's Theology of Proclamation: 1 Corinthians 4 and Greco-Roman Rhetoric* (SNTSMS 79; Cambridge: Cambridge University Press, 1994)

Lowe, John, 'An Examination of Attempts to Detect Developments in St. Paul's Theology', *Journal of Theological Studies* 42 (1941), pp. 127–42

Bibliography

Luther, Martin, *A Commentary on St. Paul's Epistle to the Galatians* (1531), trans. J. I. Packer (London: Clarke, 1953)

Luther, Martin, *Luther's Works*, vol. 28: *Commentaries on 1 Corinthians 7 and 15* (St Louis: Concordia, 1973)

Lyon, David, *Postmodernity* (Buckingham: Open University Press, 1994)

Lyotard, Jean-François, *The Differend*, trans. G. van den Abbeele (Manchester: Manchester University Press, 1990)

Lyotard, Jean-François, *The Postmodern Condition: A Report on Knowledge*, trans. Geoff Bennington and Brian Massumi (Manchester: Manchester University Press and Minneapolis: University of Minnesota Press, 1984)

Maccoby, Hyam, *The Mythmaker: Paul and the Invention of Christianity* (London: Weidenfeld and Nicolson, 1986)

McGrath, Alister, *Iustitia Dei: A History of the Christian Doctrine of Justification from 1500 to the Present Day* (Cambridge: Cambridge University Press, 1986)

Macquarrie, John, 'Philosophy and Theology in Bultmann's Thought', in Charles W. Kegley (ed.), *The Theology of Rudolf Bultmann* (London: SCM Press, 1966), pp. 127–43

Malherbe, A. J., ' "Gentle as a Nurse": The Cynic Background to 1 Thess. ii', *Novum Testamentum* 12 (1970), pp. 203–17

Marcel, Pierre, *The Biblical Doctrine of Infant Baptism: Sacrament of the Covenant of Grace*, trans. Philip Hughes (London: Clarke, 1953)

Martin, Dale B., *Slavery as Salvation* (New Haven: Yale University Press, 1990)

Martin, Dale B., *The Corinthian Body* (New Haven: Yale University Press, 1995)

Marxsen, Willi, *The Resurrection of Jesus of Nazareth*, trans. Margaret Kohl (Philadelphia: Fortress Press, 1970)

Miranda, José Porfirio, *Marx and the Bible: A Critique of the Philosophy of Oppression*, trans. J. Eagleson (London: SCM Press, 1977)

Mitchell, Margaret, *Paul and the Rhetoric of Reconciliation* (Louisville: Westminster John Knox Press, 1991)

Moltmann, Jürgen, *The Church in the Power of the Spirit: A Contribution to Messianic Ecclesiology*, trans. Margaret Kohl (London: SCM Press, 1977)

Moltmann, Jürgen, *The Coming of God: Christian Eschatology*, trans. Margaret Kohl (London: SCM Press, 1996)

Moltmann, Jürgen, *The Trinity and the Kingdom of God: the Doctrine of God*, trans. Margaret Kohl (London: SCM Press, 1981)

Moltmann, Jürgen, *Theology of Hope*, trans. J. W. Leitch (London: SCM Press, 1967)

Moore, Arthur L., *1 and 2 Thessalonians* (New Century Bible; London: Nelson, 1969)

Moore, Arthur L., *The Parousia in the New Testament* (NovTSup 13; Leiden: Brill, 1966)

Bibliography

Moores, John D., *Wrestling with Rationality in Paul: Romans 1—8 in a New Perspective* (SNTSMS 82; Cambridge: Cambridge University Press, 1995)

Morris, Leon, 'The Theme of Romans', in W. Ward Gasque and Ralph P. Martin (eds), *Apostolic History and the Gospel: Presented to F. F. Bruce* (Exeter: Paternoster Press, 1970), pp. 249–63

Moule, Charles F. D., 'Obligation in the Ethics of Paul', in W. R. Farmer, C. F. D. Moule, and R. R. Niebuhr (eds), *Christian History and Interpretation: Essays in Honour of John Knox* (Cambridge: Cambridge University Press, 1967), pp. 389–406

Moule, Charles F. D., *The Epistles of Paul the Apostle to the Colossians and to Philemon* (Cambridge Greek Testament Commentary; Cambridge: Cambridge University Press, 1957)

Moule, Charles F. D., 'The Judgment Theme in the Sacraments', in W. D. Davies and D. Daube (eds), *The Background of the New Testament and its Eschatology: Studies in Honour of C. H. Dodd* (Cambridge: Cambridge University Press, 1956), pp. 464–81

Mounce, William D., *Pastoral Epistles* (Nashville: Nelson, 2000)

Moxnes, Halvor, *Theology in Conflict: Studies in Paul's Understanding of God in Romans* (NovTSup 53; Leiden: Brill, 1980)

Munck, Johannes, *Paul and the Salvation of Mankind*, trans. Frank Clarke (London: SCM Press, 1959)

Munzinger, André, *Discerning the Spirits: Theological and Ethical Hermeneutics in Paul* (SNTSMS 140; Cambridge: Cambridge University Press, 2007)

Murphy-O'Connor, Jerome, *Paul: A Critical Life* (Oxford: Oxford University Press, 1997)

Murphy-O'Connor, Jerome, *Paul the Letter-Writer: His World, His Options, His Skills* (Collegeville, MN: Liturgical Press, 1995)

Nietzsche, Friedrich, *Beyond Good and Evil*, trans. R. J. Hollingdale (London: Penguin, 1973, 1990)

Nygren, Anders, *Commentary on Romans*, trans. C. C. Rasmussen (London: SCM Press, 1952)

Olrog, W. H., *Paulus und seine Mitarbeiter* (Neukirchen: Neukirchener, 1979)

Paddison, Angus, *Theological Hermeneutics and 1 Thessalonians* (SNTSMS 133; Cambridge: Cambridge University Press, 2005)

Pannenberg, Wolfhart, *Basic Questions in Theology*, 3 vols, vol. 1, trans. G. H. Kehm (London: SCM Press, 1970)

Pannenberg, Wolfhart, *Systematic Theology*, trans. G. W. Bromiley, 3 vols (Grand Rapids: Eerdmans and Edinburgh: T. & T. Clark, 1991, 1994, 1998)

Pierce, C. A., *Conscience in the New Testament* (London: SCM Press, 1965)

Pogoloff, Stephen M., *Logos and Sophia: The Rhetorical Situation of 1 Corinthians* (Atlanta: Scholars Press, 1992)

Polhill, John B., *Paul and his Letters* (Nashville: Broadman & Holman, 1999)

Porter, Stanley E., and Olbricht, T. H. (eds), *Rhetoric and the New Testament* (Sheffield: Sheffield Academic Press, 1993)

Reid, J. K. S., *Our Life in Christ* (London: SCM Press, 1963)

Richard, Earl J., *First and Second Thessalonians* (Collegeville, MN: Liturgical Press, 2007)

Richards, E. Randolph, *Paul and First-century Letter Writing: Secretaries, Composition, and Collection* (Downers Grove: InterVarsity Press, 2004)

Richardson, Alan, *Introduction to the Theology of the New Testament* (London: SCM Press, 1958)

Richardson, Neil, *Paul's Language about God* (JSNTSup 99; Sheffield: Sheffield Academic Press, 1994)

Ridderbos, Herman, *Paul: An Outline of His Theology*, trans. J. R. de Witt (London: SPCK, 1977)

Ridderbos, Herman, *Paul and Jesus: Origin and General Character of Paul's Preaching of Christ*, trans. David H. Freeman (Philadelphia: Presbyterian and Reformed Publishing, 1958)

Roberts, Richard, 'A Postmodern Church?', in D. F. Ford and D. L. Stamps (eds), *Essentials of Christian Community: Essays for Daniel W. Hardy* (Edinburgh: T. & T. Clark, 1996), pp. 179–95

Robinson, John A. T., *In the End, God . . .* (London: Clarke, 1950)

Robinson, John A. T., *The Body: A Study in Pauline Theology* (London: SCM Press, 1952)

Robinson, John A. T., *The Human Face of God* (London: SCM Press, 1973)

Rorty, Richard, *Objectivity, Relativism and Truth: Philosophical Papers, Volume 1* (Cambridge: Cambridge University Press, 1991)

Rorty, Richard, *Truth and Progress: Philosophical Papers, Volume 3* (Cambridge: Cambridge University Press, 1998)

Rosenau, Pauline M., *Post-modernism and the Social Sciences* (Princeton, NJ: Princeton University Press, 1992)

Rosner, Brian S., *Paul, Scripture and Ethics: A Study of 1 Corinthians* (Leiden: Brill, 1994)

Rosner, Brian S., 'Paul's Ethics', in James D. G. Dunn (ed.), *The Cambridge Companion to Paul* (Cambridge: Cambridge University Press, 2003), pp. 212–23

Roth, Cecil, *The Haggadah: New Edition with Notes* (London: Soncino, 1934, 1959)

Ryle, Gilbert, 'Achilles and the Tortoise' (1954), in G. Ryle, *Dilemmas* (Cambridge: Cambridge University Press, 1966), pp. 36–53

Sampley, J. Paul, *Walking between the Times: Paul's Moral Reasoning* (Minneapolis: Fortress Press, 1991)

Sanders, E. P., *Paul and Palestinian Judaism: A Comparison of Patterns of Religion* (London: SCM Press, 1977)

Sanders, E. P., *Paul, the Law and the Jewish People* (Philadelphia: Fortress Press, 1983)

Sanders, E. P., *Paul: A Very Short Introduction* (Oxford: Oxford University Press, 2001)

Schnackenburg, Rudolf, *Baptism in the Thought of St. Paul*, trans. G. R. Beasley-Murray (Oxford: Blackwell, 1964)

Schnackenburg, Rudolf, *The Church in the New Testament*, trans. W. J. O'Hare (Freiburg: Herder, 1965)

Schoeps, H. J., *Paul: The Theology of the Apostle in the Light of Jewish Religious History*, trans. H. Knight (London: Lutterworth Press, 1961)

Schweitzer, Albert, *The Mysticism of Paul the Apostle*, trans. W. Montgomery (London: A. & C. Black, 1931)

Schweizer, E. *Church Order in the New Testament*, trans. F. Clarke (London: SCM Press, 1961)

Schweizer, E., *Jesus*, trans. D. E. Green (London: SCM Press, 1971)

Scott, C. Anderson, *Christianity according to St Paul* (Cambridge: Cambridge University Press, 1927)

Selwyn, E. G., *The First Epistle of St. Peter*, 2nd edn (London: Macmillan, 1947)

Spicq, C., *Agapē in the New Testament*, trans. Sr Marie Aquinas McNamara, 3 vols (London: Herder, 1963–6)

Stanley, Christopher D., *Paul and the Language of Scripture: Citation Technique in the Pauline Epistles and Contemporary Literature* (SNTSMS 69; Cambridge: Cambridge University Press, 1992)

Stendahl, K., *Paul among Jews and Gentiles* (London: SCM Press, 1977), part reprinted from 'The Apostle Paul and the Introspective Conscience of the West', *Harvard Theological Review* 56 (1963), pp. 199–215

Stowers, S. K., 'Paul on the Use and Abuse of Reason', in D. L. Balch and others (eds), *Greeks, Romans, Christians* (Minneapolis: Fortress Press, 1990), pp. 253–86

Tannehill, Robert C., *Dying and Rising with Christ: A Study in Pauline Theology* (Berlin: Töpelmann, 1967)

Taylor, Vincent, *The Atonement in New Testament Teaching* (London: Epworth Press, 1940)

Taylor, Vincent, *The Person of Christ in New Testament Teaching* (London: Macmillan, 1959)

Theissen, Gerd, *Psychological Aspects of Pauline Theology*, trans. John P. Galvin (Edinburgh: T. & T. Clark, 1987)

Thiselton, Anthony C., *First Corinthians: A Shorter Exegetical and Pastoral Commentary* (Grand Rapids and Cambridge: Eerdmans, 2006)

Thiselton, Anthony C., *New Horizons in Hermeneutics* (Grand Rapids: Zondervan and London: HarperCollins, 1992)

Thiselton, Anthony C., *The First Epistle to the Corinthians: A Commentary on the Greek Text* (Grand Rapids: Eerdmans and Carlisle: Paternoster Press, 2000)

Thiselton, Anthony C., *The Hermeneutics of Doctrine* (Grand Rapids and Cambridge: Eerdmans, 2007)

Thiselton, Anthony C., 'The Logical Role of the Liar Paradox in Titus 1: 12, 13: A Dissent from the Commentaries in the Light of Philosophical and Logical Analysis', *Biblical Interpretation* 2 (1994), pp. 207–23; reprinted in Thiselton, *Thiselton on Hermeneutics*, pp. 217–28

Thiselton, Anthony C., *The Two Horizons: New Testament Hermeneutics and Philosophical Description* (Grand Rapids: Eerdmans and Exeter: Paternoster Press, 1980)

Thiselton, Anthony C., *Thiselton on Hermeneutics: The Collected Works of Anthony C. Thiselton with New Essays* (Aldershot: Ashgate and Grand Rapids: Eerdmans, 2006)

Thornton, Lionel S., *The Common Life in the Body of Christ*, 3rd edn (London: Dacre Press, 1950)

Thrall, Margaret E., *A Critical and Exegetical Commentary on the Second Epistle to the Corinthians*, 2 vols (Edinburgh: T. & T. Clark, 1994, 2000)

Unnik, Willem C. van, *Tarsus or Jerusalem: The City of Paul's Youth*, trans. George Ogg (London: Epworth Press, 1962)

Vermes, Geza, *Jesus the Jew: A Historian's Reading of the Gospels* (Philadelphia: Fortress Press, 1973)

Wagner, Günter, *Pauline Baptism and the Pagan Mysteries*, trans. J. P. Smith (Edinburgh: Oliver & Boyd, 1967)

Wanemaker, Charles A., *The Epistles to the Thessalonians: A Commentary on the Greek Text* (Grand Rapids: Eerdmans and Carlisle: Paternoster Press, 1990)

Ward, Graham (ed.), *Postmodern God: A Theological Reader* (Oxford: Blackwell, 1997)

Weiss, Johannes, *Earliest Christianity*, trans. F. C. Grant, 2 vols (New York: Harper Torch Books, 1959)

Welborn, L. L., 'Discord in Corinth', in *Politics and Rhetoric in the Corinthian Epistles* (Macon, GA: Mercer University Press, 1987), pp. 1–42

Welborn, L. L., *Paul the Fool of Christ: A Study of 1 Corinthians 1—4 in the Comic-Philosophic Tradition* (London and New York: T. & T. Clark International/Continuum, 2005)

Wenham, David, *Paul: Follower of Jesus or Founder of Christianity* (Grand Rapids and Cambridge: Eerdmans, 1995)

Whiteley, D. E. H., *The Theology of St. Paul* (Oxford: Blackwell, 1964, 2nd edn 1971)

Wibbing, Siegfried, *Die Tugend und Lasterkataloge im Neuen Testament und ihre Traditions geschichte unter besonderer Berücksichtigung der Qumran-Texte* (Berlin: Töpelmann, 1959)

Wiedemann, Thomas E. J., *Greek and Roman Slavery* (London: Croom Helm, 1981)

Wikenhauser, Alfred, *Pauline Mysticism: Christ in the Mystical Teaching of St. Paul*, trans. J. Cunningham (Edinburgh: Nelson and Freiburg: Herder, 1960)

Williams, N. P., *The Ideas of the Fall and Original Sin: A Historical and Critical Study* (London and New York: Longman, Green & Co., 1929)

Winter, Bruce W., *After Paul Left Corinth* (Grand Rapids: Eerdmans, 2001)

Wire, Antoinette Clark, *The Corinthian Women Prophets: A Reconstruction through Paul's Rhetoric* (Minneapolis: Fortress Press, 1990)

Witherington, Ben, *Women in the Earliest Churches* (Cambridge: Cambridge University Press, 1988)

Wittgenstein, Ludwig, *Philosophical Investigations* (German and English; Oxford: Blackwell, 1967)

Wittgenstein, Ludwig, *Zettel* (German and English; Oxford: Blackwell, 1967)

Wright, N. T., *Jesus and the Victory of God* (London: SPCK, 1996)

Wright, [N. T.] Tom, *Justification: God's Plan and Paul's Vision* (London: SPCK, 2009)

Wright, N. T., *Paul: Fresh Perspectives* (London: SPCK, 2005)

Wright, N. T., *The Climax of the Covenant: Christ and Law in Pauline Theology* (Edinburgh: T. & T. Clark, 1991)

Wright, N. T., *The Resurrection of the Son of God* (London: SPCK, 2003)

Yarbrough, O. L., *Not Like the Gentiles: Marriage Rules in the Letters of Paul* (SBLDS 80; Atlanta: Scholars Press, 1985)

Ziesler, John, *The Meaning of Righteousness in Paul: A Linguistic and Theological Enquiry* (Cambridge: Cambridge University Press, 1972)

Index of biblical and related references

References and pages in bold play a greater role in the argument than others.

OLD TESTAMENT

Genesis
1.1—2.3 55
1.1 44
1.26–27 **67**
1.28 101
2.8 24
2.18 **101**
2.19–24 **101**
3.1–34 80
3.8 24
4.7 75
4.13 **76**
6.8 52
9.4 69
12.3 95
15.6 **94**
15.16 76
18.3 52
18.20 76
19.17 69
44.30 69

Exodus
3.14 **156**
3.21 52
4.19 69
6.6 **83**
10.17 76
12.1–51 123
15.13 83
17.2–7 54
21.30 **83**
21.43 76
23.7 **93**
32.1–6 54
32.30–34 76
34.34 65
34.35 65

Leviticus
4.1–35 **85**
4.3 76

16.16 76
17.14 69

Numbers
7.10 69
9.6 69
16.3 **103**

Deuteronomy
4.15–20 53
6.4 **46**, 53
7.7–8 **50**
9.18 76
10.12 53
18.15–18 **141**
21.23 **85**
26.10 53
32.35 145

Joshua
7.1–26 **101**

Judges
3.7–11 **83**
3.12–30 **83**
6.34 59
14.6 59
15.14 **59**

1 Samuel
2.17 76

2 Samuel
7 43

1 Kings
12.19 76

2 Kings
1.1 76
3.17 76
7.9 76

1 Chronicles
28.8 103
28.9 55

Job
10.4 70
10.6 76
15.5 76
19.25 **83**
20.27 76

Psalms
2 43
2.37 145
8.5–8 **67**
8.6 42
8.9 55
11.4 **105**
15.13 145
22.8–28 **141**
25.7 76
40.8 55
51.2 76
51.7 76
53.1 55
74.2 83
77.15 83
79.1 **106**
116.10 113

Proverbs
8.21 76
8.22 44
17.15 **93**

Isaiah
1.28 76
2.4 14, 145
3.13–14 145
4.2–6 14
6.1 **106**
6.2–5 **49**
6.3 55
6.7 76
7.17 55
8.14 51
8.16–20 **110**
9.2–3 14

10.20–23 51,
    145
10.22–23 51
11.1 51
11.16 51
24.1–27 14
26.19 55
28.16 51
31.3 59, 70
33.2 55
37.31–32 14
42.1–6 110
42.19 110
43.1 **83**
43.2–4 **83**
43.8 110
43.10 110
43.12 110
43.18–19 **136**
43.20–21 110
43.25 76
44.6 83
46.4 76
47.4 83
48.8 76
53.4–12 **85**
53.5 **96**
53.11–12 **140–1**
53.12 76
57.15 55
60.16 83
63.14 59
65.17–25 14
65.17–19 127
65.17 14
66.1–24 14
66.6 106

Jeremiah
1.5 16
3.13 76
11.10 76
11.20 145
18.5–9 51

Index of biblical and related references

Lamentations
3.19–33   141

Ezekiel
3.12   59
8.3   59
11.1   59
36.27   143
37   14
37.1–14   **59**
37.1   59
37.9–10   143
38—39   14

Daniel
7.13   **14, 43**

Hosea
2.1   51
2.25   51
6.2   140
9.7   76
14.10   76

Joel
2.28–29   14, 60
2.28   59

Amos
4.4   76

Zephaniah
1.9–18   14

Zechariah
9—14   14
14.1–8   14

INTERTESTAMENTAL WRITINGS

Judith
10.8   52

Wisdom
1.4   76
2.12   76
8.13   76
10.2   76
10.13   76
11.23   76
13.3   76
14.8–14   **23**
15.1–6   **23**

Sirach
2.11   76
3.3   76
4.21   76
48.2   51

4 Ezra (or 2 Esdras)
3.21–23   **80**
3.35–36   80
4.30   80
7.11–12   80
7.46   80
7.68   80
7.116   80
7.117–118   **80**
8.35   80
12.32   145
12.34   145

2 Baruch (or Syriac Baruch)
64.15–18   80
64.19   80

Jubilees
1.27–28   105
1.29   145
7.20–21   129
23.27–31   145

1 Enoch
10.20   129
37–71   14
38.5   110
47.3   145
91.6–7   129
91.12–17   145
91.12   110
95.3   110
98.12   110

1 Maccabees
2.27   51
2.54   51

4 Maccabees
4.12   76
6.28–29   24
17.21   24

Qumran (Dead Sea Scrolls)
1QM 4.10   **103**
1QS 4.9–11   129

1QS 5.5   **108**
1QS 8.5–9   108
1QS 8.5–6   **105**
1QS 8.6–7   105
1QS 9.6   105
4Q 174   105
11QTª 29.7   **105**
11QTᵘ 45.12–14
   105
11QTᵘ 46.3–4
   105
CD 7.17   103
CD 11.22   103

NEW TESTAMENT

Matthew
1.22   4
2.15   4
2.17   4
2.23   4
5.27–28   3
5.29   146
6.25–34   154
7.12   6
8.17   4
8.20   154
10.10   **3**
10.39   154
11.29   4
12.17   4
12.31–32   60
13.35   4
17.20   8
18.1–6   **7**
19.3–9   **3**
20.1–15   **5**
20.4   5
20.25–28   7
21.4   4
21.33–44   **6**
21.42   114
22.34–40   6
23.31   146
24.23–31   14
24.37–39   146
25.54   4
26.17–19   **123**
26.26–29   **3**
26.26   124
27.9   4
27.35   4
28.5–10   116

Mark
1.15   **3, 17**
2.17   6
3.28–30   60
9.33–42   7
9.43   146
10.2–12   **3**
10.42–45   7
12.1–11   **6**
12.9   6
12.10–11   114
12.28–34   6–7
13   147
13.24–36   14
14.12–16   **123**
14.22–25   3
14.22   **124**
15.25–37   154

Luke
1.47   72
6.31   6
9.58   154
10.7   **3**
10.25–28   7
10.38–42   7
15.11–32   **5**
16.18   3
18.9–14   **5**
18.15–17   **7**
20.9–18   **6**
20.17   114
22.1–13   123
22.14–20   3
22.24–27   7
24.10   116
24.25–27   **140**
24.44–46   **140**

John
1.1   **48, 53**
1.3   **53**
3.16   50
20.1–18   **116**

Acts
1—5   **23**
1.15   103
2.17–21   **60**
2.36   42
2.42   103
2.46   123
3.21   145

Index of biblical and related references

4.10   141
5.15   141
5.30   141
6.1—8.40   23
6.1   103
9.1–19   16
9.2   103
9.4   71, 103
10.40   141
11.20   22
11.25–26   22
11.26   103
13.1–2   22
13.4–15   22
14.3   24
14.11–19   30
14.21–22   24
14.25–26   24
15   25, 30
15.2–3   25
15.7–11   25
15.12   25
15.13–21   25
15.36   24
16.12   25
16.22–24   25
16.31   25
17.1–15   26
17.16   26
17.32–33   137
18.1   26
18.2   114
18.6–10   27
18.12   28
18.19–23   31
19.1–7   31
19.10   31
19.23–41   31
20.1–6   35
20.1–3   31
20.3–6   35
20.33   73
20.37–38   35
21.4   35
21.11   35
21.17   35
21.20   36
21.27—25.12   36
22.3–23   36
22.3–16   16
22.3   20
22.7   71, 103
23.35   46

24.23   46
24.27   46
25.12   36
26.1–29   36
26.12–18   16
26.14   16
26.15   103
27—28   36
28.31   37

Romans
1—11   129
1—8   4
1.3–4   42–3
1.3   4, 53
1.4   40, 53, 144
1.8   50
1.10–13   34
1.16   23
1.17   4, 35, 55
1.18—5.21   119
1.18—4.25   35
1.18—3.20   161
1.18–32   23, 80
1.18   51, 76, 78
1.19–20   55
1.23   51, 78
1.25   67
1.29–31   129
2—3   81
2.1–24   23
2.2–3   144
2.2   145
2.12–13   96
2.12   145
2.16   144, 145
2.17—3.20   75
2.28   70
2.4   50, 51
3.3   18, 51
3.4   51
3.5   51, 55
3.6   144
3.9   76, 78
3.12   55
3.22–25   6
3.22–23   78
3.23   23, 87–8
3.24   89
3.25   54, 87
3.26   51
4.3   94
4.4–5   94

4.6–8   94
4.9   94
4.10   94
4.11   94
4.12   94
4.13   94
4.14   94
4.15   76
4.17   55, 136
4.21   141
4.22   94
4.23–25   94
4.24   40
4.25   40, 76, 85, 144, 157
5.1—8.39   35
5.1   96
5.5   65, 68
5.7   57
5.8   6
5.9   96
5.10   86
5.12–21   80–1
5.12–13   76
5.14   42, 76
5.15–19   42
5.15   4, 76, 82, 102
5.16–21   102
5.19   4, 82, 120
5.20   132
5.21   78
5.26   76
6.1–11   119–20
6.1–2   76
6.2   119
6.3–6   89
6.3–4   117, 119
6.3   118–20
6.4–5   133
6.4   55, 88, 119, 129, 144
6.5   120, 144
6.6   78
6.7   120
6.8   144
6.9   144
6.10   90
6.11   76, 90, 120
6.13   133
6.23   78
6.25   78
7.4   144
7.7–24   75, 80–1

7.7   76
7.8–10   81
7.11   77
7.12–13   132
7.14   77, 81
7.18   77
7.19   75
7.24   77, 79, 81
7.25   81
8.3   4, 6, 45, 54, 85
8.4   129
8.7   55, 78
8.9–11   143
8.9   58, 60–1
8.10   61
8.11   53, 62, 141, 144
8.13   57, 58
8.14   17, 58
8.15–16   53, 62
8.17   88
8.18–25   127, 137
8.19   13
8.21   77
8.23   62
8.24–25   127
8.24   57
8.26–27   60, 62
8.26   53, 65
8.27   68–9
8.28–39   102
8.31   102
8.35   102
8.38   67
8.39   57
9—11   6, 51, 97, 157
9.1—11.32   35
9.2   68
9.3–5   42
9.3   70
9.5   4, 102
9.6–9   110
9.8–13   102
9.8–11   51
9.14   51
9.16   51
9.20–22   51
9.22   51
9.24   110
10.8   18, 69
10.9   42, 141
10.14–17   155

Index of biblical and related references

11.5–6 52
11.13–24 102
11.22 51
11.26 76
11.33–36 35, 49
11.33 49
12—15 129
12.1–2 133
12.1 71, 126
12.2 68
12.4–8 112
12.4–5 103
12.9–21 130–1
12.9–20 129
12.11 40, 58, 72
13.1–7 134
13.1 69
13.8–10 7, 129, 131
13.8 132
13.9–10 42
13.10 132
13.11–14 137
13.11–12 133
13.13 129
14.7–8 38
14.8 41
14.10 45, 145
14.15 129
14.17 10
15.1–7 129, 131
15.1–3 128
15.1 131
15.2–3 42
15.3 131
15.7 128
15.8 4
15.15 51
15.19 34
15.23–24 34
15.25–27 34
15.25 34
15.30 7
15.33 51
16.1–2 8
16.3–4 8
16.3 114
16.4 69, 106
16.6 115
16.7 114
16.11 8
16.12 8, 115
16.15 8
16.16 106

16.17 8
16.20 51
16.25–27 56
16.28 34

1 Corinthians
1.1 55
1.2 161
1.4–9 50
1.7 41
1.8 145, 146
1.9 18
1.10–12 56, 111
1.11 32
1.12 154
1.13 117–18
1.14–16 27, 154
1.15 118
1.16 122
1.18—2.16 15
1.18—2.5 32, 56
1.18–25 6, 27, 158
1.18 15, 56, 82
1.19 56
1.20 15
1.23 15, 42, 56
1.31 89
2.1–5 27, 56, 155
2.5–16 32
2.6–16 56
2.6–10 66
2.8 4
2.10–16 56, 65
2.11–16 73
2.12 72
2.13 72
2.14–16 54
2.14–15 72
2.14 69
2.16 15, 16, 66, 68
3.1–4 16
3.3–5 119
3.3 7, 130
3.5–21 32
3.5–15 110
3.5 111
3.6 111
3.9 111
3.10–12 111
3.16–17 71, 105, 108
3.18–23 111
3.18–21 161

3.18 156
3.21–22 111
4.1–5 111, 150, 156, 162
4.4 75
4.5 41, 69, 111, 137
4.6–13 161
4.7 131
4.8–13 111, 140
4.9–13 13
4.10 110
4.15–16 153
4.17 9, 106
4.20 10
5.1—6.20 32
5.2 7, 130
5.5 41
5.7 4, 84
5.9 33
5.17 11
6.1–6 8
6.9–11 129
6.11 117, 120–1
6.13–14 41, 71
6.13 126
6.14 141
6.17 71
6.19 38, 71, 84, 105, 108
6.20 17, 70, 84
7.1—11.1 32
7.1 9, 32
7.3–7 131–2
7.3–5 9, 73
7.10 3
7.12–16 9
7.17 129
7.21–24 132
7.22–23 84
7.22 40
7.25–31 9
7.36–38 9
7.37 68
8.1–6 133
8.1 32
8.4–6 48, 49
8.4 10, 53
8.6 53, 56
8.7 71
8.10 71
8.11 10
8.12 71
8.13 8, 10, 133

9.1 116
9.3–18 27
9.5 4
9.12–18 154
9.14 3
9.15 10
9.24–27 71
10.4 45, 54
10.9 54
10.11 127
10.12 158
10.13 54
10.16 117
10.21 40
10.23–28 10
10.25–29 71
11.2—14.40 32
11.2 9
11.3 52
11.5 115
11.11–12 9
11.12 52
11.16 106
11.17–34 122–4
11.17 125
11.18 125
11.20–22 125
11.20 40, 117
11.21–22 7, 130
11.21 124
11.23–34 125
11.23–26 3
11.23–25 157
11.23 40
11.24 117, 123
11.25 117, 123
11.26 40, 122, 137
11.27–32 125, 158
11.29 125
11.32 40
11.36 56
12—14 112
12.3 40, 60, 66
12.4–31 107
12.4–8 54
12.4–6 66
12.4 104–5
12.7 63, 104
12.8–10 63, 100, 105
12.8 56
12.10 64
12.11 63, 104

12.12   103
12.13   61, 117, 119
12.14–26   103
12.14   103
12.15   104
12.17   104
12.19   104
12.20   103
12.21   104
12.22   103
12.23   104
12.26   104
12.27–30   104, 105
12.27   103
12.28–30   111
13   129
13.1   64, 130
13.2   8
13.4–7   7
13.4   8, 130
13.8   130
13.12   24
13.13   8
14.1–25   130
14.1–19   63
14.2–5   64
14.2   63
14.3   63
14.4   63, 64
14.7–8   64
14.14–15   68
14.24–25   63
14.25   69
14.26–27   7
14.27–33   130
14.33–36   9, 115
14.37–38   158
15   67, 139
15.1–58   17, 32
15.1–11   140–1
15.1–7   140
15.3–7   157
15.3–4   119
15.4   53, 141
15.8–11   140
15.8–9   116
15.9–10   49
15.10   95
15.12–19   141
15.12–20   14
15.15–16   141
15.17   141
15.18–19   141

15.20–34   142
15.21–22   42
15.21   4, 43
15.22   89, 145
15.23   146
15.24–28   142
15.25–28   43–4
15.28   52, 136
15.29–34   142
15.33–49   71
15.34–49   130
15.34   140, 142
15.35–58   142
15.35–39   142
15.37   143
15.38–41   143
15.39   70
15.42–44   69, 143
15.44   53
15.45–58   144
15.50   10
15.51–54   139
15.51–52   146
15.51   137
15.52   130
15.55   146
15.58   40, 76, 130, 136
16.1–20   32
16.1–4   73
16.10   40
16.15–18   9
16.15   27
16.17   32
16.18   32
16.19   106, 114
16.22   40, 137

2 Corinthians
1—9   33
1.1   55
1.3–9   112
1.3   57
1.5–11   116
1.8–9   33
1.9   90, 112, 144, 161
1.12   71
1.17–21   33
1.18–20   112
1.18   18
1.19   26
1.23—2.11   33

1.24   112
2.1–4   113
2.10–16   54
2.13   9
2.14   33
2.15   113
2.17   113
3   61
3.1–3   113
3.3   58
3.7–18   113
3.12—4.6   155
3.17   45, 65
4.2   113, 129, 154
4.4   67, 113, 154
4.5   40, 113
4.6   55, 113
4.7–18   110
4.7–14   90
4.8–10   33
4.10   90
4.14   33, 141, 144
4.15   113
4.16   55, 113
4.18   33, 113
5.2   34
5.5   62, 65
5.6   41
5.7   100, 114
5.8   41, 138
5.10   46, 145
5.11—6.10   110
5.14–18   127
5.14–17   89
5.14   114
5.15   18
5.17   18, 34
5.18   87
5.19   54, 76, 82, 87, 88, 95
5.20   18, 34, 88, 114
5.21   82, 84, 85
6.2   4
6.4–5   114
6.6–7   114
6.6   130
6.8   34
6.10   114
6.11   114
6.16   105
6.26   108
8.1–7   73
8.5   41, 73

8.9   34, 44
8.19   41
8.23   106
10—13   33
10.1   4
10.2–3   129
10.8   41
11—12   18
11.18   70
11.20   34
11.23–33   22
11.23–29   13
11.26   26
11.28   25
11.30–33   18
11.33   34
12.4–8   54
12.7–9   13, 64
12.7   70
12.8   90
12.9   34, 90
12.10   131
12.11   131
12.13   106
13.4   90
13.5   34, 158
13.10   41
13.11   34
13.13   66
13.14   54

Galatians
1.1—4.11   129
1.1   141, 144
1.2   106
1.4   82
1.5   56
1.6–24   30
1.6–9   161
1.9   82
1.11–23   161
1.11–12   21
1.13–17   16
1.13   16, 21
1.16   23, 44
1.17   21
1.18   110
1.19   4, 110
1.23   21
2.1–10   30
2.1   22, 30
2.11–20   30
2.14   83

Index of biblical and related references

2.16–17 96
2.20 89
3.1–18 94
3.1–6 30
3.1–2 68
3.6—4.7 102
3.6–7 94
3.7–29 30
3.7 102
3.8 95
3.10 132
3.13 4, 84–5
3.15—4.7 18
3.15–18 95
3.15–16 156
3.15 68
3.16 4, 102
3.19—5.12 94
3.24 132
3.26 102
3.27 117–18
3.28 74, 150
4 30
4.1–24 95
4.3–4 157
4.4 3, 4, 6, 45, 54, 84
4.5 54, 84
4.6 17, 57, 58, 60, 62
4.12—6.18 129
4.12 126
4.13–15 64
4.13 70, 126
4.14 30
4.15 10
4.19 10, 126
4.21—5.1 81
4.22–31 156
4.22–24 110
4.28 110
5.1–14 30
5.1 77
5.5 62, 96
5.6 7
5.13—6.24 30
5.13–15 90
5.14 4
5.16 129
5.20 62
5.22–23 62
5.22 7
5.24 62

5.25 61
6.1 76
6.2 7, 128
6.4 158
6.11 10, 64
6.12–13 70
6.14 82
6.17 10, 89
6.18 72

Ephesians
1—3 134
1.3–23 107
1.4 109
1.6 109
1.10 4, 145
1.11 107
1.13–14 66
1.17 57
1.20 144
1.22 106, 107
1.23 52
2.1–6 107
2.2 129
2.13–17 107
2.14–16 134
2.19–20 107
2.20 116
2.21–22 107
2.21 108
3.1 107
3.6 107
3.10 106, 107
3.14–15 57
3.17 7
3.21 56, 106
4—6 134
4.1 129
4.8 107
4.11–12 114
4.15 114
4.17—6.20 107
4.17 129
4.23 15, 68
5.2–3 129
5.8—6.9 114
5.18 65
5.23–29 106
5.25–27 107
5.26 117, 121
5.27 120
5.32 106
6.12 70

Philippians
1.3–11 47, 50
1.13 46
1.21 47
1.23–24 139
1.23 47
1.27 129
2.1 66
2.3–11 128, 131
2.3 47, 73
2.5–11 42, 44, 45
2.6–7 47
2.9–11 53
2.9–10 47
2.17 105
2.25–30 46
2.30 69
3.1–16 47
3.3–4 70
3.6 75
3.7–16 90
3.9 96
3.10–11 90
3.10 88, 90, 144
3.11–16 21–2, 137
3.11–14 17, 62
3.12 47, 90
3.17 129
3.20—4.1 136
3.20–21 137
3.20 24, 47
4.1 89
4.2–3 47
4.3 8
4.7 68
4.10–20 46, 47
4.11 73
4.20 57
4.23 72

Colossians
1.1 55
1.3–8 50
1.7 48
1.9 48
1.10 107
1.11 48
1.13 10, 16, 44, 57
1.15–20 48, 52
1.15–18 44
1.15–17 49, 55, 107
1.15 67
1.16 53, 67

1.17 67
1.18 106, 107
1.19 53
1.20 145
1.22 4, 43
1.24 91, 106
1.27 48
2.7 7
2.9 43
2.12 107, 117, 120, 141, 144
2.13 76
2.14 85
2.19 107
2.28 129
3.1 86, 107
3.10 67
3.18—4.1 134
4.3 32
4.5 129
4.10 32
4.18 32

1 Thessalonians
1.1–10 29
1.1 25, 106
1.2–9 110
1.2–3 50
1.4 50
1.5 71, 159
1.6 41, 159
1.8 50
1.9–10 44
1.9 50, 162
1.10 141, 144
2.1–20 29
2.2 50, 153
2.3–4 155
2.3 153
2.4 50, 69
2.5–6 153, 155
2.5 50
2.7 153, 155
2.8 69
2.9 50
2.11 153
2.12 10, 50
2.13 50
2.17—3.2 110
2.19 146
3.1–3 29
3.2 50
3.9 50, 71

3.10 29
3.11 50
3.12–13 41
3.13 146
4.1–14 29
4.1–9 128
4.1 50, 89, 129
4.3 50, 55
4.7 50
4.8 50
4.9 50
4.12–18 146
4.12 129
4.13—5.8 14
4.13–18 127
4.13–15 147
4.14–18 146
4.14 50
4.15—5.11 29, 136
4.15 41, 138
4.16–17 146
4.16 41, 136
4.17 29, 136
5.2–11 136
5.2 41
5.3 145
5.9 50
5.10 138, 147
5.12–28 29
5.12 68
5.14–18 128
5.14 29, 68
5.18 50
5.19 65
5.23 41, 50, 72, 146
5.24 18

2 Thessalonians
1.2 50
1.3 50
1.4–6 31
1.4 50

1.5 50, 145
1.7–10 147
1.8 50
1.11 50
1.12 50
2.1–12 31, 145
2.1 146
2.2 68
2.4 50
2.7–12 146
2.8 145–6
2.9 146
2.11 50
2.13 50
2.15–16 50
2.16–17 50
3.5 4, 50
3.6–15 31
3.11 129
3.15 68

1 Timothy
1.17 55
1.19 108
2.1–6 134
2.3 57
2.5 55
2.7 108
2.12–14 115
3.1–13 115
3.1–7 115
3.2–7 115
3.2–3 134
3.4 108
3.5 108
3.8–13 115
3.12 108
3.14–15 134
3.15 106, 108
4.1–5 134
4.1 108
4.3 108, 115
4.6 108
5.16 108

5.17–23 116
5.17 115
6.10 73, 134
6.14 146

2 Timothy
1.10 146
2.10 108
2.15 108
2.18 140
3.1–5 134
3.24 134
4.18 56
4.19 114

Titus
1.3–9 134
1.5–9 115, 116
1.13–14 108
1.13 151
1.17 57
2.1–10 134
2.10 57
2.12–14 134
2.13 57, 146
3.4 57
3.5 117, 121

Philemon
11–16 132
16 70
25 72

Hebrews
1.1 48
1.2–4 53
1.2 53
1.16 48
1.17 48
1.18 48
1.19 48
1.20 48
1.28 48
2.3 48

2.18 48
3.16 48
4.2–4 48
9.5 87
13.1–3 128

James
2.24 100

1 Peter
1.13–22 128

2 Peter
1.16 146
2.4 146
3.4 146
3.12 146

1 John
2.2 87
3.1 50
4.10 87

Revelation
4.1–11 14
5.9–14 45
17.9–18 14
19.10 45
21.3–5 14
21.9 108
22.13 108
22.20 40

EARLY CHRISTIAN
WRITINGS

1 Clement
42 115

Didache
10.6 40

Polycarp
Ep. Phil. 5 115

Index of authors

Aland, K. 122
Arndt, W. F. 87n
Austin, John L. 19n
Ayer, A. J. 160

Barr, James 65n
Barrett, C. K. 87, 112
Barth, Karl 32n, 64–5, 142
Barthes, Roland 154–5, 156
Bassler, Jouette M. 146–7
Bauckham, Richard 2, 157
Baur, F. C. 97, 98
Beaudean, John W. 155
Beker, J. Christiaan 12
Bell, Richard H. 52n
Bercovitch, S. 160
Bernstein, Richard 149
Best, Ernest 29n, 31, 103
Bonhoeffer, Dietrich 151, 161
Bornkamm, Günther 68
Bousset, Wilhelm 41–2
Brown, Alexandra R. 12, 16, 18–19, 158
Brown, Francis 76n
Bruce, F. F. 8, 30
Bultmann, Rudolf 38, 41, 50, 92, 96, 136

Caird, George B. 138
Calvin, John 93, 95, 96–7
Carrington, Philip 129
Castelli, Elizabeth A. 153
Chadwick, Henry 24
Charles, R. H. 137
Chilton, Bruce 22
Clarke, Andrew D. 154n
Collins, J. N. 112, 115
Conzelmann, Hans 50, 139
Corrington, Robert S. 160
Crafton, Jeffrey A. 34n, 116
Cranfield, C. E. B. 35n, 94n, 120
Crossan, John Dominic 2
Cullmann, Oscar 45, 122

Dahl, M. E. 141
Danker, W. F. 87
Darwin, Charles Robert 148, 149, 150
Davies, W. D. 77
Deissmann, Adolf 83
Deluz, Gaston 140
Denney, James 86
Denzin, Norman 149
Derrida, Jacques 156
Descartes, René 150
Dewey, John 160
Dix, Dom Gregory 123
Docherty, Thomas 148–9
Dodd, C. H. 21, 88, 128, 137
Donaldson, D. 160
Donaldson, Terence 98
Dunn, James D. G. 2, 41, 42, 44, 45, 55, 61, 66, 68, 86, 98, 99, 106, 119, 121

Eckstein, H.-J. 72n
Emerson, Ralph Waldo 160
Epp, E. J. 8, 114
Eriksson, Anders 10n, 140

Fish, Stanley 159, 161
Fitzmyer, Joseph A. 61n, 111n, 112
Foucault, Michel 152–3
Fowl, Stephen E. 128
Freud, Sigmund 73, 148, 149, 150, 157
Fuchs, Ernest 5–6
Funk, Robert 2, 155
Furnish, Victor P. 129n, 132

Gale, Herbert M. 17n
Gillespie, Thomas W. 32n, 63
Gingrich, F. W. 87n
Gooch, Peter D. 72n
Grayston, Kenneth 90n
Grenz, Stanley J. 74n
Grobel, Kendrick 92

Hall, David R. 32n
Hanson, Anthony T. 110, 113
Harnack, Adolf von 1
Harris, Murray J. 34n, 66, 85
Hawthorne, Gerald F. 47n
Haykin, Michael A. G. 54n, 66n
Hays, Richard B. 127, 133
Hegel, Georg W. F. 148
Heidegger, Martin 159
Higgins, A. J. B. 123
Hillel, Rabbi 2
Hock, Ronald F. 21n
Hogeterp, Albert L. P. 71n, 105n
Holland, Tom 120
Hurtado, Larry 45, 50, 52

James, William 160
Jeremias, Joachim 5n, 39n, 57, 85, 122, 123
Jewett, Robert 68n
Jüngel, Eberhard 49n

Kant, Immanuel 101, 150
Käsemann, Ernst 41, 70, 93, 97, 98, 143
Kim, Seyoon 98, 99
Knox, W. L. 137, 139
Kramer, Werner 40–1
Kümmel, W. G. 50
Küng, Hans 95
Künneth, W. 141

Leenhardt, F. J. 123
Lessing, G. E. 150
Lietzmann, Hans 122, 123
Lindbeck, George 159
Locke, John 150
Lowe, John 137
Lundin, Roger 160
Luther, Martin 93, 95, 140, 151, 161
Lyon, David 151–2

Index of authors

Lyotard, Jean-François 149, 157, 158, 159

Maccoby, Hyam 1–2
McGrath, Alister 93
Macquarrie, John 136
Malherbe, A. J. 155n
Marcel, Pierre 122n
Marshall, I. Howard 123
Martin, Dale B. 39n, 83–4, 103
Martyn, J. Louis 18
Marx, Karl 148, 149, 150, 157
Marxsen, Willi 141
Miranda, José Porfirio 92, 99
Mitchell, Margaret 103, 140
Moltmann, Jürgen 54, 55, 79, 87, 104, 109n, 135, 137, 139
Moores, John D. 161
Morris, Leon 50–1
Moule, C. F. D. 48n, 121, 123, 128
Mounce, William D. 115–16
Moxnes, Halvor 50–1
Munck, Johannes 16–17
Munzinger, André 15n, 158
Murphy-O'Connor, Jerome 21, 28

Nietzsche, Friedrich 149–50, 154, 160
Nygren, Anders 87, 96

Oepke, A. 118
Olrog, W. H. 10n

Paddison, Angus 155n
Pannenberg, Wolfhart 79, 106, 141, 157–8

Parham, Charles 119
Phillips, J. B. 13, 87, 90, 112
Pierce, C. A. 71
Prat, F. 95

Quine, W. V. O. 160

Rees, Tom 92
Reid, J. K. S. 86
Reimarus, Samuel 101, 150
Richards, E. Randolph 29n
Richardson, Alan 78, 96, 121
Richardson, Neil 41, 49, 51
Ricoeur, Paul 156
Ridderbos, Herman 3
Ritschl, Albrecht 1
Robinson, John A. T. 45, 103
Rorty, Richard 138, 151, 159–60
Rosenau, Pauline M. 159
Rosner, Brian S. 126–7
Ryle, Gilbert 139

Sampley, J. Paul 132–3
Sanders, E. P. 97, 98
Saussure, Ferdinand de 154
Schnackenburg, Rudolf 108, 117–18, 119, 120
Schoeps, H. J. 2
Schweitzer, Albert 60, 88, 97, 98
Schweizer, Eduard 3, 107n
Scott, C. Anderson 13
Sellars, Wilfred, 160
Selwyn, E. G. 128–9
Seymour, William 119
Spicq, C. 130
Stanley, Christopher D. 22–3
Stendahl, Krister 75, 97, 98
Stowers, S. K. 68n
Strauss, David F. 148

Tannehill, Robert 89–90
Taylor, Vincent 66, 85
Theissen, Gerd 64
Thiselton, Anthony C. 7n, 32n, 63n, 108n, 130n
Thornton, Lionel S. 16, 108
Thrall, Margaret E. 34n

Unnik, Willem C. van 20–1

Vermes, Geza 2
Voltaire, François-Marie Arouet 101

Wagner, Günter 120
Ward, Graham 152
Weiss, Johannes 11, 89n, 93, 97
Welborn, L. L. 20, 111n, 118n
Wenham, David 3, 6
Whiteley, D. E. H. 12, 59, 85, 91, 103, 132
Wibbing, Siegfried 129n
Wiedemann, Thomas E. J. 39n
Wikenhauser, Alfred 89n
Williams, N. P. 80
Winter, Bruce W. 61
Wire, Antoinette Clark 153
Witherington, Ben 115n
Wittgenstein, Ludwig 70, 138, 159
Wrede, William 98
Wright, N. T. (Tom) 2, 43, 66, 92, 93, 95–9, 141, 143

Yarbrough, O. L. 129

Ziesler, John 93, 94–5

Index of subjects

Important references are shown in bold print.

Abba 57, 58, 60, 61–2
Abraham 30, 94, 102
absent church members
  102–3
Acro-Corinth 26
Adam 24, 42, 79, 80, 81, 89
Adam parallel 4, 42–3, 128,
  142, 144
adoption 17
adoptionism 43–4
affection 10
affliction 114
ages 14–15; overlapping of
  the 12–13, 15–16; see also
  two ages
alienation 75, 77, 88
allegiance to Christ 118
allegory 24
ambassadors for Christ 114
ambiguity: of *pneuma*, spirit
  58, 72; of life 127
ambition 128
American postmodernism
  151, 159–61
angels 45, 48, 56, 67; see
  powers
antinomianism 132–3
Antioch 22, 24
aparchē (Greek: firstfruits) 62
apocalyptic 4, 12–18, 84,
  127, 135–6, 138, 142,
  146–7
apokatastasis (Greek:
  restoration) 136, 145
apostles 111, 116
apostleship 34, 116
apostolic tradition 10, 134,
  140, 156–8, 161
applause-seeking orators 154
Arabia 21
Aramaic 21, 43, 57
Areopagus 26
arrabōn (Greek: deposit) 62
ascension 107, 114

assembly (people of God)
  102
assistants of bishops 115
Athanasius 53–4, 57
Athens 26, 27
atonement 87–8; see also
  cross; death of Christ;
  sacrifice
atrium 124
Augustus 43
autobiography, Paul's
  writings as 11, 75
autonomy 84, 101, 150, 155
'āwōn (Hebrew: guilt,
  distorted state) 76

bandits 59
baptism 88–9, 117–22; as
  sign of adherence 118
baptism in the Spirit 61, 119
'baptismal aorist' 121
baptized for the dead 142
Barnabas 22, 29
Basil 53–4, 56, 57
begotten, not made 56–7
'being there' (at the cross)
  124–5
belonging to Jesus as Lord
  84
Beroea 26
'Beyond' who is within, the
  66
bishops 115–16
blasphemy against the Holy
  Spirit 60
boasting 18; see also law
body 15, 48, 67, 69–71,
  73–4, 78, 112, 126–9,
  140–3
body of Christ 103–5, 106–7
boldness 155
bondage 77–8
Book of Common Prayer
  117

breath see ruach
bride of Christ 107–8
brothers and sisters (church)
  103
burial of Christ 140–1

Caesar 42, 158
Caesarea 35
call 11, 39, 75
catechism 128–9
Catholic theology 94–5, 106
celebrities 110–11, 152, 162
chaburah (Hebrew:
  fellowship meal) 123–4
chatta'th (Hebrew: sin) 75–6
Chloe's people 32
Christ 33, 128; being in 33,
  35, 81, 85, 89–91, 95–6;
  dying with 86, 88–91, 111;
  as God 45–6; as human
  being 43, 46; as Lord
  38–42, 66, 70; as mediate
  Creator 46, 53; putting on
  like garment 118; and the
  Spirit 65–6
Christlikeness of God 49,
  54–5
Church 71, 98, 101–9, 110,
  134; church order 37, 108;
  community 71, 106–8
churches (local) 106–7
circumcision 70, 94, 99
Claudius 27
clay jars 113
co-agents 53–6, 66; see also
  co-workers
co-creation 53–7
cohesion, Christ as agent of
  55–6
collection of money 28, 32,
  36, 46, 73
Colossae 44
Colossians 32, 44–7, 107
coming of Christ 111, 146–7

communal enterprise:
Church as 64, 101;
ministry as 110
communal framework 63
communal gift, Spirit as 59
communal state of humanity
75
communal temple of the
spirit, people as 71
communion 63, 106, 117,
122–5
community 101–5, 151, 161
competitiveness of
Corinthian church 27–8
conceivable (God as) 18, 44,
142
conduct 40, 41
confession 39
conscience 71–2, 75
consensus 158
contentment, Paul's 73
contrariety, rule of 86
contrast between body and
soul 143
conversion of Paul 11, 16,
20–1, 44
Corinth 7, 20, 26–8, 29–31,
34, 35, 61, 115, 149, 152
Corinthians: first letter to
the 32; as God's building
111; second letter to the
33–4
cornerstone, Jesus as 107
corporate solidarity 71, 79,
81
correspondence, rule of 86
cosmic Christ 43, 44–8
cost, as metaphor 84
Council of Jerusalem 23,
24–5
count as righteous 93–4,
97
covenant 98–9, 122, 125
covenantal nomism 97
co-workers 10, 22, 50, 110
creation 48, 53, 55, 57, 67
Creator, creating 49, 53–5
creatureliness 67–8
creeds 53, 56–7
cross 55–6, 82–90, 95, 125,
127, 134, 151, 162
curse 60–1, 85, 94–5
'curse prayers' 61

Cynic moral philosophy 2
Cynics 2, 155
Cyprus 22

David 43
deacon 114–16
Dead Sea Scrolls *see* Qumran
death 77, 80, 85, 135, 142,
144, 146
death and resurrection
122–3, 125
death of Christ 82–90, 95,
122
debt 82, 85
deception 153, 155, 56
declarative verb, 'justify' as
93
deconstruction 156
deferment of meaning 156–7
deism 150
deity of Christ 45–6
deliberative rhetoric 150–1
demythologizing, Bultmann's
programme of 136
denial of the resurrection
140–2
deposit, Holy Spirit as 62
deputy to apostle 115
Derbe 24
dereliction, Jesus' cry of 55
despair 137
destiny 135–47
devotion 40, 45
Diaspora Judaism 22
'differend' 158
diolkos (Greek: paved way)
27
disguise 154–5
distance, God's 54, 77
diversity 103, 107
division 56, 95, 124
Dominical sacrament 117
dominion 43, 67
down-payment, Holy Spirit
as 62
dry bones 59
dualism 70, 145
dynamic verbs, Paul's use of
130
dynamistic 65

ekklēsia (Greek: church) 102,
105–7

economic crises 162
either-or, the view of life as
11
elders 24
enemies 78, 86
Enlightenment 79, 81, 101,
149–50
entrepreneurial opportunities,
Corinth as centre for 27
Epaphras 48
Ephesians 46, 106–8
Ephesus 28, 31
eschatological expectation
127
eschatology 3–4, 59, 127,
135–47
estrangement 17; *see also*
alienation
ethical consequences of
being in Christ 90, 95
ethics 90, 126–34; grey areas
133
Eucharist 106, 117, 122–5
European postmodernism
148–58
evil ('grammar of') 145
evil forces 79
evil impulse 80
exaltation 40, 47
exile 83
existentialism 88
Exodus 120; *see also* Moses
expect ('grammar of')
138–9, 147
expectations 4, 127, 136–9
experience 60, 113, 139
expiation 54–5, 87–9
exploitation 67
external punishment 76–7

faith 8, 33–4, 64, 99–100,
129–31, 140; reckoned as
righteousness 94
faithfulness 111
faithfulness of God 34, 111
Fall 79–81
fallibility 70
Father *see* Abba; God
fathers 153
fellowship of the Spirit 66
fellowship with God 79
fellowship with Jesus 88
Festus 36

firstfruits 57, **62**, 102, 142; as assurance of full harvest 142
first-generation church 122
first missionary journey **22–5**
flesh 62, **69–70**, 77
football 81, 82
forgiveness of sins 92, 96
formation of Christians 126
frailty, human 70
freed person 27, 39
freedom 150
fruit of the Spirit 62
fulfilment, time of 3–4
fullness of God 48, 53
future 62, 136

Galatians **29–30**, 96–9
Gallio 28
Gentiles 6, 16–17, 21, 23, 27, 30, 35, 36, 48, 73, 74, 78, 81, 99, 102, 107, 131, 134, 150
genuineness of love 130
Gideon 59
gift 94–5
gift of God 64, 74, 80, **94–5**, 107
gifts of the Spirit 59, **63–5**, 107, 111, 130; *see also* Holy Spirit, gifts
gladiator 13
glory 45, 55, 57, 65, 113
Gnosticism 71
God 12, 14, 18, 26, 39, 41, 48, **49–57**, 63, **86–9**, 92, 95–6, 140, **142–3**, 151, 154, 157; as approachable 18, 49, **54–5**; Christ and 39, **52**, 55, **86–8**, 142–3; as Christlike 49, **54–5**; as conceivable 18, **49**; eternity of 55; as faithful 18, 34, 51, 111; as Father 53, **55–7**, **87–8**; fullness of 48, 53; glory of 55–6; as good 55, 57; grace of 49, 51, 66, **86–7**, 95; love of 50, 51, **54–5**, 57, 66, 67, 78, **87–8**; as one 26, **53**, 157; of peace 51, 88; as related to Christ 49, **54–5**, 88, 151; righteousness of 55; as Saviour 57; sending his own Son 54; as sovereign 12, 14, 49, **54–5**, 140, **142–3**, 157; as suffering 54–5; as Trinity 52–5; will of, 55, 56; *see also* Abba; Holy Trinity; time; Trinity
God-fearers 17
gospel 30, 50, 63
grace 5, 15–16, 30, 35, 44, 49, 64, 66, 80, 81, 95, 102, 113, 117, 121, **130–2**; of God 49, 81, 95, 102, 128, 161; in weakness 64, 90
Graeco-Roman terminology 17
grafting 16, **89**, 120
grand narratives 157–8
gravitas 116
greed 116, 126
Greek 1, 22–3, 71–2
Greek Old Testament *see* Septuagint
Greek-speaking Church 41
Greek-speaking Jews 17, 21, 23
Greek-speaking Judaism 14, 17, 22, 23
grey areas of ethics 133
guardians 116
guilt, guilty conscience 97

healing 64
heart 64, 73, 74
Hebrew, Hebrew Bible 20, 43, 76, 156
Hellenism 1–2, 131, 137
Hellenistic-Jewish thought 2, 41
Hellenistic mystery cults 43, 52; *see also* mystery religions
Hellenistic or Greek metaphysics 1
Hellenistic world 128
hermeneutics 160
hidden years, Paul's 22
hilastērion (Greek: expiation and/or propitiation) **87–9**
historical perspective 1–3, 160
history 14, 160
holy, holiness 105, 108

Holy Spirit 17, 18, 32, 33, 35, 42, 45, **53–7**, **58–6**, 69, 71–2, 77, 81, 104–5, 108, 113, 138, 143, 146, 155, 159; baptism in **61**; and Christ 32, 42, 45, **58–9**, 65–6, 143; as gift for all Christians **60–4**; gifts, *charismata* 54, 59, **63–5**, 104–5; as personal agency 65–6; as self-effacing **64**; variety of uses 58, 69
Holy Trinity 52–7, 66, 79
hope 127, **137–8**
hospitality 115
hostility of humanity to God 78
household codes 134
household of God 107
households 115, 122
human: being 43, 46, 79, 101; effort 12; meaning of 46
humanity 67–74, 101; of Christ 79
humour **18–19**

icy cold, ice (analogy) 12, 62, 90
identity of Christian Church 120, 133–4, 161
idol, idolatry 10, 23, 44, 50, 133, 162
image of God **42–4**, 67–8, 144
'immense cut' **11–16**
immorality 140
immortality 24
imprisonment 108; *see also* prison epistles
incarnation 44
incommensurability 158
incorporation into Christ 117–18
individualism 75, 79–80, 81, 97, 101, 149
individuals **59**, 63, 75, 101; *see also* communal enterprise; communal framework; communal gift; communal state of humanity; communal temple

indwelling of Spirit 62
infant baptism 121–2
infinite pain 55
initiating cause 54
intelligible speech 63–4
internal punishment 76–7, 145
involvement of Trinity: in Jesus' baptism 86; in prayer 54
Israel 51, 54, 75, 99, **102**, 107, 110, 157
Isthmian Games 26, 27

James: as 'core' apostle 30; and Council of Jerusalem 25
James, Epistle of 93, 100
jealousy 130
Jerusalem 20–1, 23, 28, 34, 35, 73
Jerusalem conference 24–5, 30
Jesus 38–48, 128; as Christ, or as Messiah 42–3; as Lord **38–42**, 60, 66, 113; as Son of God 43, 57; see also Christ
Jesus of Nazareth 1–8, 21; Jesus and Paul 1–8; Jesus Seminar 2; sayings of Jesus 3
Jewish literature **22–4**, 76
Jewish scholars 1–2
Jews 34, 55, 74, 78, 81, 102, 131, 150
John, apostle 30
Josephus 23
Judaism **21–4**, 36, 48, 49, 73, 80, 93, 97, 105, 128
Judaizing 68, 97
Judea 23
judgement 45–6, 55, 81, 96, 97, 111, 135–6, **144–6**; the last 96, 144–6
judge 55, 83
Julius Caesar 27
Junia 8, 114
justice 92
justification by grace **4–6**, **92–8**

kērygma 119
kingdom of God 1, 12, 17, 44, 142
kinsman 83; see also redeem
knowledge 15, 160
knowledge of God 56, **142–3**

labour 134
language 154–5, 160
last days 59
last things 135–47
law 4, 6, 12, 30, 81, 84, 93–4, 97–9, **132**; different senses of 99, 132
laying on of hands by Paul 31
legal fiction 95
legalism 96–8
legitimizing narratives 149, 157–8
Letter of Aristeas 23
libation 105
liberalism 1
life 69, 138, 143–4
life-boat analogy 13, 62
lifestyle 90
limbs, members of Church as Christ's 71, 104
linear development in Paul's writings 137
literature 161
little narratives 157–8
local church 106–7
logic 60
Lord, Christ as 17, **38–42**, 60, 70, 84, 113
Lord's Supper 7–8, 32, 106, 117, **122–5**; two types of 122–3
love 6, 50, 51, 55, 62, 67, 78, 114, **129–31**
Luke 25, 31, 35, 36
Lydia 25

magic 31
make righteous 94
man of lawlessness 146
man of Macedonia 25
management 108, 115
manual worker 10
Maranatha 40
marriage 32, 131
Mars' Hill 26

material realm 77
materialism 140
media 152
mediate Creator 53
medical guild 152–3
members 71, **103**
mercy-seat 87–8
Messiah **42–3**
metanarratives 149, 157–8
metaphor 156
mind **68**, 73–4, 115
mind of Christ 16, 19, 56, 66
ministry **110–16**
miracles 64
misdirected desire 75, 79
misery of humankind 79–80
missing the mark 75
mission 110
modernity 79–80, 91
money 73, 115–16; see also collection
monotheism 45; see also God
moralism 77
Moses 24, 30, 45, 65, 118
motivation 62, 131
Mummius 26
mystery religions 43, 52, 120
myth 12, 120, 136, 148, 150, 162

narrative 53, 157–8
Nero 36, 43
New Age 59, 127
new creation **11–14**, 17, 34, 79, 84, 127, 132–3, 158
new order of existence 12, 135–6
new perspective 97–9
new world 12, 135–6

obedience 60, 128
observer **139**, 147
Old Testament 12, 14, 41, 49, 52–3, **58–9**, 66, 67, 69, 73, 75, 105, 120, 144–5
one God 26, **53**
once-for-all **91**, 121
ontology 156
original sin **79–80**

pagan deities 83–4
paganism 158

Palestinian Jewish Christians 52
paradoxes 151
parallels 35
Parousia 29, 41, 135, 138, 146–7
participant 124, **139**, 147
participation 82, **86–91**
Passover **123–5**
Passover Lamb 4
pastoral care 24, 28, 31
Pastoral Epistles 108, 115, 134
pastoral preaching 63
patience, characteristic of 130, 134
patripassianism 55
Paul: call of 11, **16**, 20, 39, 44, 49, 71, 75, **103**; his humour **18**; leatherwork 20; as pastor 24; as Pharisee 20–1; upbringing 20–1; as warm-hearted **9–10**
peddlers of God's word 113
Pelagianism 80
penal, penalty 85
Pentecost 60
Pentecostal Church 119
people of God 102; *see also* Church
perception 148, 162
performative speech 18–19
perjury 125
persecution 28, 29
Persis 114
person 65, 95
personality 110–11
personality-centred group 32, 111
pesha' (Hebrew: sin, rebellion) 76
Peter 21, 25, 30
Pharisee 5, 20–1, 24
Philemon 32
Philippi 25
Philippians **46–7**
Philo **23–4**, 80
philosophy 158
Phoebe 8, 34, 114
pioneer church 114
place of meeting **87–8**, 91
Plato 24, 70–1, 77, 140

pleading guilty (baptism as) 121
pledge, baptism as 121–2; of full harvest 142
pluralism 148, 158, 162
political language 110–11, 118
postmodernism 101, 137–8, **148–61**; as a mood 148–9; v. postmodernity 148, **151–2**
power 59, 81, 84, 113, 116, 143, **152–4**
powers 44, 56, 81, 150; *see also* angels
power-struggle 110–11, 152–4
pragmatism 151, **159–61**
pray 29, 48, **53**, 60, 62
prayer 9, 18, 45, **49–50**
preaching 15, 18, 27–8, 40, **63**, 112
pre-existence of Christ 44
prepositions, nuances of 118
presumption 137
presupposition, sacrificial system as 85
previous letter to Corinth, Paul's 33
price paid *see* redeem
priest 12
Priscilla 27, 114–15
prison epistles 32, 36, 46–7
proceeds, procession 56
process 12, **16**
proclamation 1; *see also kērygma*; preaching
progressivism 135, 137, 159–61
promise 30, 35, 51, 94, 102, 120, 142
prophecy, prophet, prophesying 9, 12, **32**, **63**, 111–12
propitiation 54–5, **87–9**; *see also* expiation
Protestant–Catholic divide 94–5
provocation in reception theory 161
psychiatry 152
psychology 11, 16
psychosomatic unity 69, 73

public acts 15, 70, 122–3, 145
public revelation 41
public sphere 122–3
public world **69–70**, **126**

Qumran 24, 105, 129

rationality 67
realized eschatology 137
reason 24, 150
rebel, rebellion 76
rebirth 121
reception theory 161
reciprocity 131
reconciliation 17, 43, **86–9**
redeem, redemption 57, **83–9**
Reformers 96
refutatio 141, 142, 150
rejuvenation 143
relationship 46; with God 74, 92, 95
religiosity 73
reliving the event of the cross **124**, **125**
remembrance of Christ **122–3**, **125**
remnant of Israel 52, 59, 102, 110
renewed mind 15
representation of God 43, 82
reputation of lord/master 39
responsibility 38, 102–3
resurrection 17, 26, 32, 39, 40, 55, 59, 71, 72, 90, 116, 135, **139–44**
resurrection of Christ 32, 43, **140–4**
revelation 15, 30, 41, 49, 54, 59, 161
rhetoric 27, 56, 148, 150–1, 153, 162
righteousness 75, **92–6**
rightful Lord 42
rights, putting to **92–5**
rock, Christ as 54
Roman citizenship 20, 25, 36
Roman colony 27, 47
Romans **34–5**, **50–1**, **94–6**

Index of subjects

Rome 21, 26–7, 34, 36, 46
ruach (Hebrew: spirit, Spirit) 58–9; see also Holy Spirit
rubbish disposal 160

sacraments 117–25
sacrifice 82, 87
salvation 12, 13, 17; three tenses of 13
salvation event 119
Samaritan woman 8
Saviour 83
Scriptures 140; see also Old Testament
second meaning, discerning in texts 156
second missionary journey 25–31
secretary, Paul's dictating letters to 29
self: self-awareness 71; self-commendation 34; self-criticism 148, 161; self-deceit 73, 130; self-destruction 78, 146; self-involvement 86; self-promotion 34; self-sacrificing 47; self-sufficiency 27
semiology 154
sentence of death 33
Septuagint 17, 22–3, 51, 58–9, 75, 76, 103, 156
Servant of God 85
sex 73, 126
shipwreck 36
signs 117
Silas 25, 29
silence (of women) 9, 115
silversmiths 32
sin 75–81, 144; as act 75; as power 76, 81; as state 75–6; universality of 77–81
sin-offering 84–5
slaves 27, 38–9, 83–4, 132; purchase of 83–4
sleep 147; see also expect; time
sociology 108, 115, 134; social construction 150, 162; social practice 160; social role 155

Socrates 25
solidarity 71–3, 79, 81, 101, 103, 138
Son of God 43–4
Son of Man 43
Sosthenes 28
soul 69, 72, 140
Spain 34, 36, 50
speech-act 19
Spirit and Christ 65–6, 144; see also Holy Spirit
spiritual 63–5, 69, 72, 143–4
spiritual gifts 63–5
stagnation of life 143
Stephanas 31
stewards 67
Stoics 26, 39, 71, 72, 126, 128
strategic centres 34
structuralism 154
structure 77
subconscious, the 68, 73
subordination passages 52
substitution 82, 86–91
suffering 13, 17, 33, 36, 54, 87, 90–1
Suffering Servant 85
sufficient sacrifice 91
supra-personal, Holy Spirit as 65
synagogues 23, 31, 131
Syro-Phoenician woman 8

Targums 21
Tarsus 20–1, 22
tasks, Christ-centred 59; different 110
technology 150
Temple 21, 36, 71, 105–6
texts 154–6
thanksgiving 33, 50
Thessalonians 29, 31; first letter to the 26, 29, 50; second letter to the 26, 31, 50
Thessalonica 25–6
thinking 73–4; see also mind
third missionary journey 31–5
thorn in the flesh 64, 70, 90
threefold ministry 112

time 138–9
Timothy 25, 29
titles 38, 40, 46
tongues 63–4
trade 20
tradition 10, 150; see also apostolic tradition
transference 16
transformation 12, 16, 18–19, 68, 72, 137–9, 143–4, 161
transparency 116
tributary, justification as 97
triclinium 124
Trinity 86–7; see also Holy Trinity
tri-theism 53, 55
Troas 25, 35
trumpet 136, 144, 146
trust 40, 60
truth 51, 113, 148, 151–2, 160–2
two ages 13, 133
two orders 13
type, typology 4, 42–3

ultimate, or first, cause 53
unconscious, the 68, 73
unity 103–4
universal Church 106–8
urgency 132

variety of imagery 82–3, 84–91
Vatican II 95
verdict 96, 99–100, 145–6
vicious circle 77
vindication 145
virtues and vices lists 128–9, 131–2
visibility 70, 117, 126
vulnerability 70

waiting 44, 62
wall, as partition 107, 134
washing, cleansing 120–1
weak, the weak, weakness 10, 17, 18, 56, 62, 103–4
welcome, as Christ 128, 131
Western thought 73
'White Mythology' (Derrida) 156

whole person, sspects of
69
wisdom 45, 46, 48, 56, 91,
162
Wisdom of Solomon 23–4
witness 57, 116
women 8–9, 47, 45

word of God 17, 18, 45, 48,
47, 73, 74, **114–15**, 131–2
word–concept error 65
works 62, 98–100
world-history 51, 157–8
world-soul 72–3
world-switch 15

worship 40, 57, 115
wrath 51, 77–9

yêtzer hâ-râ' (Hebrew: evil
impulse) 80

zeal 51